CULINA SA

Essential Food Safety Management

The Complete Food Safety Management System

Starting and running a food business
Advice on Food law,hygiene,immigration,fitness to work,allergens,cooking,training,street food,mail order,labeling plus much more.

Also includes diary sheets for a year to record food,freezer and fridge temperatures.

Praise for Culina Salus

"Very satisfied with product"
Dr N Woodruff

"Great very helpful"
Lisa Cox

"Very good book"
Chris

"Very useful at work"
John

"As a Kitchen Safety Record this book in the form of a diary is fine for daily recordings and a good reference point if you need to remind yourself of the requirements such as with the regulations around food allergens"
Scorpio Woman "Book worm"

"Much easier to use than the old system very pleased"
Alan Fox

"Best out there"
G Choi

"Ideal"
Adam Lloyd

Other titles by Culina Salus

Kitchen Safety Record 2017 Year Book: One day to a page food business diary

Kitchen Safety Record 1 year diary: Week to a page food business diary

Eating Kills: The concise guide to eating less to save your life

Eat yourself to death: How to prevent your food choices from killing you

The Winners Creed: The winners creed on how to succeed after screwing up

Dedicated to YHWH
Wambui, Kamau, Adoration
And
My big sister, Hepzibah who worked with me on the toughest catering events

First published in Great Britain in 2016 by Perseverance Works

Copyright © Culina Salus 2016

Design and layout © Perseverance Works

The right of Culina Salus to be identified as the Author of the Work

has been asserted in accordance with the the Copyright, designs and

patents Act 1988.

ISBN: 978-1537741710

All rights reserved. No part of this publication may be reproduced, stored

in a retrieval system, or transmitted, in any form or by means without the

prior written permission of the publisher, nor be otherwise circulated in

any form of binding or cover other than in which it is published and

without a similar condition being imposed on the subsequent purchaser.

Contains public sector information licensed under the Open Government Licence v3.0.

Printed and bound in the UK

Whilst every care has been taken compiling this book, the publishers

cannot accept responsibility for any inaccuracies or errors herein.

This book contains elements previously published in Good Food Good Business.

Please note the advice in this book is intended for guidance only and does not cover all areas of the law.

Contents

Introduction

Starting a food business, what every one needs to know 2
Food law inspections and your business 14
Food hygiene ratings scheme 18
Immigration law and your staff 20
Food handlers: fitness to work 23
Advice on new food allergen rules 27
Foods that need extra care 30
Good food Good business for caterers 33
Cooking 42
Good food Good business for retailers 44
Good food Good business for residential care homes 47
Good food Good business for childminders 49
Good food Good business for Asian cuisines 52
Good food Good business for Oriental cuisines 55
Dealing with waste cooking oil 58
Training for food handlers 59
Starting a food business from home 61
Starting a street food business and a pop up 66
Setting up a food mail order business 70
Food labelling and packaging 73
Employing staff for the first time 77
Essential health & safety information 78
Starting a food import business 80
Why business's fail 84
1Year week to view diary 88
Your details 89
Food business registration form 91
Return to work form 92
Hazard spotting checklist 96
Monthly probe thermometer check 102
Fire safety checklist 103
Contact list 107
Supplier list 111
Staff training record 114
Recording sheets 126
Chef's allergen menu matrix sheets 301

Introduction

Just get started

Do the right thing

Meet the challenges head on

Adapt, Improvise and Overcome

Be the best

Good luck

Culina Salus
September 2016

Starting a food business

The only reason to start a business, is to make money

Food safety procedures Get your food safety procedures right from the start, other wise you may eventually get into difficulties and in the worse case scenario, ruin your hard won reputation and even lose your business.
Key requirements: you must have written records to show, that whatever you do, make or sell, the food produced, must be safe to eat for all, especially in the case of high risk groups such as:

- Babies and infants
- The elderly
- Pregnant women
- People who are ill or have weakened immune systems

These food safety procedures mean that you must keep up to date documents and records showing your procedures and methods, there also other benefits such as:

- Being on the right side of food safety law
- Satisfied customers will keep returning as they trust your business.
- Good word of mouth about your business

You must change and adapt your procedures to reflect your changing menu and cooking methods especially, if the business gets busier and expands. What you must do, is manage food safety issues and hazards in your business. **How do you prove it**? by putting in place, food safety management procedures which are easy to use and follow, so it becomes second nature to you and your staff. Whatever procedures you use, must be written down for inspection by your local authority.

These procedures must be based on **HACCP**, what a mouthful!, what does this mean in real life? **HACCP** is another technical sounding word for *common sense*, it is a method of looking at your operation and figuring out what could go wrong and putting plans in place to make sure that problems are avoided. HACCP means Hazard Analysis Critical Control Points. This internationally recognised process helps you look at how you handle food and introduce procedures to make sure the food you produce is safe to eat.

EU Regulation 852/2004 (Article 5) requires food business operators, to implement and maintain hygiene procedures based on HACCP principles.
HACCP involves the following seven steps:
1. Single out what could go wrong (use the hazard analysis form in the 2016 yearbook or 1 year diary)
2. Identify the important points where things can go wrong (the critical control points – CCPs)
3. Set critical limits at each CCP (e.g. cooking temperature/time)
4. Set up checks at CCPs to prevent problems occurring (monitoring)
5. Determine what to do if something goes wrong (corrective action)
6. Prove that your HACCP Plan is working (verification)
7. Keep records of all of the above (documentation)

Your HACCP plan must be kept up to date. You will need to review it from time to time, especially whenever any factor in your food operation changes. You should always ask your local Environmental Health Officer for advice. Remember that, even with a HACCP plan in place, you must comply with all requirements of current food safety legislation.

Checking out your business and seeing what could go wrong

For instance,how quickly do you put delivered chilled poultry in the fridge? or does it sit on the floor waiting for the kitchen porter to come back from his third fag break of the morning?

What do you do if something goes wrong?

You come in on Monday morning and discover that fridge has packed up over the weekend with a £300 worth of fresh chicken breasts in it. You have no idea,when the fridge broke down over the weekend. Do you bin it and take the financial hit? or do you thoroughly wash the dubious smelling chicken,marinate it in strong herbs,spices and flog it,as the days special?

What do you do? What do you do?. Do the right thing.

> 4 things bacteria need to multiply: Food Warmth Moisture Time

Make sure that your food safety procedures will work,especially when you are not there. Make sure that you use this book to put food safety management procedures in place and keep the diary or yearbook up to date(and do not let your departing staff leave with it,happens very often).

Hazards
HACCAP (or common sense and honesty) is not complicated,it just a necessary routine that must be followed,like brushing your teeth in morning. Just include HACCP into your business routine to reduce and get rid of hazards. Hazards are things that can be dangerous in relation to food safety such as:

- **Microbiological**- harmful bacteria,such as the chicken mentioned earlier (waiting for the kitchen porter),usual suspects are listeria and campylobacter

- **Chemical**- rat poison,cleaning chemicals getting into foods.

- **Physical**- packaging,glass,stones getting into food(imagine crunching down on your freshly cooked burger and finding the cook's recently lost ear ring,in the salad,yes nasty)

COLOUR CODED CHOPPING BOARD SYSTEM

RED FOR RAW MEAT

BLUE FOR RAW FISH

YELLOW FOR COOKED MEAT

GREEN FOR FRUIT AND SALAD

BROWN FOR VEGETABLES

WHITE FOR BAKERY AND DAIRY

The local authorities To register your business with your local council,you need to give them **28** days notice before you start and they cannot turn you down,even if you plan to open an *eat till you can't move* buffet restaurant. Registration is free and applies to most types of food business,including restaurants,cafes,hotels,shops,canteens,market stalls,mobile catering and food delivery vans. If you have more than one premises,you will need to register all of them.

Changing your information
Once you have registered your food business,you only need to notify the council if:
- The business changes ownership,the new owner must complete a new application form
- The nature of the business changes
- The address at which movable premises(vans and stalls) are kept,changes

You can register,using the food business registration service at www.gov.uk/food-business-registration or via your local authority website. You can also use the application form,in the 2016 yearbook or 1 year diary,which you can photocopy,fill in and send off to your local council. Remember to inform the council about significant changes in business and keep them updated with information about your premises. For example that complaining resident living in the flat on top of your business,who always whines about the smells from your kitchen,moves out and you decide to buy the space and open a dining room up there instead.

Licences Licences for sale or supply of alcohol are now dealt with by your local environmental health department,not the Magistrates Court. If you wish to sell alcohol and do not already have a licence,you need to contact your local

council. A licence will be required from your local authority for the following:
- Selling or supplying alcohol
- Selling hot food between 11pm and 5am
- Providing live music,theatre or cinema
- Selling food from a stall or van

Food hygiene regulations The most important food hygiene regulations for your business are regulation (EC) No 852/4004 which covers the hygiene of foodstuffs and the food hygiene (England) regulations 2006 (as amended) and equivalent regulations for the rest of the UK. These cover basic hygiene requirements for your food business such as premises,facilities and staff.

Premises Along with food costs and staff wages,your rent will be one of your highest bills. To serve hot food,you will need an A3 planning licence. They are normally in high demand and may also have a premium attached. (depending on location). The premium is a fixed sum of money,required at the beginning of the lease,paid to the landlord or outgoing tenant and usually covers things like equipment,fixtures,stock and for existing trade,if the business is already established and profitable. The premium will run to thousands,so look out for this when searching for a premises.

Try to maximise all space in your newly acquired premises,as you are paying for the total square footage available,for example, a very large basement might be great for storage but you can jazz it up,put in more tables and chairs and turn it into a productive, profitable area. Your premises
- Goes without saying: your business premises must be clean,in good condition.
- The layout,design,site,construction,size must allow for maintenance,cleaning and disinfection.
- It should avoid or minimize airborne contamination.
- Provide enough working space to carry out all tasks properly,even a small burger van must allow the cooks to carry out all tasks in a hygienic manner.

- Must protect against dirt,toxic material,prevention of crap falling into food(contamination) and prevention of mould on walls (which means that you probably have poor ventilation)
- Make sure that it allows for effective pest control.
- Must provide best conditions for handling and storing food at appropriate temperatures.

Being optimistic and thinking long term about the premises,is there room for growth and expansion? To avoid headaches,loss of money,hassle,WTF! situations,consult local experts such as commercial agents,surveyors and solicitors and your local authority first,before you buy,lease or rent any premises. Gather as much information as possible,even before buying an existing catering business,research the name of the business on google,you may find that they have a good reputation or you may discover a history of improvement notices with a terrible local reputation. Will the sign 'Under new management' be sufficient to tempt back customers?

Renting premises Every situation is different but these are the kinds of things to expect:
- The rents are based on the open market rental value and you should work out in your business plan,if your turnover can pay the rent(and other overheads) and still leave you a decent profit.
- Rent reviews at the end of leases tend to be in an upward direction.
- You may be responsible for all repairs,decorations and maintenance of services for the premises.
- Factor in costs for dilapidations;an amount payable to the landlord at the end of the lease for repairs
- You will be responsible for the payment of all utility bills and business rates.
- Do not forget surveyor's and legal fees in connection with the letting process and preparation of the lease.
- Buildings insurance may be covered by the landlord,if not,another bill for you to pay.
- A rent deposit equivalent to anything from 3 to 12 months rent (depends on what you negotiate with the landlord) is payable on all new lettings,this significant amount of money is normally held throughout the term of the lease. Also normally three month's rent in advance is payable on completion of the lease.
- If you are an individual without a business track record and insubstantial personal assets,the landlord may want a guarantee that you can meet the rent costs. In most instances a bank guarantee will be fine,however some landlords may want a cash deposit or they may insist on taking a charge on your personal property. Think carefully before agreeing to this,business failures happen to the best.
- The rent is normally payable quarterly in advance.

- Break clause: a date in the lease, agreed by you and the landlord, where the lease can be 'broken' without anyone facing a penalty. You need to give your landlord 2 months notice that you are using the break clause.

These are classes of property planning use which are as follows:
- A1: a retail shop
- A2: professional and financial services (e.g. estate agency, bank)
- A3: restaurant or café
- A4: drinking establishments (e.g. pub or bar)
- A5: the sale of hot food for consumption off the premises

In certain circumstances, it may be possible to change the use of the property. You may also have to make an application to the local council for planning permission to change the use.

Turnover rent

Turnover rents enable landlords and tenants to share the risk and reward of a tenant's business. A turnover rent arrangement usually involves the tenant paying a base rent (usually between 70 – 80 %) of the open market plus a turnover 'top-up' which is based upon a percentage of the tenant's turnover and which is payable only to the extent that it exceeds the base rent. Landlords will want to ensure that your turnover includes everything from physical products to online orders. Your accounts will be independently certified and the landlord is entitled to review the documentation. Make sure terms are negotiated, so all parties are happy.

Hand washing facilities and toilets in your business
You should have an adequate number of toilets for men and women

Number of People at work	Number of toilets	Number of washbasins
1 to 5	1	1
6 to 25	2	2
26 to 50	3	3
51 to 75	4	4
76 to 100	5	5

- The toilet should not open directly into the food handling areas.
- Provide adequate washbasins that should only be used for washing hands.
- The washbasins must have hot and cold water, soap and material for drying hands.
- Never wash food in hand washbasins, get a different sink.

Ventilation

- Toilets must have ventilation either natural or mechanical.
- If you do have ventilation systems, it must be easy to clean with good access to replace parts and filters.
- Make sure that your premises has enough ventilation, just imagine a hot kitchen on the hottest day of the year, with poor or non existent ventilation.

Other requirements

- Adequate lighting goes without saying, who needs waiters carrying trays of food, stumbling around in a poorly lit environment or even more scary; chefs holding very sharp knives.
- Drainage facilities must be adequate and should not be a source of contamination.
- Changing rooms are required for the staff, or do you expect them to change in the toilet?
- Only a fool would store cleaning chemicals in the same area where food is handled! make sure nobody does foolish things in your kitchen.

The Kitchen

- **Floors**- must be without saying, in tip top condition, easy to clean and disinfect.
- **Walls**- must in a good condition, easy to clean and disinfect.
- **Ceilings**- must prevent dirt and particles from building up, reduce condensation and mould.
- **Windows**- must prevent dirt from building up, must open onto the outside and do not forget to fit insect screens that can be easily removed for cleaning.

- **Doors**- easy to clean and disinfect.
- **Surfaces-** all kitchen surfaces, especially where food is prepared must be in sound condition, easy to clean and disinfect.

Always try to choose kitchen surfaces that are smooth, washable, corrosion resistant and non-toxic- Why do you think the best kitchens are full of equipment and surfaces made out of stainless steel?

Washing equipment All equipment and utensils will need to be cleaned using either a dishwasher or in a sink. The number and size of sinks in your business will depend on the size of your operation. At least two sinks are needed, one for washing, and one for rinsing and disinfecting. You must have adequate facilities for washing food, with hot and cold water available. The water must be potable. It is strongly recommended that a separate sink is provided if raw meat and/or poultry is defrosted and prepared and a separate sink for use for vegetables and salads. These areas must be kept clean and easy to disinfect.

Transport
Vehicles and container used to transport food must be clean and in good condition to protect food from contamination. Food containers must not be used for carrying anything else other than food. If your van has to carry other items than food, or different types of food, you must keep them separate. Do not forget to clean out the vehicle after each load in such instances to avoid the risk of contamination. The food containers used, must be capable of keeping food at appropriate temperatures for example, raw chicken must be kept chilled (5°C) or cooked prawn madras must be kept hot (63°C)

Equipment All kitchen equipment must be cleaned properly and disinfected as necessary. Must be made of appropriate materials, kept clean and in good condition. All your equipment should be installed in a manner that allows their proper cleaning and of their surrounding areas, for example, you must be able to move your fridges to allow sweeping and cleaning under and behind them. Gas appliances should be connected to the supply by flexible hoses, this allows equipment to be moved for cleaning. Make sure where necessary, that all temperature sensors are fitted and working, especially to check fridge/freezer temperature readings.

Food Waste Make sure that you have enough bins in your kitchen and they are emptied regularly to prevent rubbish from building up. External bins should also be provided with close fitting lids and be easy to clean. These must not allow pests or animals access to the contents inside. Engage a contractor to remove refuse and used cooking oils on a regular basis (see chapter 14 on waste oil removal)

Water supply   You must have an adequate supply of potable(posh word for drinking)water. Where non-potable water is used such as fire control, steamers, it must have its own circulation system completely separate from drinking water. Ice used for human consumption must have a potable water source supplying the ice making machine.

Personal hygiene Everybody working in the kitchen must have and maintain a very high level of personal cleanliness, who the hell wants an unwashed, dirty, smelly, unkempt, nose picking slob preparing their food?

- All food handlers must take a shower daily.
- Staff should wear protective footwear, with steel toe caps and slip resistant soles
- Uniforms must be changed daily
- Uniforms should preferably made of breathable fabrics

It goes without saying that while touching food, you and your staff should not pick your nose, spit or sneeze over the pizza or even touch your face. Anyone found chewing gum or smoking in the kitchen should be disciplined and probably sacked. I know you are working in a food preparation area, creating all kinds of delicious food but:
NO EATING IN THE KITCHEN. NO HAND TO MOUTH ACTION

All staff must keep hair tidy, tied back if necessary, better still wear a hair net, you may look like a dork but this is serious food preparation not a fashion show.

Nobody wants hair in their soup.
Keep all bling,watches out of the kitchen,only wedding bands are allowed. Watches and jewellery can collect and spread crap into food. Use tongs,ladles and spoons to handle food,this will prevent unnecessary hand contact.

The following are not fit for work:
- Any one suffering a transmittable disease
- Anyone with infected wounds and sores
- Anyone with food poisoning or diarrhoea.

Anyone suffering from any of the above should tell their line manager and stay away until they have no symptoms for 48 hours. Especially those with vomiting and diarrhoea.
For more information,see chapter 5 food handlers,fitness to work.

Hand washing

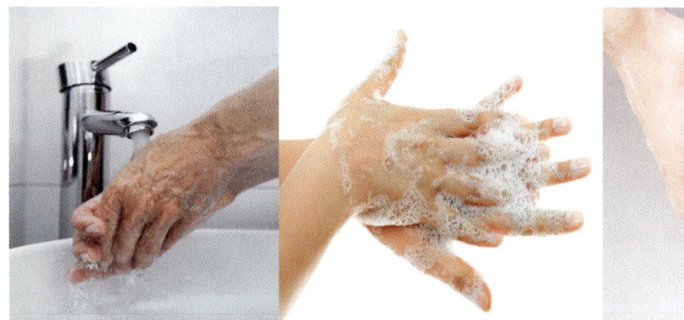

All staff who work with food must wash their hands properly. Common sense really, but when was sense ever common?
After a break - **wash your hands**
Before leaving the kitchen - **wash your hands**
After visiting the toilet - **wash your hands**
Before touching food and kitchen equipment - **wash your hands**
After touching raw food like poultry and unwashed vegetables - **wash your hands**
After emptying the bin - **wash your hands**
After cleaning - **wash your hands**
After blowing your nose - **wash your hands**
After eating- **wash your hands**
After touching a cut or dressing - **wash your hands**
After shaking hands with a customer,pleased with your food - **wash your hands**
After handling cash, touching door handles,the office phone - **wash your hands**

Wash your hands! Wash your hands! Wash your hands! Wash your hands!

This is probably the most important food safety procedure.

True life story

E coli struck 142 takeaway customers after staff did not wash hands

Owners of aKebab shop in Hyson Green, Nottingham admit hygiene offences after a court heard that staff did not wash their hands after going to the toilet. More than 100 takeaway customers were sick for up to two months with a rare strain of *E coli.*Nottingham crown court was told that **142** customers of the Khyber Pass in Hyson Green,had nausea,vomiting and diarrhoea after the outbreak in June 2014. In one case, a 13-year-old girl spent four nights in hospital,with a consultant saying the infection could have been fatal if it was not treated.
The takeaway owners,pleaded guilty to seven food hygiene offences and were sentenced on Wednesday the 23rd of September 2015. Bernard Thorogood, prosecuting, said it was only the second recorded case in Europe of this strain of *E coli.* He said: "**Its only known reservoir is the human gut**. You realise the way it was transmitted was by use of incorrect hand-washing after using the lavatory to defecate. A cough can't do it, a handshake could if it's an infected hand,which means it was not washed after using the lavatory." He added that nine of the 12 members of staff who handle food at the takeaway were found to have traces of the bacteria, and one of the defendant's daughters fell ill.

The owners were both given four months' prison sentences suspended for a year, as well as being ordered to do 250 hours of unpaid work each. Breaches included selling food unfit for human consumption,poor personal cleanliness of food workers and inadequate hand washing facilities and drainage. Judge Jeremy Lea also said the defendants should pay each of the victims **£200** compensation as well as paying costs of **£25,752.36**. He said: "If you make money by supplying cooked food to members of the public,you owe a real duty of care to ensure that people will not be made unwell by your disregard for food safety and hygiene regulations. This is not simply red tape that you have failed to comply with." The judge said he was "not blind to the consequences", which included adding burdens to the NHS,employers who had to cover for sick employees and parents and children who fell ill. "One or two individuals indicate they have never felt so ill and thought they were going to die," he said. "Some of them were made so unwell they had to go to hospital and one 13-year-old was so unwell the medical evidence was clear that, notwithstanding medical treatment, she may well have died."

Paul Dales, from Nottingham City Council's food, health and safety team, said: "This was a significant and serious food poisoning outbreak affecting a large number of people,some of whom developed severe symptoms. "It's fortunate there were no fatalities, as this is a strain of **E. coli** rarely found in the developed world, this being only the second confirmed outbreak in Europe." The same strain of **EIEC** was found in lettuce prepared by food workers at the takeaway. "It's clear that hand-washing practices by some workers were wholly inadequate and this led to food becoming contaminated," he added.

Your customers may want side dishes,they sure as hell do not want a side serving of your harmful bacteria.

Cleaning Surfaces and equipment must be cleaned down before disinfecting. Always follow the manufacturers instructions. Ensure that you always have an adequate supply of cleaning chemicals and equipment. Keep your premises clean and tidy all the time,mop up spills as they happen and remember to place a warning sign informing people of the wet floor. Whilst cleaning out your fridge,transfer the food to another fridge to maintain the required temperature during the cleaning time. This will prevent bacteria from growing.

Foodstuffs Steer clean of contaminated or adulterated food not fit or meant for human consumption. Horse meat anyone? Food must be protected from all sources of contamination and deterioration,for example just delivered chilled raw chicken must go straight into the fridge and not wait until someone can be bothered to put it into the fridge. Keep pets and pests away from food preparation and storage areas. Insects and rodents must not be unpaid members of staff,roaming around your kitchen.

Temperature Rules
Cold food storage: **8°C** degrees or below- **a legal requirement.**
Cold food storage: **5°C** degrees or below- **best practice**
Hot food storage **63°C** degrees or above
Cooking and reheating core temperature must reach **75°C** (at least for **2** minutes)
Frozen **-18°C to -23°C** degrees (at this temperature,bacteria will survive but not multiply)
Get a temperature probe to do it right and record the results in the 2016 yearbook or 1 year diary. Job done.
Hot should be **Hot**
Chilled should be **Chilled**
Frozen should be **Frozen**
Lukewarm food does not belong in a professionally well run kitchen.
Temperature danger zone
Between the temperatures **8°C** and **63°C**,bacteria can multiply quickly and at **37°C** (body temperature) can double in numbers every 10 to 20 minutes.
Cold food can be kept above **8°C** degrees for up to **4** hours. **1** time only.
If any food is left after this time,bin it or keep it chilled at **8°C** degrees or below until it is used.
Hot food can kept below **63°C** degrees for up to **2** hours. **1** time only.
Any left overs must be reheated to **75°C** and returned to the hot plate or cool it as quickly as possible to **8°C** degrees or below or bin it.

Chilled storage and display
Certain foods must be kept cold to remain safe,to prevent the growth of harmful bacteria. Please note some condiments used in your business,need to be refrigerated such as ketchup - modern versions contain less salt which is a natural preservative. Soy sauce, mustard,mayonnaise,Tabasco all need to be kept in fridges. Read the labels for guidance such as '**keep refrigerated**'. Food marked with a '**best before**' or '**best before end**' date should be removed from sale by the end of that day.

It is illegal to sell food after its 'use by' date

Do not overfill chilling equipment or load the food above load lines and **always** store and display wrapped raw meat, poultry, fish and eggs **separately** from other food. If things go wrong and the fridge/freezer breaks down and food has began to defrost,take the hit,be safe,do not refreeze,throw the food away unless it is a 'thaw and serve' product like cakes,cookies, donuts and muffins. Most fridges and freezers will have a digital display to show the temperature,use a clean needle probe thermometer to double check the readings by inserting into the centre of food. Clean the needle probe,every time,you insert it to check food temperatures.

It is essential to keep the probe in good working order,kept clean and regularly tested. The readings in iced water should be between **-1°C** to **+1°C**,if outside this range the unit should be replaced or returned to the manufacturer to be recalibrated. The reading in boiling water should be between **99°C** and **101°C**,if outside this range the unit should be replaced or returned to the manufacturer to be recalibrated.

Defrosting
Food should be thoroughly defrosted before cooking (unless the manufacturer's instructions tell you to cook from frozen). Pouring hot water over frozen food is a no no. Just put it under a tap running cold water,to help to speed up defrosting. Ideally all defrosting should take place in a fridge. This will minimise the risk of harmful bacteria growing.

Packaging food
Whatever you use for wrapping and packaging food,must not be a source of contamination,so do not use that free newspaper left behind on the bus to wrap food. All food containers and packaging,must be kept clean and stored in areas safe from contamination,for example pests running over plastic food containers,cups,cutlery etc.
Training
Make sure that all your staff are well trained,otherwise they will drop you in it (and it will be your fault). A member of staff without the proper food hygiene training can cause a whole heap of trouble and ruin your hard earned reputation in the process. They may just get fired,if they are lucky but you will have sort out the mess and deal with the damage to your reputation. At least make sure they have **Level 1 Food Hygiene and Safety training** and a certificate to prove it. If they do not,protect yourself,spend the money,get them trained. Properly. Keep records of all training undertaken by you and your staff, handy when the heavy mob(aka enforcement officers from your local council) come round to inspect your premises. Use the training record in the 2016 yearbook or diary to record training undertaken by your staff.See chapter 15; Training for food handlers.

Movable feasts
Market stalls,mobile vans,marquees,vending machines must all be clean and in good condition.You need to consider the following:
- Proper facilities for cleaning of equipment and food,using hot and potable cold water,not forgetting personal hygiene facilities which including hand washing,toilets and changing areas.
- Make proper arrangements to get rid of your rubbish. Read Chapter 17 Starting a street food business for more information.

Unwrapped food
Food must be stored at the appropriate temperatures (hot food at **63°C** and cold food **5°C**) and unwrapped foods must be displayed in a way that avoids contamination. Examples of unwrapped foods are:
- Cold,cooked meats from the deli counter
- Salad bars
- Pick and Mix
- Buffets

Barbecues Your barbecued jerk chicken should not be displayed in a manner that allows prospective customers to sneeze,spit or cough over uncovered food. Food on display should be placed out of reach of customers. Work surfaces,equipment must be properly cleaned before unwrapped foods are placed on them.

The Law (best not to provoke their ire or adopt the Boys scout motto: "Be Prepared")
Your local council is responsible for enforcing food hygiene laws. The environmental health officer aka the "Food police" are pretty powerful: they have the right to enter your premises,at any time without telling you first,take samples and photographs of food,the kitchen,inspect your records or remove suspect foods. If you and your staff have not been doing the right things, they can also serve you with a notice,such as a **hygiene improvement notice** or even worse a **hygiene emergency prohibition notice** (more details of these in the Food law inspections and your business chapter 2).
They could use their nuclear option and recommend **prosecution**. If prosecution is successful,you could face a fine or imprisonment,or both. You could also be banned from using certain processes,premises or equipment,or from managing a food business. So adopt the boy scouts motto: **BE PREPARED**,get up to date with your food safety procedures,as part

of your business practices,so get busy one time and do what's right. You have been warned.

True life story

A pub chef and manager have been jailed after a woman who ate a Christmas meal they served died from food poisoning. The court heard that on Christmas day,2012 the pub served lunch to 128 customers. Thirty-three of them suffered food poisoning. The two were found guilty of perverting the course of justice and jailed for between **12** to **18** months. They had fabricated food safety records at the Hornchurch hotel relating to the cooking of turkey meat. The turkeys which had been prepared the day before were not cooled properly after cooking and not adequately reheated before being served to the guests. **Clostridium perfringens bacterium**,a common cause of food poisoning,was later found in samples taken from the diners who fell ill. Food safety records had not been filled in so the manager and the chef retrospectively filled in due diligence logs before health inspectors could carry out an investigation. The prosecution said it was "highly likely that other food-related records were fabricated". The Judge said the chain which owned the pub took "manifestly inadequate steps" to address the risks of inadequate cooking, cooling and reheating of turkey and were fined £1.5 million for placing unsafe food on the market.
Source: www.bbc.co.uk/news

Health and Safety
The health and safety of your employees and customers must be taken into consideration whilst you are running your business. Once you have five or more employees,you must have a written health and safety policy for your business. See chapter 21 on Health and Safety.

Hazardous Substances
It is your duty to minimise your employees and customers exposure to hazardous substances. Cleaning chemicals for example are generally safe but may be hazardous if used incorrectly. Always follow the manufacturers' instructions. Chemicals must not be mixed and must be left in their original containers. Staff should be clearly instructed and must be provided with protective clothing (e.g. rubber gloves) as specified by the manufacturer's instructions. Hazardous chemical data sheets should be available from your supplier and should be read by your staff.

Gas Safety
Defective gas fired appliances can emit carbon monoxide which is highly toxic. All gas fittings and flues must be maintained in a safe condition. An annual safety check must be carried out on each gas appliance by a "Gas Safe" registered engineer. The inspection report must be kept for two years.

Fire safety
Being a business owner,you must carry out a fire risk assessment and take safety precautions for your premises,which should cover the following:
- Controlling fire risks, preventing fire in the first place.
- Early warning in case of fire.
- Adequate escape routes.
- Knowledge of meeting points.
- Adequate training and information for staff.

For more information: www.gov.uk/workplace-fire-safety-your-responsibilities

Fire Risk Assessment
Performing a risk assessment is simple,but it must be updated on a regular basis.(See form in yearbook or 1 year diary)

Five steps you need to take:
- Identify potential fire hazards such as ignition sources and fuel
- Identify people at risk such as your staff,customers and visitors to your business premises.
- You must do a walk about your business to evaluate,remove or reduce hazards,and protect the occupants. Identify what could be done to control the hazard if the existing arrangements are insufficient.
- Staff must be aware of your fire safety measures,this requires regular staff training sessions to cover all aspects of fire safety within the premises. New members of staff should be made aware of your measures during induction.
- Keep the assessment under review and revise as and when necessary

Manual Handling

Repeated or incorrect lifting by staff of heavy or awkward loads can cause back injury. Manual handling should be minimised and you should ensure that staff have been trained to lift items safely.

First Aid and Accidents Adequate first aid provision for employees is essential. Provide a properly equipped first aid box and nominate an appointed person to take charge when someone is injured and to keep the first aid box fully stocked. All accidents at work must be recorded in an accident book. You should have **Public Liability Insurance**, which covers owner's liability to guests and others for injury, loss and damage on your premises. If you employ staff you must also have Employer's Liability Insurance as well. Type *Public Liability Insurance for food business* into google for a list of suppliers.

Suppliers and deliveries Do not buy any foods from off the back of a lorry, spend the required amount of money, think sensibly and source all your goods from a reputable, established and safe supplier. Use the KSR yearbook or 1 year diary to keep records of all the contact details of your supplier's. Your business reputation is in the hands of your suppliers, if their provenance is dodgy, when trouble hits the fan, your reputation and business may be destroyed. Stick to long established suppliers with a good reputation, google their name and see what the internet throws up, check out reviews, do your due diligence, as the buck stops with you. When food is delivered, do not just store it away, check the following:

- The packaging is not damaged.
- It is what you ordered.
- The brand you asked for has not been substituted for a different one, this is important as you will have to carry out due diligence to check the label for ingredients especially in relation to allergens in foods.
- Frozen and chilled food is delivered at the correct temperature, use a probe to make sure (chilled food should be below **5°C**, frozen foods should be at or below **-18°**) You get warm raw poultry delivered, you do not check it, cook it, serve it and give food poisoning to the wedding guests, your name will be mud, splashed all over the social networks and newspapers, long before the supplier's (who may never be mentioned).

If any deliveries are not fit for purpose, reject them immediately and contact the supplier to complain. Keep all invoices and receipts in a folder, in case you need them in the future. If you supply food yourself to anyone, keep complete and up to date records.

Product withdrawal and recalls Keep up to date as a supplier may have supplied your business, food that that is harmful to health, unfit to eat and it may have neighed instead of mooed. Withdrawn or recalled products must **not** be sold, but immediately removed from the shelves and not used in your kitchen. The food is not safe to eat as it may contain:

- Bacteria which may make people sick.
- There may have been a discovery of a physical contamination such as glass or metal.
- Mislabelling of food, a food may contain an allergen, such as nuts but does not appear on the label.

Make sure that your staff are aware of such products and know what to do. If in doubt: always ask your local Environmental health officer for advice.

Menu's Make sure that all your prices, service charges are clearly displayed. If you run a business where you sell high tea for £45 or more, your customers should not have a shock when they are handed the bill. Do not use terms like **'freshly made'** or **'home made'** in a misleading manner. Pictures and descriptions of food must be accurate, if you say that you are selling battered cod and chips, it better be cod and not cheaper whiting or catfish.

True life story

A chip shop owner who tried to make extra profit by passing off catfish as cod has instead found himself **£2,000** worse off. The owner was prosecuted after a tip-off to trading standards investigators by a customer who suspected the 'cod' was in fact a cheaper alternative. The shop in Bourton-on-the-Water sold Pangasius Hypophthalmus, a type of catfish masquerading as cod.
Source: www.dailymail.co.uk

If someone with an allergy asks about the ingredients in a particular item, give the customer the correct and precise information, do not guess. If your food contains genetically modified soya or maize then it should be clearly displayed. You can also display the calorie content of your dishes to help your customers make informed choices. This is not a legal requirement.

VAT To charge or not to charge? that is the question, it all depends on a number of factors:
- Are you selling hot or cold food?
- Do you need to register for VAT?
- Do you sell products like crisps, bottled water where VAT always applies?

The main regulation that, you need to take notice of is **VAT Notice 709/1: catering and take-away food / VAT Notice 701/14**

Starting your own business aka the roller coaster
A business plan is absolutely essential and has many functions from securing funding,to measuring the success of your business. Your plan must include details of your objectives,strategy,sales,marketing,social media profile and financial forecasts. Get an effective,memorable business name at the same time,explore logos and domain names for your website and availability of email addresses. Starting up any type of business requires capital – either through savings,a bank loan,grants,crowd funding or business angels. This task of securing investment is notoriously difficult,full of rejections and setbacks,but always remember the following words:

"Nothing in the world can take the place of persistence. Talent will not; nothing is more common than unsuccessful men with talent. Genius will not; unrewarded genius is almost a proverb. Education will not; the world is full of educated derelicts. Persistence and determination alone are omnipotent. The slogan Press On! has solved and always will solve the problems of the human race."-Calvin Coolidge the 30th President of the United States of America

Types of business entity
You must choose a legal structure for your business. This structure will define your legal responsibilities,such as:
- Paperwork you must fill in,to get started i.e. a limited company.
- Taxes you will have to manage and pay.
- Paying yourself from the profit your business makes.
- Your personal responsibilities if your business makes a loss.
-

There are **3** main types of legal structure:
- Sole trader- self employed individual.
- Partnership-with another person or even more people.
- Limited company.

You will need to choose your structure before you start,you can always change it after you have started.
You can register a private limited company online at www.gov.uk/register-a-company-online,It usually takes 24 hours and costs £15 (paid by debit or credit card or PayPal account).
You will need:
- The company's name and registered address
- Names and addresses of directors (and company secretary if you have one)
- Details of shareholders and share capital

Record keeping AKA red tape
Which ever business structure you choose ,you have now entered the world of endless paperwork:
- Income records
- Expenses
- Tax returns
- Employees details
- Bank statements
- Bills
- Work place pensions

The list never ends but you will have to get with the program,so update your records regularly,keep all receipts,pay your employees tax and national insurance contributions etc. You must keep records for at least 5 years. You will need to be aware of employee rights,minimum wages,equal opportunities,immigration status etc. Get an accounting and cash-flow system set up to maintain accurate,up-to-date information about cash-flow is absolutely essential from the start. You need to keep on top of all these and run your business successfully,if all this sounds like too much,then you might be better off working for someone else for a living and forget your outrageous dream of running your own successful food business.

Dig deeper
www.fpb.org/business-resources
www.gov.uk/starting-up-a-business/start-with-an-idea
www.gov.uk/alcohol-licensing
www.food.gov.uk/news-updates/news/food-alerts
www.hse.gov.uk/workers/employers

www.gov.uk/renting-business-property-tenant-responsibilities
www.gov.uk/rates-of-vat-on-different-goods-and-services
www.startups.co.uk/10-steps-to-starting-a-business
www.smallbusiness.co.uk/starting-a-business
www.startupdonut.co.uk
www.knowledge.hsbc.co.uk/business_plan
www.fsb.org.uk federation of small business
www.simplifythelaw.co.uk
www.lawdonut.co.uk
Equipment:
www.nisbets.co.uk
Amazon.co.uk
Ebay.co.uk

Food law inspections and your business

An inspector calls............

Food law inspections and your business

If you run a business that makes or prepares food,it will be inspected to make sure that you are following food law. The inspectors from your local council can enter your premises,without notice or warning and no, you cannot refuse them entry. They could be carrying out a routine inspection or visiting as a result of a complaint from a customer. It is a **criminal offence to obstruct** an authorised officer in the course of their duty.

How often are businesses inspected by Environmental Health Officers?

It depends on the risk associated with the particular business,which in turn depends on the kind of business,a restaurant will be visited **more often** than a corner shop selling pre-packed sandwiches. Inspection intervals can range from every six months to every five years. Some premises have never been inspected like canteens hidden away on large factory premises. The inspectors will check if your business produces food that is safe to eat. They will look at the kind of food you prepare and most importantly your food safety management system. The inspectors will also look at how you describe,the food you sell, for example on a menu or label, to make sure the description is not misleading.

What happens during an inspection?

You can expect the inspectors to show you their identification badges,when they arrive and be polite throughout the visit. They will always give you feedback on an inspection. This means they will tell you about any problems they have identified and advise you about how they can be avoided.
They will:
- Talk to staff about your quality control systems and practices.You would be using a safety management system,such as this book.
- Inspect all parts of your premises and equipment
- Talk to you about staff training,controlling hazards and temperature control.

The inspector may also request relevant documentation including recipes,food temperature records,food safety management systems,staff sickness records. Inspectors may also take samples and swabs as part of a routine inspection. If inspectors advise you to do something,they must tell you whether,you need to do it to **comply with the law**,or whether it is **good practice**. If you are asked to take any action as a result of the inspection,you must be given the reasons in writing. If the inspectors decide that you are breaking a law,they must tell you what that law is. The inspectors should give you a reasonable amount of time to make changes,except where there is an immediate risk to public health.

Due Diligence What would happen if a customer complained to their local environment health officer,they had eaten chicken liver pate at your restaurant and had food poisoning as a result? When the environmental health officer (EHO) arrives to investigate the allegation,are you able to show the following? :
- Full documentation of the delivery of the livers from the supplier-was the temperature taken?

14

- Do fridge temperature records exist?
- Was the cooking temperature recorded? did it reach the required **75ºC** ?
- What was the chilling temperature? Was it recorded?
- Is all your equipment working properly?
- Are all your records up to date?
- Did you do, everything to ensure that proper food safety procedures were followed?

Once the EHO sees that every aspect of the route from delivery to finished product was recorded and can see your past record keeping is impeccable and up to date, then the conclusion has to be that you have been diligent. Due diligence can be used as **defence** under food safety legislation, if an allegation of food poisoning is made against your business.
Inspectors taking action against your business
When they think it is necessary, inspectors can take 'enforcement action', to protect the public. For example, they can:
- Inspect your records
- Take samples and photographs of food
- Write to you informally, asking you to put right any problems
- Detain or seize suspect foods They can also serve you with a notice.

There are three main types of notice:
Hygiene improvement notice which sets out certain things that you must do to comply, if your business is breaking the law

True life story of a hygiene improvement notice
The owner of an Inn in Wilberfoss, appeared before Beverley Magistrates' Court and plead guilty to a total of 17 charges under regulation 19(1) of the Food Safety and Hygiene (England) Regulations 2013. Magistrates heard how inspectors from East Riding Council's food safety team visited the Inn in January 2014, following a complaint from a diner who had found dog excrement on the floor in the restaurant. The court heard that a number of inspections were carried out by officers who found that food in the kitchen, was mouldy and unfit for human consumption, a large quantity of food was being served to the public that had exceeded its **use by date**, raw meat was being prepared in **direct contact** with ready to eat salad items, posing a serious risk of **cross contamination**. Inspectors also found kitchen equipment was in an unhygienic condition due to disrepair and there was a failure to carry out **regular disinfection and cleaning** while food safety systems, monitoring checks and procedures were not in place and food handlers consistently demonstrated a lack of understanding of food safety issues. The owner also admitted failing to comply with a **hygiene improvement notice** requiring food hygiene training for his staff. In his defence, he said he had taken over the running of the business with no knowledge of running a kitchen or a restaurant but said he had worked in pubs and bars "with no problems before" and he had been "naive" and had been led to believe the chef had the right qualifications relating to food hygiene.
Source: www.pocklingtonpost.co.uk

Hygiene emergency prohibition notice which forbids the use of certain processes, premises or equipment and must be confirmed by a court.

True life story of a hygiene emergency prohibition notice
Harlow council gained an emergency prohibition order against an Indian takeaway, in Edinburgh Gate, following a routine food hygiene inspection by the environmental health team. The inspectors found:
- Active **cockroach infestation** noted in all areas of the premises including in food containers, live cockroaches were seen on food contact surfaces.
- **No hot water supply** to the wash hand basins and sinks in the food preparation areas
- A wash hand basin was not connected to the drain
- A risk of **cross contamination** in the refrigerator, raw foods were **stored directly above cooked food** and ready-to-eat food, presenting risks of **contamination from dripping juices** from the raw food onto the ready-to-eat food below
- Food preparation surfaces and equipment were **visibly dirty**, including chopping boards, oven and microwave
- Poor temperature control with **uncovered cooked chicken**, left cooling in the kitchen and in an oven encrusted with burnt on fat
- Staff had little **understanding of food hygiene and seemed unconcerned** over the conditions

The business was closed immediately by environmental health officers and was served with a hygiene emergency prohibition notice. An officer returned to the business to lay cockroach traps to monitor the infestation. Live cockroaches were still evidenced near the bin area. 3 days later an officer returned to check the premises and, although some cleaning and repairs had been carried out, found the traps that had been laid contained more than 100 cockroaches. As a result the business remained closed. The council made an application to Chelmsford Magistrates Court for an emergency prohibition order, which was granted. The order makes it an **offence for a food business to operate from the premises** until the council is satisfied, that it is hygienic and that no health risk exists. A local councillor said: "This is not action we take lightly but the hygiene offences and the numbers of cockroaches were so extreme we had to act due to the risk the premises posed to the public.
Source: www.harlowstar.co.uk

A convenience store in Walsall that was closed down by environmental health officers after they found **mouse droppings and partly eaten food** has been ordered to pay over £1,000 by the council. The store was issued with a

Hygiene Emergency Prohibition Notice, requiring its **immediate closure**, following a visit by environmental health officers in November 2014. As a result of the conditions found legal proceedings were instituted against the store owner. He plead guilty to all four charges and was subsequently fined **£170** for each of the offences totalling **£680** and also ordered to pay **£1,096.86** costs, with a victim surcharge of **£20**, a total of **£1,796.86**, by Walsall Magistrates. The convenience store was ordered to close its doors after mouse droppings were discovered throughout the shop, along with **gnawed food, including cakes.** Officers identified external and internal holes in the building providing rodents access to the shop.
Source: www.walsalladvertiser.co.uk

Remedial action notice forbids the use of certain processes, premises or equipment, or imposes conditions on how a process is carried out – it is similar to a hygiene emergency prohibition notice, but it does not need to be confirmed by a court.

True life story of a hygiene remedial action notice
A South Ayrshire takeaway was pulled up by inspectors for the second time in 7 months. Food hygiene inspectors found critical failings including staff who **did not know where the food thermometer was**. Over-use of food colours, which puts children at risk of hyperactivity and poor concentration, was found in the outlet's Pakora batters. Failure to do so would result in further action being taken against him by the local council. The inspectors found food being stored at **temperatures which could breed disease**. Food handlers were not wearing clean protective clothing and temperature monitoring records were not available. The raid comes after a similar operation in August 2014, when 25 stomach churning failings were found in the store:**filthy cloths and cheese slices were found alongside mould, dirty ovens and mops** on that visit.
Source:www.carrickherald.com

Prosecution Inspectors can also recommend a prosecution, in serious cases. If a prosecution is successful, the court may forbid you from using certain processes, premises or equipment, or you could be banned from from being a food business operator or from participating in the management of a food business. It could also lead to a fine or imprisonment.

True life story of a food safety prosecution
A Southport chip shop owner has been fined **£2,000** after he was found to have breached food health and safety rules. He plead guilty and was charged with two food hygiene offences at Sefton Magistrates Court relating to the condition of the chip shop. The prosecutor for Sefton Council, said the owner failed to keep the Chippy clean after inspectors visited the premises on August 28, 2014. They found the inside of the microwave that was used to heat up mushy peas and beans to be **coated in grime**, as well as the can opener being covered in **'brown grime'** and the top lid of the chest freezer in the potato preparation room to be covered in flour and 'not sufficiently cleaned or maintained.' Another charge said that the owner had failed to clean and maintain the flooring in the rear preparation room, the floor around the drain in the yard, the corridor leading to the servery and the flooring underneath the frying range. Inspectors also found **insufficient hand washing facilities**, with the bottom of the wash basin covered in grime and no soap or hand drying facilities available. The prosecution for Sefton Council noted a 'tennis-ball sized hole' in the wall which led out onto the yard, which inspectors said would be an access point for vermin into the kitchen and preparation areas - although there was no evidence to suggest there were any on the premises. **Cigarette butts** were found on the floor of a food storage area - indicating that people were smoking on the premises - where canned drinks and cans of beans and mushy peas were kept. The defence, for the owner noted that he had managed to clean up the chip shop to an acceptable standard within four days and has since spent approximately £10,000 for renovations for the shop, which are due to be completed soon. The owner was charged on two separate breaches of The Food Safety and Hygiene (England) 2013 Act. He was fined **£1,500** for each, reduced to **£1,000** for his early guilty plea. He was also made to pay **£1,048.83** in prosecution costs and a **£120** victim surcharge.
Source: www.southportvisiter.co.uk

Making an appeal Every local authority has a formal procedure to deal with complaints about its service. So if you do not agree with action taken by an inspector,you should contact the head of environmental health or trading standards services at your local authority,to see if the problem can be resolved by further discussion and negotiation. If you still disagree after that,you could approach your local councillor. If you think your local authority is applying the law in a different way from other authorities, you can seek advice from the Local Authorities Co-ordinators of Regulatory Services(LACORS), or the Scottish Food Co-ordinating Committee, either through your trade association or your local authority. You can appeal to the magistrates' court(or a Sheriff in Scotland) about a local authority's decision to issue a hygiene improvement notice or remedial notice, or not to lift a hygiene emergency prohibition order.
When there is a ban on an individual,this can **only be lifted by the court**. When inspectors impose a hygiene emergency prohibition notice on premises,a process, or a piece of equipment,they must apply to the court(or a Sheriff in Scotland)for confirmation within a specified period of time. Food that has been seized by an inspector can only be condemned as unfit for human consumption on the authority of a Justice of the Peace (or a Sheriff). You can attend the court hearing if you want to. If the court decides that premises have been shut without proper reason,or food has been wrongly seized or detained,you have a right to compensation.

True Life Stories

Mice droppings, cockroach infestations and cooking utensils caked in fat are just some of the horror stories behind the 58 Greater Manchester restaurants given zero ratings by food hygiene inspectors.
A bar and takeaway in Bolton town centre was slapped with a zero rating after inspectors found a rodent infestation in its store room and droppings on the kitchen floor.
A Salford takeaway in Pendlebury, was found to have a microwave encrusted with burnt food debris, utensils caked in fat and raw meat was found next to ready to eat food such as bread buns and coleslaw.
A Cheetham Hill takeaway, was voluntarily closed to undergo a deep clean after inspectors discovered a mouse and cockroach infestation.
Source: Manchester Evening news

A £45-a-night, three-star hotel, in Swindon, was prosecuted for a dozen separate breaches of food hygiene rules after inspectors found the kitchen in a shocking state. Kitchen surfaces were smeared with grease and **fridges were piled high with unwrapped raw meat**. **Juices from meat-filled containers almost spilling over on to other food**. Cooked food was being **stored with unwrapped raw chicken** and bacon, while preparation areas were soiled, smeared with grease and encrusted with old food. The hotel was also found to be selling **out-of-date** sandwiches. The hotel's director and manager were fined a total of **£20,100** and ordered to pay **£7,500** costs after admitting to all **12** breaches.
Source: Daily Mail

Food safety inspectors found bird excrement on a rafter from which hams were hanging, when they visited a restaurant in York city centre. At York Magistrates Court today, the restaurant's owner admitted **9** offences and was fined **£14,626** including costs.
Source: The Press

Three people have appeared in court after inspectors allegedly found a host of food hygiene failings at a Croydon town centre restaurant including **mouse droppings in a bag of rice**. The restaurant was accused of **36** breaches of food hygiene regulations namely: **16** counts of failing to comply with a food hygiene improvement notice, one of breaching duty to an employee, seven of contravening health and safety regulations, two of failing to prevent someone from smoking on the premises, and ten of failing to comply with Food Hygiene (England) Regulations 2006.
Source: Croydon Advertiser

A tale of one restaurant
Then: September 2011
Doctor's cafe dream to transform landmark pub
A town centre pub is being reinvented as a cosmopolitan cafe bar and restaurant. Run-down Arkwright's Wheel, in North End, had a reputation as the watering hole of choice for Croydon's undesireables. But now the pub is being given a makeover by the new owner, who hopes to transform it into a landmark. The retired doctor and property developer, who paid £1.7 million for the pub – £100,000 more than the asking price – said:"Many people have told me that I am taking a big gamble. But I paid more than expected because it is in a prime position and could be one of the nicest buildings in Croydon. I think the new direction will go down well here because Croydon is a diverse place and combination of pub and restaurant offers something different." He admits,that he and his business partner are losing up to £10,000 a month while the venue, now called **Babylon Inn**, is refurbished. Half of the building will continue to be a pub,while the other will be a buffet and grill serving Middle Eastern and Oriental food in the evening and breakfast and coffee in the morning. The extensive renovation is due to be finished within six weeks, with the restaurant to open at the end of September.
Source:Croydon Advertiser

Now:October 2015
Owner of filthy rodent and cockroach-infested restaurant admits breaking hygiene rules
A retired doctor who owned a filthy rodent and cockroach-infested restaurant in south London has admitted a litany of safety and hygiene offences. Food inspectors found mouse dropping in a bag of rice. He paid £1.7 million in 2011 to buy the former pub in a "prime position" in Croydon town centre and dreamt of making it "one of the nicest buildings" in the area. But despite his grand ambitions,the all-you-can-eat buffet Babylon Inn was kept in an **"appalling" state and overrun by pests.** The 2 owners were convicted at Camberwell Green Magistrates' Court. A series of inspections by council officers revealed **infestations of cockroaches,rats and mice,dodgy electrics,mouldy ceilings and a failure to follow basic health and hygiene practices,including protecting food against contamination and properly cleaning kitchen equipment.** Speaking about one visit in 2013, a council spokesman said: **"There was an ongoing active infestation of rodents,with mouse and rat droppings found throughout the kitchen and food storage areas in the basement,and a live mouse was seen in the small food preparation area in the basement."** The doctor who lived above the premises,pleaded guilty to **21** offences including **breaches of food safety and hygiene,health and safety and smoking regulations.** The other owner of was convicted of **19** offences after a trial.Councillor Mark Watson,Croydon's cabinet member for communities, safety and justice,said: "Such appalling conditions in an establishment serving food to members of the public, on what is arguably Croydon's busiest shopping street, is completely unacceptable. "The full weight of the law should be brought down on those responsible, while others serving the public should take heed and realise that such flagrant disregard of the food safety laws will not be tolerated in Croydon."The pair will be sentenced in November. Babylon Inn is no longer operating. Source:The Standard
Conclusion:Laziness is the food business proprietors greatest enemy

Food Hygiene Ratings

"The aim of the Food Hygiene Rating Scheme is to drive businesses to improve their standards and, as a result,reduce the number of cases of food poisoning in the UK. The scheme wants to help consumers judge for themselves whether the hygiene standards of a food outlet are good enough. That is why it is a legal requirement for businesses to clearly display their ratings." - Ali Thomas Leader of Neath Port Talbot Council

Food Hygiene Ratings

Your business will be given a hygiene rating following a planned inspection by a food safety officer from your local authority. Your hygiene rating depends on the standards of hygiene found **at the time** of the inspection. Your business can be given one of six ratings. These are on a scale from '**0**' at the bottom, which means that urgent improvement is necessary, to '**5**' at the top, which means that the business was found to have 'very good' hygiene standards at the times of the visit.

Calculating your rating
The rating you are given will depend on the following:
- How hygienically the food is handled – how it is prepared, cooked, cooled, stored, and what measures are taken to prevent food being contaminated with bacteria.
- The condition of the structure of your premises, including cleanliness,layout,lighting, ventilation, equipment and other facilities.
- How you manage and record what you do,to make sure food is safe. The environmental health officer will explain to you if there are any improvements needed, what they are and how you can achieve a higher rating.

All food business should be able to reach the top rating. The food hygiene rating is not a guide to food quality, for that,you need the Michelin guide.
Advertising good hygiene to your customers
You can tell consumers how good your hygiene standards are by putting your rating sticker in the window or your

certificate on display – you will be given these by your local authority. This means that your consumers can easily see your food hygiene rating when they visit your business. Your customers will also be able to look up your hygiene rating online at www.food.gov.uk/ratings. I am sure you will not be displaying your 0 rating sticker,that you deserved to get.

Making sure the scheme is fair You can appeal if you think your hygiene rating is wrong or unfair – in other words it does not fairly reflect the hygiene standards found at **the time** of your inspection. You must lodge an appeal with your local authority within 14 days of being told what your hygiene rating is. You have a '**right to reply**' if you've improved hygiene standards since your inspection, or if there were unusual circumstances at the time of the inspection and you want to explain this to your customers. You should submit this to your local authority and it will be published with your hygiene rating at www.food.gov.uk/ratings. You can ask for another visit to get a new rating, if you make the improvements to hygiene standards that the local authority food safety officer told you about at your last planned inspection. You will need to do this in writing and supply evidence of the improvements made. The food safety officer will re-assess hygiene standards and give you a new rating – this could go up but it could stay the same or it could go down. You can find out more about these safeguards at www.food.gov.uk/ratings.
Find out about your competitors
Each business is given a hygiene rating following its inspection by a food safety officer from the local authority. Is there a food business near you with better hygiene standards? Find out at food.gov.uk/ratings

True life story
Two takeaways in Port Talbot have been fined for failing to display a valid food hygiene rating sticker in the proper way. Neath Port Talbot Council environmental health officers issued fixed penalty notices of £200 to a Chinese takeaway at Victoria Road in Port Talbot on April 16 and another to a Tandoori Indian Takeaway, at Commercial Road, Taibach on January 23. Leader of Neath Port Talbot Council Ali Thomas said: "The issuing of these fixed penalty notices demonstrates how serious the council is about promoting food hygiene, and ensuring fairness amongst all food businesses.
Source:www.southwales-eveningpost.co.uk

More information:
www.food.gov.uk/business-industry/caterers/hygieneratings

Immigration law and your staff

Obtain
Check
Copy

Immigration law and your staff You **must check all** your employee's immigration employment status. There are document checks you **must** carry out to find out, if a person has both the right to work in the UK and the right to carry out the type of work you are offering.

Remember three key words when conducting a right to work check:

Obtain- Obtain original versions of one or more acceptable documents.
Check- Check the document's validity in the presence of the holder
Copy- Make and retain a clear copy, and record the date the check was made.

Make sure the correct checks are carried out, that is your responsibility, It is the Home Offices job to catch people working illegally. It is not recommended that you participate in any sting against people working for you.

List of documents to prove eligibility to work in the UK
The following list of documents proves an potential employee eligibility to work in the UK when provided on their own:
- **Passport** showing that they are a **British citizen**, or have a **right of abode** in the UK.
- Document showing that they are a **national** of a European Economic Area (EEA) country or Switzerland. This must be a national passport or identity card.
- **Residence permit** issued by the UK to them as a national from an EEA country or Switzerland.
- Passport or other document issued by the Home Office which has an endorsement stating they have a current **right of residence** in the UK as the family member of a national from an EEA country or Switzerland.
- Passport or other travel document endorsed to show they can stay **indefinitely** in the UK, or that they have no

20

time limit on their stay.
- Passport or other travel document **endorsed** to show that they can stay in the UK, and that this endorsement allows them to do the type of work you are offering, if they do not hold a work permit.
- **Application Registration Card** issued by the Home Office to an asylum-seeker stating that they are permitted to take employment.

If they are able to supply one of the documents listed above, then there is **no requirement to provide any other documentation** to prove their eligibility to work in the UK.

Other ways to prove eligibility

If the potential employee does **not hold** any of the documents shown in the list above, they can prove their eligibility by providing **one** of the combinations of documents shown below.

Please note that the combinations will only prove their eligibility to work if they provide them within the same combination – they will not be able to prove their eligibility by providing one document from the first combination with a document from the second combination.

Combination 1

- A document that shows **National Insurance** number and name - an example of this would be a recent P45, P60, National Insurance Card or a letter from a government agency.
- In addition to this document, plus one of the following:
- **Full birth certificate** issued in the UK which includes the names of the holder's parents.
- **Birth certificate** issued in the Channel Islands, the Isle of Man or Ireland.
- **Certificate of registration** or **naturalization** stating they are a British citizen.
- Letter issued by the Home Office which indicates that they can stay **indefinitely** in the UK, or have no time limit on staying in the UK.
- **Immigration Status Document** issued by the Home Office with an endorsement indicating that they can stay indefinitely in the UK, or that they have no time limit on their stay.
- Letter issued by the Home Office which indicates that they **can stay** in the UK and which states that they are also allowed to do the type of work you are offering.

Combination 2

They must provide a **work permit**, or other document showing approval to take employment that has been issued by Work Permits UK. Along with a document issued by Work Permits UK, they must also provide one of the following documents:

- **Passport** or other travel document endorsed to show that they are **able to stay** in the UK and can take employment.
- **Letter issued by the Home Office** confirming that they are able to stay in the UK and can take employment.

You may need to ask the Home Office to check an employee's or potential employee's immigration status if:
- They cannot show you their documents, e.g. they have an outstanding appeal or application with the Home Office.
- They have an Application Registration Card
- They have a Certificate of Application

You will need to get the employee or potential employee's permission to make the check and also the following details:
- Full name
- Date of birth
- Nationality
- Job title
- Hours worked per week
- Home address
- Home Office reference number or case ID

You need to see their original **Application Registration Card** or a **Certificate of Application** if this is what you are checking. You will also need to provide your:
- Business name
- Business type
- Business contact information

Penalties for employing illegal workers

You can be fined up to **£20,000** per person for employing illegal workers. Illegal workers include:
- Students with expired visas, or students working more hours than they are allowed to.
- People who work on a visitor's visa.
- People who have entered the UK illegally

If you are caught employing an illegal worker You will get a 'referral notice' to let you know that:

- Your case is being considered
- You may get a fine (also known as a civil penalty) of up to **£20,000** for each illegal worker
- You will not have to pay a fine, if you can show a valid reason for employing an illegal worker.
- You will be sent a 'civil penalty notice' if you are found liable and you will have 28 days to respond.

The penalty notice will give you your payment options and tell you what do next. It will also tell you how to appeal if you want to. Your business's details may be published by Immigration Enforcement as a warning to other businesses not to employ illegal workers.

You can be sent to jail for up to 2 years and receive an unlimited fine if you are found to have 'knowingly employed' an illegal worker.

Get help and advice

Contact the Home Office if you need more help with making sure your employees are entitled to work in the UK.

Employers helpline
0300 123 4699

Monday to Thursday, 9am to 5pm
Friday, 9am to 4:30pm

True Life Stories

Takeaways, off-licences and restaurants were slapped with **£108,000** in fines after being found employing dozens of illegal immigrants. The businesses have paid out thousands after the Home Office discovered their employee's had entered the UK illegally or overstayed their visas. Ten men were deported from the UK after they were found working in the businesses in Merseyside.
Source: Liverpool echo.co.uk

Three illegal immigrants from China have been caught at a Sunderland takeaway following a raid by Home Office staff. The takeaway has been served with a notice warning that a civil penalty of up to **£20,000** per illegal worker arrested will be imposed unless proof is provided that the correct right-to-work checks were carried out, such as seeing a Home Office document or passport.
Source: Sunderland echo

A restaurant on Lea Bridge road, Leyton which employed illegal immigrants on two separate occasions has had its **licence to sell alcohol revoked**. The decision was made by the licensing committee at Waltham Forest Council after an application from the Met Police. People working in the country without permission were found to be employed at the restaurant.
Source: Waltam Forest Guardian

More information:
www.gov.uk/employee-immigration-employment-status

Food handlers fitness to work

Sick note/Fit note/Self certification

Food handlers: fitness to work This section helps managers and staff to prevent the spread of infection by advising which illnesses and symptoms staff should report and what managers need to do in response.

What to watch out for: Diarrhoea and/or vomiting are the main symptoms of illnesses that can be transmitted through food. Staff handling food or working in a food handling area **must** report these symptoms to management immediately. Managers must exclude staff with these symptoms from working with or around open food, normally for **48** hours from when symptoms stop naturally. It is possible to be infected but not have symptoms so staff who handle food and who work around open food must always: **Wash and dry their hands before handling food, or surfaces likely to come into contact with food, especially after going to the toilet.**

The Law The law requires that in all food businesses:
"No person suffering from, or being a carrier of a disease likely to be transmitted through food or afflicted, for example, with infected wounds, skin infections, sores or diarrhoea is to be permitted to handle food or enter any food-handling area in any capacity, if there is any likelihood of direct or indirect contamination."
"Any person so affected and employed in a food business and who is likely to come into contact with food is to report immediately the illness or symptoms, and if possible their causes, to their manager or supervisor."
Food handlers who are ill, can also contaminate food by spreading bacteria for example, to surfaces that food will come into contact with, e.g. work tops and food packaging before it is used. They can also contaminate other surfaces such as door handles which can then contaminate the hands of people who handle food directly for example.

Infections

Bacteria The risk of bacteria spreading is highest when the infected person has diarrhoea and vomiting because there are lots of bacteria in vomit and stools. Vomit or liquid stools are more likely to contaminate hands and other things. Food may be contaminated with harmful bacteria, either directly by an infected food handler, or indirectly through contact with a food contact surface that has been contaminated by an infected food handler. Foods which will not be cooked before being eaten like salads are of greater risk because cooking is a process that would kill many of the bacteria present. (see chapter on **foods that require extra care**) People can also have infections without showing any symptoms.
- This can be because they are long-term carriers of infectious bacteria
- They just have very mild infections
- They are only in the early stages of illness and symptoms are not yet apparent.

This is one reason why it is important for food handlers to always follow the hand-washing guidance in the first chapter

Viruses Some viruses can be transmitted through food and spread in much the same way as bacteria,with similar effects. The main differences are that viruses **cannot multiply on food but can survive on food for long periods**. Viruses can spread via contaminated hands and some can also spread through the air, especially when an infected person vomits.

Symptoms of gastrointestinal infection
The most common symptoms of an infection are:
- Diarrhoea.
- Vomiting.
- Stomach cramps or pain.
- Nausea
- Fever.

What to do Managers must exclude any person from food handling duties and food handling areas,if they have an infection of the stomach or gut. The length of the exclusion is usually **48** hours from when their symptoms stop. It follows that the affected member of staff could be given work elsewhere in the premises,such as warehouse operations where only packaged food is handled,although they should practice good personal hygiene,especially **washing their hands thoroughly** after using the toilet,so as not to spread the infection to other workers. On the other hand,excluding infected food handlers from the entire premises is also an option,as this will remove the potential risk of contamination of food via other staff who may use the same facilities,e.g. toilets or canteens,as the infected person.

Penalising staff for being ill, for example by not paying them when they are excluded from work, could lead to them working whilst ill and may lead to food safety problems

Anyone working in a food business who is likely to come into contact with food poisoning must report to their manager immediately,if they have an illness that is likely to be passed on through food or if they have certain medical conditions that could lead to this. They should immediately seek to exclude themselves from food handling duties and areas if they develop such symptoms at work.

It is also a legal requirement for every person working in a food handling area to maintain a high degree of **personal cleanliness** and to wear suitable, clean and, where necessary, protective clothing. The key action is to: **Ensure you wash and dry your hands thoroughly with soap and warm water before working with or around food, especially after using the toilet.** Your hands can also come into contact with bacteria and viruses from other sources,such as from other people,raw foods or even yourself.

It is also very important to wash your hands after:
- Handling raw food,such as meat and poultry.
- Changing a dressing or touching open wounds.
- Any contact with other people's faeces or vomit, e.g. changing nappies,working in a care home.
- Touching animals / pets.
- Handling waste and touching bins.
- Cleaning.
- Breaks.

As we have said before: **Wash your hands!,Wash your hands!,Wash your hands!,Wash your hands!**,is that crystal? Also dry your hands thoroughly because wet hands spread bacteria more easily. Just imagine someone shaking their wet hands over a salad or sandwich.

Anti-bacterial gels Anti-bacterial gels only work on clean hands,they can kill bacteria not the norovirus. Gels will not work properly on dirty or oily hands. So you need to wash your hands properly before you use the anti-bacterial gel.

Gloves Gloves are not a substitute for good personal hygiene and hand washing. Gloves can become contaminated with bacteria in much the same way as hands can, even when they are new, and should be kept clean and sanitised in a similar way to your hands.

Contaminated food Managers should assess the risk to food safety of anyone found to have been working with or around food whilst ill. The likely consumers of the food could also be a factor if known,e.g. producing food for young children,or the elderly will require a high degree of precaution. If any unsafe food is still on the market,the food business operator must notify their local authority immediately.

Returning to work after an illness In most cases of infection, bacteria and viruses can still be found in someone's faeces after symptoms stop. It is therefore important that managers continue to exclude food handlers for a period of time after this. **48** hours is the recommended length of time. This is counted from the time that symptoms(mainly diarrhoea) stop of their own accord or from the end of any treatment of the symptoms with medicine such as anti-diarrhoea drugs (if they are used). For example,symptoms end from 6pm Tuesday,so the person can safely resume work from 6pm Thursday. You can count from the time of the first normal stool,if you are not sure when symptoms ended. Extra care should be taken over personal hygiene practices on return to work though, especially hand washing. Managers should interview all staff on return to work to assure themselves that they have received all the relevant information.

Infections
The following is a list of infections(not exhaustive) that if contracted by a member of staff, they need to be excluded from food production and handling duties.

- Salmonella (except Salmonella Typhi and Salmonella Paratyphi A, B or C)
- Campylobacter
- Vibrio (except Vibrio cholerae O1 and O139)
- Yersinia
- Bacillus
- Staphylococcus aureus
- Clostridium perfringens
- Protozoa, e.g. Cryptosporidium, Giardia lamblia (except Entamoeba histolytica)
- Shigella sonnei (but not Shigella dysenteriae, flexneri, and boydii)
- Worms (except Thread worm and Taenia solium)
- Salmonella Typhi and Salmonella Paratyphi A, B or C (Enteric fever)
- Verocytotoxin-producing Escherichia coli (E. coli)
- Norovirus
- Hepatitis A

Infected or injured skin
Damaged skin or sores caused by injury or disease, e.g. boils and septic cuts, can become infected with bacteria such as Staphylococcus aureus, which can cause food poisoning. Symptoms of infection include scaling, weeping or discharge from lesions. It is usually acceptable to continue working with food as long as the infected area is completely covered, e.g. by use of a distinctively coloured, waterproof dressing.

Instances when not to exclude staff due to non-infective causes

Infections are not the only cause of diarrhoea, vomiting and exclusion is not required where there is good evidence of a non-infective cause. For example:

- Morning sickness during pregnancy.
- Inflammation of the bowel including diverticulitis, ulcerative colitis, and Crohn's disease.
- Irritable bowel syndrome.
- Cancer of the bowel.
- Malabsorption syndromes (e.g. coeliac disease and cystic fibrosis).
- Dietary indiscretion consuming too much alcohol, spicy food, or taking part in a man versus food competition.
- Chest and respiratory diseases
- However, it is quite common for people to have bacteria such as **Staphylococcus aureus** in their nasal passages, mouth or throat, which can contaminate food if they sneeze or cough on it. If food handlers are unable to work without coughing or sneezing on open food, then they should work elsewhere until their symptoms subsides.
- People with blood-borne infections, such as hepatitis B, hepatitis C and HIV, are not a hazard to food safety as long as they are otherwise in good health.
- Other people, a food handler who has someone in their household suffering from diarrhoea and vomiting does not always require exclusion, but they should inform their manager and take extra precautions, such as more stringent personal hygiene practices. If they start to feel unwell at work they should report this immediately to their manager or supervisor. Cases that may require exclusion are where the contact has enteric fever, **E. coli O157** and **Norovirus**

The list above is not exhaustive.

For staff members
Your Responsibilities when you may be or are ill.
You can pass on illnesses when you work with or around food, to prevent this:

- Tell the manager immediately if you are ill, as bacteria or viruses can come from you.
- Wash and dry your hands with soap and warm water, especially after going to the toilet.
- You can affect the safety of food when working with or around food.
- Your hands and clothes can spread harmful bacteria or viruses to food or surfaces that will come into contact with food.

Tell the manager if you have:

- Diarrhoea or vomiting.
- Stomach pain, nausea, fever or jaundice.
- Someone living with you with diarrhoea or vomiting.
- Infected skin, nose or throat.

If you fall ill at work: remove yourself from the food handling area and tell your manager what has happened.

Returning to work after an illness:

- Take extra care when washing your hands.
- Wash and dry your hands thoroughly with soap and warm water before working with any food, especially after going to the toilet.

Managers and business owners Your Responsibilities when your staff may be or are ill.

The law requires you to **exclude** anyone from work, if they have an infection that can be passed on through food and there is any likelihood of them contaminating food directly or indirectly. This would apply to people employed as food handlers or to other staff working in areas where open food is handled. Diarrhoea and/or vomiting are the main symptoms of infections that can be transmitted through food. Other symptoms can include stomach cramps or pain, nausea and fever. Skin infections are also a problem. This is because some infections, mainly from bacteria and viruses, can spread in faeces and vomit. This can contaminate infected persons' hands when they have diarrhoea or vomiting. Vomiting can also spread it directly. If an infected person contaminates food or food contact surfaces, in many cases the infection can spread to people who eat the food.

Action to take Ensure that all staff handling food and anyone working in a food handling area knows to report the symptoms of infection and if they have close contact with someone with these symptoms. Exclude staff with these symptoms from food production and handling duties

Returning to work The exclusion period is normally 48 hours from when symptoms stop naturally. When excluded staff return to work ensure that they take extra hygiene precautions, particularly hand washing. People can have infections without symptoms so it is important that you ensure that everyone washes and dries their hands regularly at work, especially after using the toilet. Managers should assess the risk to food safety of anyone found to have been working with or around food whilst infectious and take the appropriate action to ensure that unsafe food is not released to the public, which can create a nightmare for your business. If you are not sure what to do in any situation, you can seek advice from the environmental health officer at your local council. You can find a copy of the return to work form in the yearbook and 1 year diary, which you can photocopy, to use as required.

More information:
www.rcplondon.ac.uk/resources/infected-food-handlers-guideline

Food allergen rules and your business

"Are we allergic to food or are we increasingly allergic to what has been done with it"
-Robyn O'Brien

Advice on new food allergen rules

Allergen information for loose foods Since 13th December 2014 the EU Food Information for Consumers regulation (EU FIC) came into force. These new regulations are backed up by the UK Food Information Regulations 2014(FIR). What is a "**loose**" food ? - All foods that are not pre-packed. These new regulations affect you,if you run a cafe,take away,restaurant,bakery and cater in schools, hospitals, staff canteens, home caterers and care homes. This also includes foods that you wrap yourself, such as sandwiches, cakes, pies and foods from deli's,even food sold on websites and delivered to homes,basically:wherever **food is prepared for and sold to members of the public.** Allergic reactions can cause severe illness and in some cases death. As there are no cures for food allergies,so those who suffer, have to stay away from foods that cause them.

You,the food producer must tell your customers,if there are any allergens in the food that you make and sell. These new rules, mean that you must provide precise allergen information about the food that you make and serve. Oh,you are also legally responsible for the information that you provide. Better get it right! Nearly 2 million people in the UK,who suffer from allergic reactions to certain foods,are relying on you. The new EU law has listed **14** allergens which must be identified in a meal. Since December 2014,you must provide details of the allergic ingredients in the food that you sell.

The 14 Allergens
1 Celery. Celery stalks,leaves,seeds, celeriac. **Found**: Celery salt(obviously!) salads,stock cubes,and some meat products - **this list is not exhaustive**. Celery powder is naturally rich in nitrate,without nitrite, cured meats like ham and salami will not have their unique taste and appearance

2 Cereals. containing gluten- Wheat,rye,barley and oats. **Found:** Flour,batter,baking powder,bread,cakes,couscous,pasta,pastry,sauces,soups, foods dusted with flour - **this list is not exhaustive.**

3 Crustaceans. Crabs,lobster,prawns and scampi. **Found:** in shrimp paste, rice dishes, soups- **this list is not exhaustive.**

4 Eggs. Found: Cakes,mayonnaise,pasta,quiche,sauces, some meat products, meringues,pancakes egg glaze on pastry,bread & butter pudding – **this list is not exhaustive**.

5 Fish. Found: Fish sauces,relishes,fish fingers,stock cubes,paella,Worcestershire sauce – **this list is not exhaustive**.

6 Lupin: Garden flower which produces seeds,which can be crushed in flour. **Found:** Baked goods such as pastries,pies,pancakes and in pasta – this list is not exhaustive. Not commonly used in the UK. Mainly used in mainland Europe in bread,cakes and pastries.Lupin flour is high in protein,up to 40%.

7 Milk: Butter,cheese,cream,yogurt and milk powders. **Found:** Soups,sauces,foods glazed with milk – **this list is not**

exhaustive.

8 Molluscs: Mussels,land snails,squid and whelks. **Found:** Oyster stews,fish stew, paella– **this list is not exhaustive**.

9 Mustard: Liquid mustard,powder and seeds. **Found:** Breads,curries,marinades,soups,relishes,salad dressings – **this list is not exhaustive**.

10 Nuts,also know as tree nuts as they are harvested from trees. Almonds,Hazelnuts,Walnuts,Cashew nuts,Pecan nuts,Brazil nuts,Pistachio nuts,Macadamia nuts. **Found:** Breads,cakes,biscuits,crackers,ice cream,cakes,marzipan,nut oils,sauces curries and stir fries– **this list is not exhaustive**.

11 Peanuts,also know as groundnuts as they are grown in soil. **Found:** Biscuits,cakes,curries,sauces like satay,desserts,oils and flour– **this list is not exhaustive**.

12 Sesame seeds. Found: Bread,burger buns,houmous,tahini and sesame oil used in stir-fry – **this list is not exhaustive**.

13 Soya: Bean curd, edamame beans,flour,tofu. **Found:** Soya milk, ice cream,meat products,sauces and vegetarian products – **this list is not exhaustive**.

14 Sulphur dioxide: This a sulfite which prevents foods from becoming discoloured, and has antimicrobial properties to discourage the growth of bacteria. Additionally, they can soften dough or bleach foods. **Found:**Dried fruits soft drinks and alcoholic beverages such as wine and cider– **this list is not exhaustive**.

Consequences of not complying with the law
Giving inaccurate or incomplete information about allergens in foods that you sell,would be a breach of the regulation. If **incorrect information** is given in relation to more than one of the products that you sell, then this could result in multiple charges being laid against your business. Any business found guilty of any offences is liable to a fine of up to **£5,000** per charge. Ignorantia juris non excusat or "Ignorance of the law excuses no one". Now you know about the **14,** You cannot say **you don't know what allergens are in the food you serve.** You also cannot say that your food **may** contain an allergen. No! you have to get your stuff together,be precise and tell your customers which allergens are in your food.
Recording Information
- Please list the type of allergen used in a particular dish in the **chef's allergen menu matrix** section in the 1 year diary or 2016 Yearbook.
- Always read the ingredients label on products that you use.
- Make sure you and your staff do not **deviate** from the standard recipe ingredients.
- Keep a copy of all ingredient information on labels.
- All containers must have up to date ingredient information labels.
- Check your deliveries,to make sure that you are getting what you asked for. Also check that your chosen brand has not been swapped for another.

Providing information to your customers:
FOOD ALLERGIES and INTOLERANCES
Please speak to our staff about the ingredients in your meal, when making your order.
 Thank you.
Make sure that all your staff are trained,and fully informed, so that when a customers asks; **what is in the food**? they must be able to provide the information by telling the customer or giving them an up to date recipe or ingredients card. (cards are handy if your staff have communication issues). The allergen information can also be on the menu,chalkboard or your website. Takeaways will need to put that information on the flyers,they drop through people's letterboxes.
Finally
- If someone asks you, what ingredients are in a dish? **DO NOT GUESS OR LIE**. Always check and provide the correct information.
- Make sure your recipes cards,ingredient sheets,allergen control sheets are up to date and easy to access by staff and members of the public.
- If you change menu,recipes or ingredients,you need to update all the relevant sheets.
- As always be careful of cross contamination via chopping boards,utensils and thoroughly clean work surfaces and equipment,and wash hands before making food for someone with an allergy.

If in doubt; **ASK THE CUSTOMER,**they also have a responsibility to ask for information and relay their dietary needs to the person providing the food.

True life story
THE owner of a string of award-winning Indian restaurants has appeared in court,charged with the manslaughter of a

customer who ate a takeaway curry. He was accused of the manslaughter of a father who suffered a fatal allergic reaction to peanuts after eating a takeaway from the restaurant, in Easingwold. The customer suffered a severe anaphylactic reaction and died after buying a curry from the restaurant in January 2014. The owner was charged with manslaughter by gross negligence over the tragedy. It was the first time a caterer has faced such a charge. The head of the Crown Prosecution Service complex casework unit, said following a 14-month investigation, it had concluded there was sufficient evidence, and that it was in the public interest to charge, the proprietor, who was also been charged with perverting the course of justice and an employment offence under the Immigration, Asylum and Nationality Act 2006.

Source: www.thenorthernecho.co.uk

True life story

A celebrity chef's restaurant chain was fined after staff served the wrong kind of pasta to a woman with **coeliac disease**, which means she is unable to digest **gluten**. The customer suffered an allergic reaction after being served regular pasta. She was violently sick for around five hours after the meal in Portsmouth. A court heard how she told staff **three times** she needed a **gluten-free tagliatelle** but in a misunderstanding, she was unknowingly served regular pasta. The restaurant admitted that she had been served wheat pasta. Environmental health officers from the local council, visited the premises, revealing 'lamentable failures' over food allergy issues. Eventually the restaurant plead guilty to selling food **not of the nature, substance or quality demanded by a purchaser.** The offence is a breach of the Food Safety Act 1990. The chain had failed to exercise due diligence and take all appropriate precautions that meals were served as requested. The waitress thought the customer had ordered a vegetarian, rather than gluten-free and vegetarian option. A judge today fined the eaterie **£8,000** for breaching food safety laws and ordered it to pay **£9,212** costs as well. The customer also reached an out of court settlement with the restaurant chain.

Source: www.dailymail.co.uk

Foods that need extra care

Handle with care

Foods that need extra care

Some foods need to be treated with extra care to make sure they are safe to eat.

Ready-to-eat food Ready-to-eat food will not be cooked or reheated before serving. These include salads,cold meats,smoked fish,desserts, sandwiches,cheese and food that you have cooked in advance to serve cold.
To protect food from harmful bacteria:
- Keep ready-to-eat food completely separate from raw meat,poultry,fish,eggs and unwashed vegetables. Use the appropriate chopping board for the right job.
- Make sure work surfaces,chopping boards,knives etc.are clean and disinfected if you have prepared raw food.
- Keep ready-to-eat food covered at all times during preparation and storage

Why? This is to prevent harmful bacteria getting onto the food. This is especially important for ready-to-eat food because it will not be cooked or reheated before serving.

When preparing fruit, vegetables and salad ingredients:
- Peel,trim,or remove the outer parts,as appropriate
- Wash them thoroughly by rubbing vigorously in a bowl of clean water
- Wash the cleanest ones first, **wash your hands before and after** handling fruit and vegetables. If you have prepared vegetables that have dirt or soil on the outside, clean and then disinfect chopping boards and work surfaces before preparing other food.

Why? The dirt on vegetables and salad ingredients can contain harmful bacteria. Peeling and washing helps to remove the dirt and bacteria.

Make sure ready-to-eat food stored in the fridge and cold display units must be kept between **1°C** to **4°C**.
Why? If these types of food are not kept cold enough, harmful bacteria could grow.

Do not use ready-to-eat food after the '**use by**' date, if there is one.
Why? You should never use food that has passed its '**use by**' date because it might not be safe to eat.

Slicing cooked meats-follow the manufacturers instructions and do not handle meat with bare hands, **wear disposable gloves or use tongs.**
Why? Meat slicers need careful cleaning and disinfecting to prevent dirt building up and to stop harmful bacteria growing, in particular on the slicing blade. Hands can easily spread harmful bacteria onto food.
You should not use the same machinery and equipment,such as vacuum packing

30

machines,slicers and mincers for both raw and ready-to-eat food. This is because,it is not possible to clean equipment thoroughly enough to be sure all harmful bacteria have been removed. Any bacteria could then spread to ready-to-eat food. If you are preparing both raw and ready-to-eat food, you should make sure where possible this is done in separate clean and disinfected areas. If this is not possible, surface and utensils used must be thoroughly cleaned and then disinfected between tasks. Make sure staff **wash their hands thoroughly between tasks**,especially when working with raw and ready-to-eat food. This stops bacteria being spread onto foods, surfaces and equipment.

Trouble If you think that a food delivery has not been handled safely,reject the delivery.
- If ready-to-eat vegetables,fruit or salad ingredients have not been washed properly,wash them properly and clean any work surfaces etc.they have touched.
- If ready-to-eat food has been prepared on a work surface or with a knife that has been used for raw meat,poultry, fish, eggs or unwashed fruit and vegetables,**throw the food away**.
- If ready-to-eat food has not been chilled safely,**throw the food away**.

If you do not think a supplier handles food safely,consider changing to a new supplier. After all it is your business and reputation at risk, if something goes wrong.

Eggs

Cook eggs and foods containing eggs thoroughly until they are **steaming hot.**
Why? Eggs can contain harmful bacteria. If you cook them thoroughly this kills any bacteria. Use pasteurised egg (not ordinary eggs) in any food that will not be cooked, or only lightly cooked e.g. mayonnaise and mousse.
Why? Pasteurisation also kills bacteria,which is why pasteurised egg is the safest option.

Do not use eggs after the '**best before**' date. Make sure you rotate stock and use the oldest eggs first.

Why? After this date, there is a greater chance of harmful bacteria growing in the eggs

Rice When you have cooked rice, make sure you keep it hot until serving or chill it down as quickly as possible and then keep it in the fridge. The problems tend to arise as rice is cooked in large batches,cooled too slowly,then not reheated to **75ºC**.
Why? Rice can contain spores of **Bacillus cereus** that may not be killed by cooking or reheating.
You can make rice chill down more quickly by dividing it into smaller portions, spreading it out on a clean tray, or running it under cold water (make sure the water is clean and drinking quality).
Why? If cooked rice is left at room temperature, spores can multiply and produce toxins that cause food poisoning. Reheating will not get rid of these.

Pulses Follow the instructions on the packaging on how to soak and cook dried pulses, such as beans.

Why? Pulses can contain natural toxins that could make people ill unless, they are destroyed by the proper method of soaking and cooking. Save yourself the hassle,get tinned pulses,they will have been soaked and cooked already.

Shellfish Make sure you buy shellfish from a reputable supplier
Why? If you do not use a reputable supplier,you cannot be confident that shellfish have been caught and handled safely. Crabs, crayfish and lobster should be prepared by someone with specialist knowledge.
Why? Some parts of these shellfish cannot be eaten and some are even poisonous,so it is important to know how to remove these parts safely.

Shellfish such as prawns and scallops will change in colour and texture when they are cooked. For example,prawns turn from blue-grey to pink and scallops become milky white and firm. Langoustines (also called scampi or Dublin Bay prawns) are pink when raw and the flesh becomes firm and pink-white when they are cooked. If you use ready-cooked (pink)prawns, serve them cold or reheat them until they are piping hot all the way through.
Before cooking mussels and clams,throw away any with open or damaged shells.

Why? If the shell is damaged or open before cooking, the shellfish might not be safe to eat.

To check that a mussel or clam is cooked, make sure the shell is open and that the mussel or clam has shrunk inside the shell. If the shell has not opened during cooking,throw it away.

Fish

Make sure you buy fish from a reputable supplier. If you buy fresh fish make sure you store it between **0°C** to **4°C**. If you buy frozen fish then keep it frozen at **-18°** until you are ready to use it.
Why? Certain types of fish, such as mackerel, tuna, anchovies and herrings, can cause food poisoning if not kept at the correct temperature.

Raw chicken: Do not wash raw chicken

Do not wash raw chicken, as splashing water from washing chicken can spread campylobacter. Campylobacter is the most common cause of food poisoning in the UK. Campylobacter can be spread easily and just a few bacteria could cause illness. This could come from raw or undercooked chicken, or from contamination due to washing raw chicken. Campylobacter infections typically cause abdominal pain and diarrhoea for between two and five days.

Cover raw chicken and store at the bottom of the fridge so juices cannot drip on to other foods and contaminate them.

Thoroughly wash and clean all utensils, chopping boards and surfaces used to prepare raw chicken. Wash hands thoroughly with soap and warm water, after handling raw chicken. This helps stop the spread of campylobacter by avoiding cross contamination.

Make sure chicken is steaming hot all the way through before serving. Cut in to the thickest part of the meat and check that it is steaming hot with no pink meat and that the juices run clear. Thorough cooking to **75°C** will kill any campylobacter present.

Good Food Good Business for caterers

The catering business is not for the faint hearted

Good Food Good Business for caterers This section is recommended for **ALL** kitchens to comply with food hygiene regulations including hotels,bed & breakfast, restaurants, schools,colleges, hospitals,care homes,takeaways,cafes,mobile catering vans,home caterers,church and community halls-**wherever food is prepared for members of the public.**

What you need to know before you start working with food
- Always wash your hands,before touching food,after going to the toilet,after every break,after emptying bins,after touching mobile phones,cash tills,door handles.
- Wear clean clothes
- Wear an apron,if handling unwrapped food
- Tell your manager if you have vomiting or diarrhoea.
- Take off your watch and jewellery
- Wear a hat or hairnet
- No smoking,eating or drinking in the food preparation area
- Avoid touching your face,coughing or sneezing over food
- Cover cuts with a blue waterproof plasters
- Wash your hands thoroughly with soap under warm running water. Make sure your finger nails are cut short,as dirt can gather under finger nails.
- Dry your hands thoroughly on a disposable towel. Turn off the tap with the towel in your hand and then throw the towel away.

Cross-contamination Cross-contamination is one of the most common causes of food poisoning. It happens when harmful bacteria are spread onto food from other food,surfaces,hands or equipment. These harmful bacteria often come from raw meat/poultry,fish,eggs and unwashed vegetables. So it is especially important to handle these foods carefully.
Other sources of bacteria can include:
- Staff
- Pests
- Equipment
- Cloths
- Dirt or soil
- Physical contamination such as broken glass or pieces of packaging

- Chemical contamination such as cleaning products or pest control chemicals.

Personal hygiene Staff must follow good personal hygiene practices to help prevent bacteria from spreading to food. This is probably the most important point,when it comes to providing food to members of the public. Staff should always wash their hands thoroughly before preparing food.
Why? hand washing is one of the best ways to prevent harmful bacteria from spreading.

Make sure all staff are trained to wash their hands PROPERLY before preparing food.

All staff should wear clean clothes when working with food. They should change into clean work clothes before starting work and must not wear these clothes outside food preparation areas.

Why? Clothes can bring dirt and bacteria into food preparation areas. Wearing clean clothes helps to prevent this.

Staff should change aprons after working with raw food e.g. meat, poultry, eggs or unwashed vegetables,because they are working hard in kitchen,all the food preparation does not need to show up on their uniform.

Why? Aprons help to stop dirt and bacteria from getting onto work clothes and they can be removed easily for washing,or thrown away if they are disposable.

Staff must wear a hat or hairnet when preparing food.

Why? If hair is not tied back or covered,it is more likely to fall into food and staff are more likely to touch their hair.

Staff should not wear watches or jewellery when preparing food (except a wedding band).

Why? Watches and jewellery can collect and spread dirt and harmful bacteria, or fall in the food.

Staff should not smoke,drink,eat or chew gum while handling food. Staff should also avoid touching their face or nose,or coughing and sneezing.

Why? All of these lead to staff touching their face or mouth. Harmful bacteria can be spread from someone's face or mouth to their hands and then onto food.

Kitchen Cloths- These are one of the top causes of cross-contamination in the kitchen. A study from the University of Arizona found just that 89 percent of dishcloths and kitchen sponges had some kind of bacteria. Simply washing the towels in the sink with some detergent will not be effective because bacteria like E.coli and Salmonella are resilient. A dirty kitchen cloth would actually be spreading hundreds of thousands of bacteria around your kitchen.
Source: Bacterial Occurrence in Kitchen Hand Towels. Food Protection Trends. 2014.

Do not muck about,just use kitchen roll,for cleaning,wiping surfaces,hands etc. Use and dispose. For holding hot items,do NOT use paper towels or kitchen roll,use oven cloths or oven gloves.

Separating foods

Delivery and collection Plan delivery times so that, if possible, raw foods arrive at different times to other foods. If you collect food from shops yourself, make sure it is kept at the correct temperature when you collect it and transport it at the proper temperature (1°C to 5°C, if chilled). Make sure that raw and ready-to-eat food are kept separate. Unload deliveries in a clean, separate area, remove outer packaging and throw it away, before you do this, make a note of any cooking instructions or ingredient information, if you need to.

Why? This helps to prevent harmful bacteria spreading from raw meat/poultry to other foods. This will also prevent dirty outer packaging or leaks from deliveries from spreading bacteria in your kitchen, Packaging can also harbour pests.

Storage Best practice:

- Store raw and ready-to-eat food in separate fridges, freezers and display units.
- If you have to store foods in the same unit, store raw meat, poultry, fish and eggs below ready-to-eat food.
- Unwashed fruit and vegetables should also be kept separate from ready-to-eat food and above raw meat.
- Cover cooked foods and other ready-to-eat food always.

Why? This helps to prevent harmful bacteria spreading from raw food to ready-to-eat food.

Defrosting Keep foods that are defrosting in the fridge, in a covered container, below ready-to-eat food, or in a separate area of the kitchen away from other foods.

Why? When foods are defrosting, the liquid that comes out can contain harmful bacteria, which could spread to other foods.

Preparation Prepare raw meat/poultry and other foods, such as salads in different areas. If this is not possible, separate by preparing them at different times and clean and then disinfect thoroughly between tasks.

Chopping boards Never use the same chopping board or knives for preparing raw meat/poultry and for ready-to-eat food. Use the colour coded chopping board system. This system is widely accepted in all catering establishments and kitchens at home. The colour coding system is not a legal requirement but good practice to avoid cross contamination.

> **Colour coded chopping boards**
>
> **RED FOR RAW MEAT**
> **BLUE FOR RAW FISH**
> **YELLOW FOR COOKED MEAT**
> **GREEN FOR FRUIT AND SALAD**
> **BROWN FOR VEGETABLES**
> **WHITE FOR BAKERY AND DAIRY**

Why? This helps to prevent harmful bacteria spreading from one food to another. Harmful bacteria from raw meat and poultry can spread from chopping boards and knives to other foods. Colour coding allows your staff to identify quickly which chopping boards, knives and utensils should be used for a specific task. Always use separate equipment, such as vacuum packers, slicers or mincers, for raw and ready-to-eat food.

Why? It is not possible to remove harmful bacteria **completely** from complex machinery and these bacteria can spread to food.

Physical and chemical contamination Always follow the manufacturer's instructions on how to use and store cleaning chemicals. Store cleaning chemicals separately from food and make sure they are clearly labelled.
Why? This is to prevent these chemicals getting into food.

Keep food covered.

Why? This helps to stop things falling into the food.

Make sure you control pests effectively.

Why? This is to stop insects, droppings etc. getting into food, as well as preventing the spread of bacteria.

Make sure that any chemicals you use to control pests are used and stored in the correct way and clearly labelled.

Why? This is to prevent chemicals getting into food and drink.

Always clear and clean as you go and take care to throw away packaging, string etc as soon as you remove it.

Why? Keeping surfaces clear and clean will help prevent chemicals and objects getting into food, as well as preventing the spread of bacteria.

Repair or replace any equipment or utensils that are damaged or have loose parts.

Why? Loose parts may get into food by accident.

It is a good idea to have a rule of no glass in the kitchen.

Why? This helps to prevent broken glass getting into food.

Hand washing
Wash your hands thoroughly with soap under warm running water. Dry your hands thoroughly on a disposable towel. Turn off the tap with the towel and then throw the towel away.

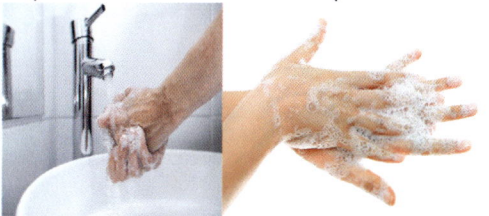

When to wash your hands:

When entering the kitchen e.g. after a break or going to the toilet.

After touching or emptying bins.

After any cleaning.

After touching a cut or changing a dressing.

After touching items such as phones, light switches, door handles and cash registers.

Disposable gloves

If you use disposable gloves in your business, they should never be used as an alternative to proper hand washing. If using disposable gloves make sure you:

- Wash your hands thoroughly before putting them on and after taking them off.
- Always change them regularly, especially when handling raw and ready-to-eat food.
- Throw them away after use or if damaged.
- Hygienic hand rubs and gels can be useful when used as an additional precaution, but should never be used as replacement for effective hand washing.

Cleaning effectively
Effective cleaning is essential to get rid of harmful bacteria and stop them spreading. Cleaning needs to be carried out in two stages. **First** use a cleaning product to remove visible dirt from surfaces and equipment, and rinse. Then **disinfect** them using the correct dilution and contact time for the disinfectant, after rinse with fresh clean water.

Why? Chemical disinfectants only work, if surfaces have been thoroughly cleaned first, to remove grease and other dirt.

Follow the manufacturer's COSHH safety data sheets, on how to use cleaning chemicals. Disinfectants merchandisers should meet BS EN(British Standard European Norm) standards.

Why? This is important to make sure that chemicals work effectively.

Wash work surfaces and equipment thoroughly between tasks, follow the manufacturer's cleaning instructions if there are any. Wash and then disinfect surfaces after preparing raw food.

Why? This will help prevent dirt and bacteria spreading onto other foods from the surface or equipment.

High-priority cleaning
Regularly wash/wipe and disinfect all the items **people touch frequently**, such as work surfaces, sinks, taps, door handles, switches, can openers, cash registers, telephones and scales.

Why? This will help prevent dirt and bacteria being spread to people's hands and then to food or other areas.

Wash and disinfect fridges regularly, preferably at a time when they do not contain much food. Transfer food to another fridge or a safe cold area and keep it covered.

Why? To clean a fridge thoroughly, you should take out all the food and keep it cold somewhere else. If food is left out at room temperature, bacteria could grow.

Pay special attention to how often you clean pieces of equipment that have moving parts.

Why? These can be more difficult to clean, but it is important to clean equipment properly to stop bacteria and dirt building up.

Ideally use a dishwasher. If you do not have dishwasher, wash plates, equipment etc in hot soapy water using diluted detergent. Remove grease and any food and dirt. Then immerse them in very hot, clean water. Leave to air dry, or dry with disposable kitchen roll.

Why? Dishwashers wash items thoroughly at a high temperature so this is a good way to clean equipment and kill bacteria.

Items that do not touch food are not as high a priority but they should still be cleaned effectively. Examples include dry storage areas and floors.

Why? This prevents dirt and bacteria building up in the kitchen.

For equipment or areas that are hard to clean, you may wish to employ a contract cleaner to carry out a deep clean.

Why? Contract cleaners have special equipment and experience of more difficult cleaning.

They can also provide specific canopy, structural and extraction cleaning to help ensure meticulous standards are maintained, and compliance with legislation is upheld. They can also deep clean all kitchen equipment such as brat pans, ovens, deep fat fryers, ovens, ducts and filters. Following each visit, they can provide a full report which will include the sanitation specification check list, risk assessment, method statements and COSHH (Control of Substances Hazardous to Health Regulations) details about all the products used.

Clear and clean as you go. Keeping your kitchen clear and clean makes it safer. Take off outer packaging from food and throw it away before you bring food into the kitchen or storeroom.

Why? Outer packaging could have touched dirty floors etc. when it has been stored or transported before.

Take extra care with how you throw away packaging and food waste from raw food. If packaging from raw food touches work surfaces, make sure you wash and then disinfect them afterwards.

Why? Packaging and food waste from these foods are more likely to spread harmful bacteria to food and surfaces.

Keep your kitchen free from clutter and rubbish. Clear away dirty kitchen equipment as soon as possible.

Why? Work surfaces are easier to keep clean when they are not cluttered. It is also important to clear away used equipment to prevent bacteria spreading from it to surfaces or food.

Keep sinks clear and clean them regularly.

Why? This stops dirt building up and helps prevent bacteria from spreading.

Wash or wipe away spills as soon as they happen. Clean and then disinfect work surfaces after wiping up spills from raw food.

Why? This stops dirt building up and helps prevent bacteria from spreading.

Wash work surfaces thoroughly between tasks. Use kitchen roll to clean work surfaces before preparing ready-to-eat food.

Why? This will help prevent dirt and bacteria spreading onto other foods from the surface.

Pest control
Effective pest control is essential to keep pests out of your premises and prevent them from spreading harmful bacteria.

Check your premises regularly for signs of pests.

Why? Pests carry harmful bacteria

Check deliveries thoroughly for signs of pests. Do not accept delivery if it shows signs of pests such as gnawed packaging or insects, e.g. beetles.

Why? Pests could come into your premises in a delivery

Keep external areas tidy and free from weeds. Make sure bins have close-fitting lids and are easy to clean.

Why? Weeds and rubbish can attract pests and provide them with food and shelter.

Type of pests

Rats and mice

Rats and mice are most active between dusk and dawn,it is often easier to spot signs of a problem,rather than an actual rodent.

Signs: Small footprints in dust, droppings,holes in walls and doors,nests, gnawed goods or packaging, grease or smear marks,urine odour and stains on food packaging

Flies and flying insects e.g. moths

Signs: Bodies of insects,live insects,webbing,nests and maggots.

Cockroaches

Signs: Eggs and egg cases, moulted 'skins',the insects themselves, droppings

Ants

Signs: Small piles of sand or soil,the insects themselves,flying ants on hot days

Birds

Signs: Feathers,droppings,nests,noise,the birds themselves

Beetles and weevils

Signs: Moving insects,particularly in dry food,small maggots

What to do if things go wrong
If you see signs of a pest infestation,call a pest contractor immediately. Write the contact details for your pest contractor on the contacts list in the diary or yearbook,also make your pest checks more frequent. If you think any equipment,surfaces or utensils have been touched by pests,they should be washed,disinfected and dried to stop harmful bacteria from spreading.

Improve staff training on recognizing signs of pests and encourage them to report problems immediately. If you think food has been touched by pests in any way, throw it away immediately. Make sure food or dirty plates etc. are left not out at night – these are a source of food for pests. The kitchen must be sparkling clean after a shift.

Never let pest control bait/chemicals, including sprays, come into contact with food, packaging, equipment or surfaces, because they are likely to be poisonous to people

Maintenance
Effective maintenance is essential to allow you to clean properly and keep pests out. Repair structural damage as soon as it happens e.g. damp/chipped plaster,broken tiles,holes in walls or windows.

Why? Structural damage can make your premises harder to clean and can attract pests.

Check extractor fans and filters regularly to make sure they are working properly and are free from grease and dirt.

Why? This is to make sure the fans and filters can do their job properly.

Replace chopping boards that are scratched,pitted or scored.

Why? Dirt and harmful bacteria can collect in any areas where the board is not smooth.

Repair or replace any equipment or utensils that are damaged or have loose parts.

Why? Dirt and harmful bacteria can collect in damaged equipment/utensils. Loose parts may fall into food.

Throw away any cracked or chipped dishes and other tableware

Why? Dirt and harmful bacteria can collect in cracks or chips.

Make sure your cooking,hot holding and chilling equipment is well maintained and working properly.

Why? If it does not work properly,food may not be kept safe.

Temperature probes should be checked regularly to make sure their readings are accurate.

Why? If your probe is not accurate,then it will not give a reliable measure of whether food is at a safe temperature.

Chilling
Chilling food properly helps to stop harmful bacteria from growing. Some foods need to be kept chilled to keep them safe,such as sandwiches,chilled meals,diary products,desserts and food with a **'use by'** date and food that says **'keep refrigerated'** on the label. This section tells you about storing and displaying chilled food,chilling down hot food,freezing and defrosting.

Chilled storage and displaying chilled food
Harmful bacteria can grow in food that is not chilled properly. It is recommended that fridges and chilled display equipment should be set at **8°C** or below. The requirement applies to the temperature of the food,not the surrounding air. This is to make sure that chilled food is kept at the

appropriate temperature . This is a **legal requirement** in England,Wales and Northern Ireland and recommended in Scotland.

Cold food storage: 8°C degrees or below- **a legal requirement.**
Cold food storage: 5°C degrees or below- **best practice**
You **must** check the temperature of your chilling equipment at least once a day starting with your opening checks. To ensure that your chilling equipment is working effectively,you can use a temperature probe to check food as a one-off test to prove that your equipment keeps food at a safe temperature.

Certain foods need to be kept chilled at 5°C degrees or below to keep them safe e.g.

- Food with a **'use by'** date
- Food that says **'keep refrigerated'** on the label
- Food you have cooked and will not serve immediately
- Ready-to-eat food such as sandwiches,salads and desserts

Why? If these types of food are not kept cold enough harmful bacteria could grow.

Make sure that you **do not use** food after its **'use by'** date. For dishes you have prepared or cooked,it is a good idea to use stickers to keep track of when food should be used or thrown away.

Why? Food with **'use by'** dates,cooked dishes and other ready-to-eat food have a limited shelf life. If you keep them too long,they might not be safe to eat.

Follow the manufacturer's instructions on how to use fridges and chilled display equipment

Why? It is important to use equipment properly to make sure food is kept cold enough.

- Make sure the unit is switched on and well chilled before you put food in it.
- Only put on display as much food as you think you will need.
- Display food for the shortest time possible.

Why? It is important to keep chilled food cold while it is on display to prevent harmful bacteria from growing in the food.

Chilled food must be kept at 8°C or below, except for certain exceptions

When you display cold food, e.g. on a buffet, you should use suitable chilled display equipment to keep it at 8°C or below. If this is not possible,you can display food out of chilled storage for up to 4 hours,but you can only do this once. Food that has not been used within 4 hours can be put back in the fridge and kept at 8°C or below until it is used. If it has been out for more than 4 hours,it should be thrown away. If you do take food out of chilled storage to display it,remember **not to mix** new food with the food that is already on display. This could lead to the older food being left out for too long.

Trouble If your fridge or display equipment breaks down,use other equipment,or move the food to a cold area. If you cannot do this, or you do not know how long the equipment has been broken down,contact the environmental health service at your local authority for advice.

If food on display has not been kept chilled for more than 4 hours,throw it away. Better safe than sorry.

Chilling down hot food Harmful bacteria can grow in food that is not chilled down as quickly as possible. If you have cooked food that you will not serve immediately,chill it down as quickly as possible and then put it in the fridge.

Why? Harmful bacteria can grow in food that is left to chill slowly.

Avoid cooking large quantities of food in advance, unless you need to.

Why? Large quantities of food are more difficult to chill down quickly, especially solid food.

Options for chilling down food
You can use one or more of these methods.
Divide food into smaller portions.

Why? Smaller amounts of food chill down more quickly.

Cut joints of meat into smaller pieces.

Why? Smaller pieces of meat will cool more quickly.

Cover pans of hot food and move them to a colder area e.g. a storage room, or stand them in cold water. You can also add ice to the cold water to speed up chilling.

Why? This will make the contents of the pans chill more quickly.

Stir food regularly while it is chilling down.

Why? Stirring helps food chill more evenly.

Cover hot food and move it to a colder area.

Why? Food will chill more quickly in a colder place.

Spread food out on a tray e.g. rice.

Why? Spreading the food out will help it cool more quickly

Use a blast chiller or shock freezer to chill down food.

Why? A blast chiller or shock freezer is specially designed to chill down hot foods quickly and safely. Chilled air is blown at a high velocity for rapid cooling. Cooked foods at **70°C** are cooled down to below **3°C** quickly. Shock freezers act in the same manner and bring cooked food down rapidly to **-18°C**. Blast chillers allow the core temperature of food items to move through the danger zone faster than they would in a standard commercial refrigerator or freezer.
If food has not been chilled down safely, re-cook it, if appropriate, or throw it away.

Review your chilling methods to make sure they are working properly. If appropriate, try out different methods and choose the one that best meets your needs. Train staff on this safe method.
- Make sure you always allow enough time and make portions small enough.
- Improve staff supervision.

If you chill down lots of hot food in your business, you may wish to consider using a blast chiller or shock freezer.

Defrosting
Harmful bacteria can grow in food that is not defrosted properly. Food should be thoroughly defrosted before cooking (unless the manufacturer's instructions tell you to *cook from frozen*). If food is still frozen or partially frozen, it will take longer to cook. The outside of the food could be cooked, but the centre might not be, which means it could contain harmful bacteria. Think chicken or turkey.

Options for defrosting food
Ideally, plan ahead to leave enough time and space to defrost small amounts of food in the fridge.
Why? Putting food in the fridge will keep it at a safe temperature while it is defrosting.
If you cannot defrost food in the fridge, you could put it in a container and then place it under cold running water.
DO NOT USE HOT WATER.
Why? Cold water will help to speed up defrosting without allowing the outside of the food to get too warm.
If you use the sink to defrost some foods, make sure the sink is clean and empty. The sink should be cleaned properly and then disinfected after being used for defrosting.
Why? Cold water will help speed up defrosting or you could defrost food in the microwave on the 'defrost' setting. Nothing is faster than a microwave or safer.
If necessary you can defrost food at room temperature. Follow the manufacturer's defrosting instructions. Food should be left out at room temperature for the shortest time possible. **Ideally, defrost all foods in the fridge.**
Why? Foods will defrost quite quickly at room temperature, but harmful bacteria could grow in food if it gets too warm while defrosting. When you think food has defrosted, it is important to check to make sure that it has defrosted fully, with no ice crystals, on any part of the food. Cook the food to **75°C** within 12 hours.

Freezing
It is important to take care when freezing food and handling frozen food safely, so put frozen food in the freezer as soon as it is delivered.

Why? If frozen food starts to defrost, harmful bacteria could grow.
If you are freezing fresh food, freeze it as soon as it has been delivered or prepared. Freeze hot food as soon as it has been properly chilled down.
Why? The longer you wait before freezing food, the greater the chance of harmful bacteria growing.
Divide food into smaller portions and put it in containers or freezer bags before freezing.

Why? Smaller portions will freeze more quickly. The centre of larger portions takes longer to freeze,allowing harmful bacteria to grow. Using containers and freezer bags prevents cross-contamination. When you freeze food,make a note (e.g. on a sticker) of the date/month/year,it is frozen and the date when it is removed for defrosting. Once food has been defrosted you should use it immediately.

If you find that your freezer is not working properly,you should do the following things:

- Food that is still frozen(hard and icy) should be moved to an alternative freezer straight away. If there is no alternative freezer,defrost food in the fridge.
- Food that has begun to defrost(starting to get soft and/or with liquid coming out of it) should be moved to a fridge to continue defrosting.
- Fully defrosted food(soft and warm) should be cooked, if appropriate e.g. raw meat and poultry must cooked,until it is piping hot all the way through. After cooking,use the food immediately,chill or freeze it safely straight away. If this is not possible, throw it away.
- Food that has to be kept frozen e.g. ice cream cannot be re-frozen once it has started to defrost. You will have to use it immediately or throw it away.

Cooking

A good chef has to be a manager, a businessman and a great cook. To marry all three together is sometimes difficult
- Wolfgang Puck

Cooking It is essential to cook food properly to kill any harmful bacteria. If it is not cooked properly, it might not be safe for your customers to eat. It is also very important to handle ready-to-eat food carefully, to protect it from harmful bacteria. Read chapter 7, **Foods that need extra care**. This is because it will not be cooked or reheated before serving. This section includes information on cooking safely, reheating and hot holding.
Where appropriate **always follow** the manufacturer's cooking instructions for food products.

Why? The manufacturer has tried and tested safe cooking methods specifically for its products.

Preheat equipment such as ovens and grills before putting in food.

Why? if you use equipment before it has preheated, food will take longer to cook. This means that recommended cooking times in recipes or manufacturers instructions might not be long enough.

Do not let raw food touch or drip onto cooked food e.g. when adding food to the grill/barbecue. Never use the same utensils, plates or containers for raw and cooked or ready-to-eat food.

Why? Raw food can carry harmful bacteria, which could spread onto cooked food and stop it being safe.

If you serve beef, rare, whole cuts such as steaks and whole joints only, make sure all of the outside surfaces are fully cooked, e.g. by sealing in a pan.

Why? This will kill harmful bacteria on the outside of the meat. Pork and rolled joints should not be served rare. To check a pork joint or rolled meat joint, insert a skewer into the centre until juices run out. The juices should not have any pink or red in them. Even better still use a temperature probe to make sure the food reaches the optimal cooking temperature of **75°** degrees. Liver and offal must be cooked all the way through. When preparing dishes, such as liver pâté or parfait, the liver should be cooked until there is no pink meat left.

Why? Harmful bacteria can be found in the centre of liver as well as the outside.

Turn meat, pork, poultry, fish, processed meat products, such as sausages, burgers, kebabs and chicken fillets to ensure they are evenly cooked.

Why? This helps it cook more evenly, ensuring the meat is steaming hot all the way through with no pink or red in the centre. Tuna steaks can be served 'rare' as long as they have been fully seared on the outside. To check fish is cooked through, cut into the centre of fish, or by the bone if there is one, to check that the colour and texture has changed.

Make sure liquid dishes, e.g. soups and sauces, are simmering and stir them frequently.

Why? This is to make sure the food is hot enough to kill bacteria. Stirring will help make sure the food is the same temperature all the way through. Check that liquid dishes bubble rapidly when you stir them.

Reheating

It is very important to reheat food properly to kill harmful bacteria that may have grown since the food was cooked. Remember, **reheating means cooking again to 75°C**, not just warming up. Always reheat food until it is steaming hot all the way through (you should only do this once). Do not put food into hot holding without reheating it properly first.

Make sure you use equipment that reheats/cooks food effectively and follow the equipment manufacturer's instructions
Why? If equipment is not suitable for reheating, or is not used properly, the food might not get hot enough to kill bacteria. Preheat equipment such as ovens and grills before reheating.

Why? Food will take longer to reheat, if you use equipment before it has preheated. This means that recommended reheating times in recipes or manufacturer's instructions might not be long enough. If you are reheating food in a microwave, follow the product manufacturer's instructions, including advice on standing and stirring.
Why? The manufacturer has tested its instructions to make sure that products will be properly reheated. Standing and stirring are part of the process of cooking/reheating in a microwave and help make sure the food is the same temperature all the way through.

If you use a microwave to reheat food that you have cooked yourself, it is a good idea to stir it at stages while reheating.
Why? When food is microwaved, it can be very hot at the edges and still be cold in the centre, stirring helps to prevent this. Serve reheated food immediately, unless it is going straight into hot holding.
Why? If food is not served immediately, the temperature will drop and harmful bacteria could grow.

Hot holding

It is very important to keep food hot until serving to prevent harmful bacteria from growing. If you need to keep food hot before serving, you should use suitable equipment

Why? It is difficult to hold food at a consistent, safe temperature without suitable equipment, use a temperature probe to make sure the food is kept at **63°C** or above.
Bain marie, soup kettle and chafing dishes. Make sure food is piping hot and steaming all the way through, from the moment it is cooked, to the moment it is served.
Preheat hot holding equipment before you put any food in it.
Why? Putting food into cold equipment means it might not be kept hot enough to stop harmful bacteria growing.

Food must be cooked thoroughly and steaming hot, before it is decanted into any hot holding vessels

Why? Hot holding equipment is for hot holding only. **It should not be used to cook or reheat food.**

Trouble If a dish is not hot enough at any point during hot holding: Reheat it until it is steaming hot and put back into hot holding (you should only do this once) or chill down the food safely (see the 'Chilling down hot food' safe method in the Chilling section) and reheat it later before serving.
If you cannot do either of these things, throw the food away.

Good Food Good Business For retailers

A nation of shopkeepers..............

Safer Food Better Business for Retailers
This section is for retail shops that sell food that needs to be chilled,in order for it to be safe to sell.
This includes:
- Pre-packed items that need to be kept chilled for example,ham,milk and dairy products.
- Sandwiches.
- Bake off pasties,sausage rolls
- Cooking a limited range of items,such as eggs,bacon and sausages,rotisserie chicken.

You must be able to show that all the food you sell and prepare is safe to eat and keep written records to prove it. (Use the Kitchen Safety record 1 Year diary or 2016 Yearbook to record the information),essentially you need to keep a daily diary to record temperatures,cleaning routines and when things go wrong. You do not need to record tons of information, just fill in the daily sheet.

The Law
It is a legal requirement to keep full details of the food you brought,who from,the quantity and date, best set up a filing system to keep all the invoices and receipts,so no more getting those cheap chicken breasts from the market stall,paying cash.

Be safe and get it right
Repair structural damage on your premises,immediately – pests can enter thorough broken windows. Repair and if necessary replace broken and faulty equipment- broken parts can get mixed into food.If equipment is not working properly,get it fixed immediately. Make sure that all your staff have been trained to use and operate catering equipment properly.

All freezers,fridges and chilling units must be in proper working order- it they are not,it could possibly mean that food is not being stored at the appropriate temperatures.

Chilled foods,for reasons of safety and quality,are designed to be stored at refrigeration temperatures at or below **5°C** for cold foods and below, **-18°C** in the case of frozen foods.

Poor or inadequate temperature control of food is one of the main causes of food poisoning,you should employ temperature probes to double check the readings on chilled and frozen displays.

Physical contamination
Use cereal dispensers,cake domes,food covers,foil and cling film to keep unwrapped food covered from objects falling into the food,pests and people sneezing,coughing and touching the food.

44

Chemicals Store them according to manufacturers instructions,keep them stored away and make sure are clearly labelled. Use manufacturers COSHH sheets as guides to use them safely.
Equipment
Make sure all equipment is working properly,used properly and regularly maintained. Electrical equipment should be PAT tested annually.

Hand washing Make sure that all staff who work with food,wash their hands properly before preparing food. Harmful bacteria can spread from hands to equipment,to work surfaces,to food,into customers which can cause food poisoning. Make sure your premises has warm water,soap and paper towels.

Staff training Use the staff training sheets in the 1 Year diary or 2016 yearbook to record all the training your staff have received. You need to show them what to do,question them afterwards,ask them to repeat the action,so you know that they know how to complete the task properly. If they require more training then get it done. When the member of staff is competent and comfortable in carrying out the task,get them to sign the training sheets in the diaries.

Customer feedback

Listen to all complaints carefully,take them seriously,they may just reveal an underlying issue with a product or a particular procedure in your business. You may resolve the issue,and end up creating a better selling product or service. On the other hand you may just have an unhappy customer. Since you are in the food business,it may be a food poisoning complaint,you will need to investigate carefully,check all your safe methods and you may even need to contact your suppliers and even your local environmental health officer.

Handling unhappy customers Remain calm. When a customer starts yelling or being otherwise rude, there is absolutely nothing to be gained by responding in a similar manner.
Do not take it personally
Pay attention
Listen actively
Show empathy with the customers complaint
Apologize sincerely
Propose a solution
Take a few minutes on your own afterwards to calm down

Stock control Carry out a stock check before placing an order.
Order the stock you need,to last until the next delivery.
Make sure all stock delivered is within its **'use by'** date and has been delivered at the correct temperature. Use your probe to make sure and record the information in your diary.
Make sure the packaging is not damaged,blown,ensure all seals are intact,the stock must be in perfect condition,if not reject it. Record any issues in the your diary.
Older dated stock must always be sold first.
Rotate stock and throw away stock that has passed its **'use by'** date.
Record stock checks in the diary.
Use price reductions to clear out old stock that is nearing its used by date.
Eggs; must be sold at least seven days before 'best before' date,it is illegal to sell eggs after this date.

Cooking If you prepare and sell sandwiches,cooked meats,cream cakes,desserts and salads,it is very important to handle such food safely as they will not be reheated to kill off any harmful bacteria. Make sure all your surfaces,and equipment are clean before you start work.
Prepared sandwiches should ideally be sold in packaging,this will enable you to put dates on them.
Cooked meats should be sliced onto wrapping and handled with tongs. Slicers should be cleaned carefully after every time,it is used by trained staff.

Salads Salad ingredients must be thoroughly washed to rid them of soil, especially items like spring onions, soil can sometimes carry harmful bacteria like E.coli, although producers clean vegetables, the risk can never be entirely eliminated. Washing to remove any soil is important. When you wash vegetables, do so in a bowl of fresh water. Start with the least soiled items first and give each of them a final rinse.
Remember: sandwiches, cooked meats, cream cakes, desserts and salads need to be kept at the right temperature Storing them at the incorrect temperature can lead to food poisoning.
It is your responsibility to ensure these ready to eat foods are refrigerated at the recommended temperature of 5°C or colder.

Par-baked and Bake off products

Make sure that your equipment is suitable for baking, reheating and hot holding, to ensure that the products are cooked properly and kept at a safe temperature which is **63°C** degrees or above. Preheat the hot cabinet before you put any food into it.
Do not use the hot cabinet to cook or reheat food

Follow the product manufacturers instructions on times and temperatures for cooking, reheating and standing to ensure that food emerges from the oven thoroughly cooked. Hot food should be transferred straight from the oven to hot cabinet which must be kept above **63°C**. You can take it out of the hot cabinet and display it for up to **2** hours, you can only do this one time. **If food has been out of the hot cabinet for over 2 hours, bin it.** If you have not sold it, you can heat it until it is steaming hot and put back into the hot cabinet or quickly chilled down to **5°C** or below by using a blast chiller or covering it and moving it to a colder area, then later put it the fridge. **Use a clean temperature probe to ensure all the required temperatures are reached.**
If you are in a situation where you cannot reheat food or chill it down, then bin it. Better safe than sorry.

Breakfast items

Bacon, sausages and eggs need to be cooked and handled properly as they may contain harmful bacteria, which can be killed by thorough cooking. Be careful not to let raw food drip onto cooked whilst you are cooking. Sausages and bacon must be cooked till the colour has changed and is steaming hot. Make sure sausages are cooked in the middle. Eggs must be cooked until the **white and yolk is solid** (This is the safest option for any food seller to take). You can always use your probe to ensure the correct temperature is reached which is **75°C**.

Rotisserie Chicken First things first, **wash yours hands before and after handling raw poultry and meat.** To check to see if chicken is properly cooked: Pierce the thickest part of the leg between the drumstick and the thigh, meat should not be red or pink and all juices should run clear. Better still use a temperature probe to make sure. If you use a probe to check that the correct temperatures are reached during cooking, you should record the details in the temperature log section of the 2016 Yearbook or 1 year diary.

Good Food Good Business for Residential care homes

Keep calm and help the elderly

Residential care homes Older adults,aged 65 and over,are more vulnerable to food poisoning,so food handlers need to take extra care handling their food. **The elderly are more likely to suffer from food poisoning and become ill.**
Why? As adults age, their immune systems weaken,making it harder to fight off bacteria infections and serious illness, conditions they would have brushed off in their younger years. The elderly also have less stomach acid to control their bacteria and probably suffer with weakened kidneys,which are not as effective in filtering bacteria from the blood. Large portions of the older population have been diagnosed with one or more chronic conditions such as high cholesterol levels,hypertension,cancers, kidney disease,and suffer from medication side effects. These factors may weaken the immune system, causing older adults to be more susceptible to contracting food poisoning.
This section gives advice for residential care homes that provide food for short or long term residents, covering kitchen safety issues such as:
- Food brought in either through donations or by visitors
- Heightened Vigilance in regards to food safety
- Mini kitchens

You need to read chapter 8,**good food good business for caterers** section first and apply the advice there in conjunction with this section.
Food brought in either through donations or by visitors
Make sure visitors are aware of your policies regarding any food,brought in for residents,it is a good idea to put posters up in your facility and in residents rooms explaining which are the lowest risk foods to bring in for the residents.

Since you cannot be sure that any food brought in by family and friends is safe,it is **best to discourage such practices** and encourage them to bring in low risk foods only such as packaged items like biscuits, chocolate,snacks and washed fruit or even fruit that does not require washing like bananas.
Make sure that all visitors and staff know how strongly you feel about contraband on your premises, **make it crystal clear.**

- Friends and family should avoid bringing in cooked meals,even if it is the residents favorite meal.
- They should not use raw eggs,especially in foods like icing and desserts.
- Clean containers must be used to bring in food stuffs,these containers will also keep out bacteria,pests,insects and wandering unwashed hands.

Keep an eye on **use by dates,**do not serve any food after this date,no matter how good it looks or smells,serving it is just asking for trouble. **Best before date:** generally safe to eat but I ask you **is it worth the risk to your residents and business,if something goes wrong?**
Foods that require chilling must be kept in the fridge to avoid the growth of bacteria.
Remember it is in your interest to judge how strongly you want to enforce these rules,after all if anything goes wrong,you will be the one responsible for clearing up any mess.

Food donations Only accept food donations from well run and reputable organisations with strong due diligence,which means:
- Is the food stored,packed and transported in a hygienic manner?
- They are not giving you the crappy unwanted,unsellable stuff,they would refuse to give to their pets.
- Everything must be within the use by date.
- Chilled and frozen foods are delivered chilled and frozen. Check the temperatures. Always.

Basically they should deliver food to you as if they were delivering to Buckingham Palace. If your donations come 'off the

back of a lorry' refuse them.
All donated food should come with paperwork,as part of your due diligence. You must have a clear record of where the food came from. **There should not be any mysteries in your kitchen.**
All food donors should be recorded in the supplier section of the 2016 Year book or 1 Year diary.
If you have any reservations about the safety of any food donated to you,feel free to bin it after the donor has left the building.

Continually review your procedures.

Heightened Vigilance in regards to food safety in care homes

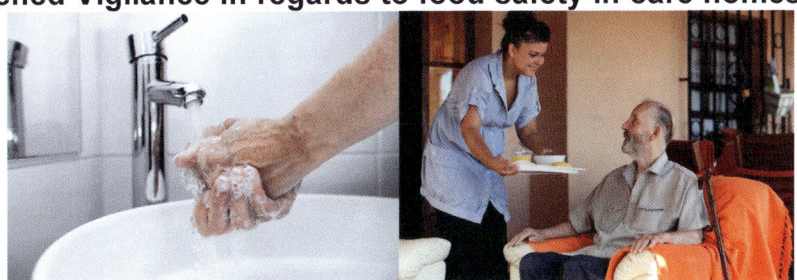

Wash your hands It has been said a thousand times before,everyone who works with with food **must** wash their hands before touching food or utensils. In a residential home,you have more factors to consider.

- Wash your hands after helping a resident use the toilet
- Wash your hands after handing a bed pan and medical equipment
- Wash your hands after touching soiled,dirty clothes and bed linen
- If you have to clean up after an accident like vomiting or diarrhoea,do it immediately to prevent harmful bacteria being spread about, wear a disposable apron and wash your hands afterwards
- Wash your hands after shaking hands with visitors,thanking you for looking after their dearest one
- Wash your hands before serving food or helping to feed residents
- Visitors should wash their hands before helping to feed residents. These helpful visitors are not allowed in the kitchen
- Wash your hands,Wash your hands,Wash your hands,Wash your hands,is that crystal?

After all how do you think infections get spread? by people of course, the viruses do not jump around onto people by themselves

Food Storage Do not use any food past its use by date. Make sure that all your fridges and freezers are working at their required temperature range. (**-18°C** for freezers,**5°C** for fridges) Follow the storage instructions on food labels,for example ketchup should be kept in the fridge after opening. These actions will help protect residents from bacteria that cause illness.

Common sense

Only use disposable paper towels in the kitchen, provide an adequate supply. Equipment for the kitchen should only be used in the kitchen, for example the kitchen mop should not be used to clear up vomit or diarrhoea. Dirty soiled laundry has no place near a food preparation area, make sure that it does not happen.

Mini kitchens If your care home has smaller kitchen premises located around your premises used by residents or members of staff. These need to be cleaned on a daily basis,just add them to the cleaning schedule.

True life story
Operators of a care home where 15 people aged 73 to 100 years old suffered with food poisoning were fined more than £20,000. Elderly people ate minced beef pies made from meat that had been reheated and cooled several times. source:www.gazettelive.co.uk

A pensioner died after contracting food poisoning from an undercooked chicken Kiev. The 86-year-old grandmother started to suffer from sickness and diarrhoea the following day. Doctors believed her organs started to fail after she contracted campylobacter – the most common cause of food poisoning. Tragically she later died.
Source Daily mail.

More information:
www.cqc.org.uk
www.careinspectorate.com

Good Food Good Business for Childminders

Handle with extra special care

Good Food Good Business for Childminders This section is for you, if you are a childminder and you give food to a child or baby in your care, the food hygiene legislation applies to you. This includes all food, from a drink of fruit juice to a fully cooked meal. It goes without saying that you must comply with food safety and hygiene regulations. **You must be able to show that the food you provide for the children and babies in your care is safe to eat**

You must also have the paperwork to back it up. Which means that you must keep records. If you own or run a nursery, then you need to also read chapter 8, **Good food Good business for caterers** first. If a child's parent or guardian has prepared the food and you are only responsible for storing it, the food hygiene legislation **does not** apply. Since the 1st of January 2014, childminders no longer need to register with local councils separately as a food business. Now, they only need to register with Ofsted. Ofsted will share any relevant information with the council, if required. In all circumstances, it is prudent to contact the environmental health officer at your local council for advice and guidance. **It is strongly recommended that all childminders complete the basic food hygiene training course, to ensure they are up to date and providing the best care for children in their care.**

What you need to know The basics of safe food hygiene are the **4 C's: Cross contamination, Cleaning, Chilling** and **Cooking**. Four simple rules that will help you to stay safe from food-borne illnesses in the kitchen.

Cross contamination Cross contamination is the main culprit when it comes to food poisoning. Dangerous bacteria can be spread from food to hands. They can move to equipment, to other food, the sources could be raw chicken (do not wash raw chicken as splashing water will just spread more bacteria around), unwashed vegetables ,people, pets, nappies, chemicals, objects and even you.

Cleaning Make sure all surfaces, equipment and hands are cleaned properly.

Chilling Cold temperatures can prevent bacteria from growing, keep all food chilled according to the manufacturers recommendations, check the packaging for details. Also be careful when defrosting foods. Especially with foods that can be cooked from frozen which need to be cooked until it's piping hot all the way through. Use a food temperature probe to ensure that the food reaches the recommended **75°C**.

Formula milk Unused made up formula,should be kept in the fridge until it is required. Use within 24 hours. Any left over formula after a feed,**must be thrown away,** just do the right thing because bacteria from the baby's saliva breeds quickly in warm milk. As we have said many times before,clean work surfaces and wash your hands before you make up baby feed. Before you start make sure that all bottles and teats are clean and sterilised following manufacturers guidelines.
Cooking
As we just mentioned all food must be properly cooked to kill any harmful bacteria. The optimum safe cooking and reheating temperature is **75°C** (at least for **2** minutes).
Formula milk
Use freshly boiled drinking water from the tap,do not use a microwave to make or warm up infant formula as it can heat the food unevenly and may burn the baby's mouth.

Breast milk Once again,the microwave is not recommended as using it,can cause hot spots in the milk,which may cause burning,just place the bottle in lukewarm water. **NEVER** boil breast milk as this will destroy valuable nutrients in the milk. Use an electric bottle warmer instead.

Baby food Follow the manufacturers instructions,if it is ready made.All home made baby food needs to treated safely, follow the advice in chapter 8.

Foods not to give babies and infants

Honey
Honey is not suitable for children under a year old as honey may contain the potentially deadly bacteria Clostridium botulinum.

Fish
Fish such as Shark,Swordfish,King Mackerel,or Tile fish are not suitable for children under a year old as they contain high levels of mercury,the most noted effect on human health is the impairment of neurological brain development in infants and children

Shellfish
Raw shellfish can contain harmful bacteria which can increase the risk of food poisoning so it's best not to give it to babies.

Nuts
Apart from allergic reactions,whole nuts,including peanuts,should not be given to children under five as they can choke on them.

True life story
Two British babies contracted a rare life-threatening disease triggered by eating honey. The boys,aged three months and five months,had to be put on life-support machines suffering from infant botulism. The younger boy had eaten honey,while the older one had been given a homeopathic treatment that may have contained honey,which can carry the potentially deadly bacteria. The disease is caused by the bacteria Clostridium botulinum,which lives in the environment,especially soil. If bees pick it up they can infect honey.
source:www.dailymail.co.uk

Personal hygiene Make sure anyone who makes food for babies and children is a picture of cleanliness,and not just understands the importance of excellent personal **hygiene** but lives it as well. An unkempt,unwashed smelly individual is not likely to be any better when it comes to handling food. Make sure,cleanliness is lived and staff do not just say yes and later cough onto the freshly made fruit salad. Make it crystal. Never be afraid to ask someone to wash their hands if necessary, it is better to be safe than sorry.

Make sure children wash their hands after going to the toilet and before eating. Ensure that you have a never ending supply hand washing soap,hand sanitizers and disposable paper towels.

Nappies: if your washing machine is situated in the kitchen, do not bring dirty laundry into the kitchen,whilst food is being prepared. Yes I know you are very careful but accidents happen and dirt,or even worse stuff can spread to food. It goes without saying that your nappy changing facilities should be far away from food preparation areas as possible. Remember to wash your hand properly afterwards.

Wash your hands,Wash your hands,Wash your hands,Wash your hands,is that crystal?

Pets

Yes I know that the UK is nation of pet lovers, but Max the dog,Tigger the cat and Pookie the hamster should be kept away from food, food equipment and children whilst they are eating. They are cute and lovable but you do not want their bacteria in you,the children and babies in your care.

Food Allergies The foods that most commonly cause an allergic reaction in children are:
Milk
Eggs
Peanuts
Tree nuts such as almonds,coconuts and walnuts to name few
Fish
Shellfish

Keep a record for children with allergies,this will be useful when it comes to food preparation. Become a labels reader,check the ingredients,do not assume anything or you will find yourself calling 999 for the ambulance,panicked because a child in your care has had an allergic reaction,because you could not be bothered to notice the line on the packaging that said **"made in a factory where nuts are handled"**. That phrase **"made in a factor where nuts are handled"** is an admission by manufacturers that cross contamination **may** have occurred.So before preparing food for a child with allergies,clean down all surfaces and equipment thoroughly. If the child brings a packed lunch, make sure that it is clearly labelled with the child's name to prevent any mix ups.

What to do if a child in your care has an allergic reaction

- Call 999 immediately as the child may start to have difficulty breathing,or becomes lethargic.
- Do not try to make the child vomit,if the allergic reaction was caused by food.
- If the child is unconscious but breathing, place the child in the recovery position. This will ensure that their airway remains clear and open. It also ensures that any vomit or fluid will not cause them to choke.
- Perform cardiopulmonary resuscitation (CPR) if the child's breathing or heart stops.
- Keep the child calm and keep calm yourself.

How is anaphylactic shock treated? When the ambulance arrives,the child will probably be given an injection of adrenaline. It works almost instantly by raising the child's blood pressure,easing any breathing difficulties and swelling.

Further information
www.nhs.uk/conditions/food-allergy

Good Food Good Business for Asian cuisines

Britain's favourite food

Good Food Good Business for Indian cuisines This section is for restaurants and takeaways serving Indian,Pakistani,Bangladeshi or Sri Lankan food.

Cooking Always follow the manufacturers cooking instructions as they have tried and tested the best cooking methods for their products.
Preheat equipment such as grills and tandoor ovens before cooking starts. When adding raw meat,chicken and prawns to the grill or tandoor oven,make sure that its liquid does not drip onto cooked food.

Remember raw food,especially chicken can carry harmful bacteria.
If you are reheating food in a microwave,follow the manufacturers instructions. You should stir food during reheating, as stirring and standing are part of the safe methods to ensure the food is reheated thoroughly all the way,as microwaved food tends to be hot around the edges and cooler in the centre.

REHEATED FOOD MUST BE STEAMING HOT ALL THE WAY THROUGH
ONLY REHEAT FOOD 1 TIME.

Sauces and Gravies Make sure all sauces,gravies are stirred during cooking and are boiling hot,reaching the required temperature of **75°C** for at least 2 minutes, use a clean temperature probe to check,if you are not sure.

Curries Cut meat,chicken into small size chunks to ensure that all the pieces take the same amount of time to cook. The cooked meat, chicken should not have any pink or red in them. Cook of course,to the minimum temperature of **75°C**

Tandoori Chicken,Chicken Tikka, Prawns and Kebabs

Tandoori chicken,prawns make sure that the middle is steaming hot,the insides should not be pink,or even raw and the juices should not have any pink or red in them.
Seekh,Shami kebabs,Keema nan and koftas which are minced meat products must be well cooked,all the way to the centre,which must not have any raw uncooked meat.

Combination dishes

Pilau and Biryani dishes, the classic combination dish of spices,vegetables,rice,chicken,lamb or prawns,make sure that the rice and meat is steaming hot. Make sure that the core temperature of the food reaches **75°C** or above,to ensure that harmful bacteria are destroyed. Examples of other combination dishes,where the inside must be be cooked to the appropriate temperature are samosa's and keema nan.

Fish and Prawn curry

Make sure that the fish is thoroughly cooked and centre has changed colour and texture.

Hot holding and delivery
Serve hot food immediately or put it immediately into a hot cabinet.
In a well run kitchen,food should be either hot or cold, warm food does not belong in a professionally run kitchen
Preheat the hot cabinet before you put any food into it, **never** put hot food into a cold cabinet. Remember the hot cabinets purpose is to keep hot food hot, to maintain the correct temperature above **63°C**,do not use it to reheat food or even cook food. For example putting fresh fish in the hot cabinet hoping that over time, the heat will cook the fish. Food must be thoroughly cooked and steaming hot when placed into the hot cabinet.
Exceptions
On a buffet for example,hot food must be kept above **63°C,** you can take it out of hot holding to display for up to **2** hours. You can only do this **once.** After this you can reheat the food back to **63°C,**or chill it down to **8°C** or below, or bin it.
Do not mix new and old food on display

Takeaway and delivery
Make sure that the food is kept hot until it is collected by the driver or customer, keep it in the hot cabinet,do not leave it on a table in the middle of the kitchen. Use an insulated bag or box when transporting food to customers homes. Keeping the food hot will prevent harmful bacteria from growing,also your customers will enjoying tucking into a just delivered steaming hot Indian takeaway without having to use the microwave to reheat it.

Ready to eat foods
Salads,garnishes,mint sauce,yoghurt's,chutneys,ice cream, basically foods that will not be cooked or reheated before serving.
What to do with ready to eat foods:
- Keep them away from raw meat,chicken and eggs
- Make sure that all equipment such as chopping boards and knives are clean and disinfected.
- Keep ready to eat foods covered.
- Follow manufacturers instructions which are written on the product labels.
- Vegetables and salads- peel and remove outer parts
- Wash salad ingredients properly in clean drinking water to get rid of

dirt,spinach (if you use fresh) and spring onions come to mind.
- Clean all equipment once again after preparing vegetables.

Salads,garnishes,mint sauce and yoghurt's should be kept chilled at **8°C** or below until time of serving.

Do not use chutneys after **use by date**,only decant into serving dishes before use. If a customer dining in your restaurant,does not use the chutney,please throw it away, because it looks untouched does not mean that it is safe, they may have coughed or sneezed over it.

Rice Cooked rice can be responsible for food poisoning, rice forms the basis of many ethnic foods and meals containing rice are frequently implicated in food poisoning episodes. It is common for restaurants and takeaways to prepare large quantities of rice,a day ahead of use and leave it to cool slowly at room temperature, before heating and serving the next day. **Such practices are simply not safe.**

Rice must be handled safely, as it can contain harmful bacteria such as Bacillus Cereus. If cooked rice is left at room temperature, this bacteria could start growing,producing toxins that will **not be killed** by reheating the dishes. These bacteria will multiply and may produce poisons that cause vomiting and diarrhoea. So **DO NOT** leave rice out at room temperature. When rice is cooked make sure it is steaming hot and cooked all the way through. If you cook rice to serve later or use in a biriyani,then it needs to be properly chilled or kept very hot.

Methods of chilling If you chill down rice, it needs to be done within an hour of cooking.
- Remove immediately from hot container,rice cooker or steamer.
- Use a blast chiller(if you have one)
- Divide rice into smaller portions
- Spread it out on a clean shallow tray
- Put a container of hot rice in a larger container filled with cold water or ice.
- If you chill down rice, it needs to be done within an hour of cooking.

When reheating rice ,stir it, to **make sure** it is steaming hot all the way through to **75°C**,well stirred,without any cold spots. If rice has not been chilled down safely; throw it in the bin. Yes,it is money wasted but if you had followed the correct procedures,you would be counting profits instead.

DO NOT REHEAT RICE MORE THAN ONE TIME

How do you check to make sure that the food you serve has been cooked properly? Safest method; get a temperature probe to check and record the readings in the 2016 Yearbook or 1 Year diary.

Colours in restaurant and take-away foods Excess artificial colours in food pose a potential long term health hazard to consumers who may,as a result,suffer a skin rash,gastric problems,vomiting or a worsening of asthma etc. Foods sold from restaurants and takeaways are **not required to be marked with lists of ingredients** or to declare the presence of additives. Rules apply to commonly sold food include the following: Meat, Fish and Shellfish may not be directly coloured (however, accompanying sauces and seasoning's may contain colour).Tandoori chicken is **not permitted** to contain colour - except by virtue of the Tandoori/curry spice mixes used which themselves may contain no more than 500mg/kg of artificial colours. Rice is only able to contain colour introduced by ingredients added to it, such as seasoning's. Raita may contain colour no more than 500mg/kg of which may be artificial colours.

Good food Good business for oriental cuisines

No 9
No 38
No 49
No 93
The perfect combination

Good food Good business for oriental cuisines This section is for catering businesses serving oriental cuisine, such as Chinese and Thai restaurants and takeaways.

Cooking Always follow the manufacturers cooking instructions as they have tried and tested the best cooking methods for their products. Preheat equipment such as steamers and deep fat fryers before cooking starts.
If you are reheating food in a microwave, follow the manufacturers instructions. You should stir food during reheating, as stirring and standing are part of the safe methods to ensure the food is reheated thoroughly all the way, as microwaved food tends to be hot at the edges and cooler in the centre.
Reheated food should be steaming hot all the way through
Only reheat food **1** time.

Sauces and Gravies Black bean, Szechuan, Satay, Curry, Black Bean, Plum, Oyster etc. Make sure all sauces, gravies are stirred during cooking and are boiling hot and have reached the required temperature of **75°C**, use a clean probe to make sure.

Stir frys Cut meat, chicken into small size chunks to ensure that pieces take the same amount of time to cook. The meat, chicken should not have any pink or red in them once cooked.

Roast Pork, Duck

Make sure that the middle is steaming hot, the meat should not be pink, or even raw and the juices should not have any pink or red in them.

Combination dishes

Spring rolls,Stir fries,Chicken,Prawn & Pork balls,Dim-sum,Dumplings,Fried rice, Noodles,Chow mien,Foo yung,Chop suey must be properly cooked and steaming hot. These meals tend to be a combination of foods that cook thoroughly at different times,so make sure **All** ingredients are properly cooked. Use a temperature probe to be sure,**75°C** is the recommended target.

Fish,squid,shrimp and prawn dishes Make sure that the seafood is thoroughly cooked and the centre of the fish has changed colour,texture and is steaming hot.

Eggs When you are making egg fried rice or any other dish such as foo yung that requires using fresh eggs,add the egg to the wok first and make sure it is thoroughly cooked before adding rice or other ingredients. Never add raw egg to the cooked rice as you will never be sure,that the egg has been properly cooked. **Do not use the same spoon for adding raw egg to the wok and for serving cooked food, e.g. when making egg foo yung.**

Precooked items Food that has been pre-cooked cooked and requires reheating e.g. Char sui pork,Spare ribs,Pork,Prawn & Chicken balls,need to be thoroughly cooked until they are steaming hot at **75°C**.

Hot holding and delivery Serve hot food immediately or put it straight into a hot cabinet,operating at **63°C**.

In a kitchen,food should be either hot or cold, warm food **does not belong** in a professional kitchen.

Preheat the hot cabinet before you put any food into it, never put hot food into a cold cabinet.
You can keep rice hot,in a rice cooker if you leave it on.
Remember the hot cabinet's purpose is to keep hot food hot, to maintain the correct temperature above **63°C**,do not use it to reheat food or even cook food. For example putting fresh fish in the hot cabinet,hoping that over time,the heat will cook the fish. Food must be thoroughly cooked and steaming hot when placed into the hot cabinet.

Exceptions

On a buffet for example, hot food must be kept above **63°C**,You can take it out of hot holding to display for up to **2** hours. You can only do this **once**. After this,you can reheat the food back to **75°C**, other wise know as steaming hot. Or chill it down to **8°C** or below or bin it. **Do not mix new and old food on display**.

Takeaway and delivery Make sure that the food is kept hot until it is collected by the driver or customer,keep it in the hot cabinet,do not leave it on a table in the middle of the kitchen. Use an insulated bag or Insulated boxes,when transporting food to customers homes. Keeping food hot will prevent harmful bacteria from growing, also your customers will enjoying tucking into a just delivered steaming hot takeaway,without having to use the microwave to reheat the food.

Ready to eat foods Salads,garnishes,ice cream basically foods that will not be cooked or reheated before serving.
What to do:
- Keep them away from raw meat,chicken and eggs
- All equipment such as chopping boards and knives are clean and disinfected.
- Keep ready to eat foods covered.
- Follow manufacturers instructions,which are on the product labels.
- Vegetables and salads- peel and remove outer parts
- Wash salad items properly in clean drinking water,to get rid of dirt,fresh spinach and spring onions come to mind.
- Clean all equipment once again after preparing vegetables.
- Salads,garnishes,should be kept chilled in the fridge until time of serving.

Rice Cooked rice can be responsible for food poisoning. Rice forms the basis of many ethnic foods and foods containing rice are frequently implicated in food poisoning episodes. It is common for restaurants and takeaways to prepare large quantities of rice, a day ahead of use and leave it to cool slowly at room temperature,before reheating and serving the next day. Such practices are simply not safe. Rice must be handled safely as it can contain harmful bacteria such as bacillus cereus. If cooked rice is left at room temperature,this bacteria could start growing,producing toxins that will not be killed by reheating the dishes,regardless of the temperature. These bacteria will multiply and may produce poisons that cause vomiting and diarrhoea.
- **NEVER** leave rice out to cool down at room temperature.
- When rice is cooked,make sure it is steaming hot and cooked all the way through.
- If you cook rice to serve later or use in a combination dish such as king prawn fried rice,then it needs to be properly chilled or kept very hot.
- If you chill down rice,it needs to be done within **an hour** of cooking.

Methods of chilling
Remove immediately from hot container,rice cooker,steamer
- Use a blast chiller(if you have one)
- Divide rice into smaller portions
- Spread it out on a clean shallow tray
- Put a container of hot rice in a larger container,filled with cold water or ice.
- When reheating rice,**make sure** it is steaming hot all the way through,well stirred to ensure no cold spots.

If rice has not been chilled down safely; throw it in the bin. Yes it is money wasted but if you had followed the correct procedures, you would be counting profits instead.

DO NOT REHEAT RICE MORE THAN ONE TIME

How do you check to make sure that the food you serve has been cooked properly? Safest method :get a temperature probe to make sure all your cooking achieves the required temperature of **75°C** and write the readings in the 1 year diary or yearbook.

Waste cooking oil

Never down the drain

Waste cooking oil from catering premises Since 31 October 2004 **waste/used** cooking oil from catering premises can no longer be used as an ingredient in animal feed. Waste cooking oils from food manufacturing,fresh or unused cooking oil, can continue to be used in animal feed. This change has been introduced as a measure to **safeguard animal health** and the subsequent food chain under the Animal By-Products Regulation EC 1774/2002 (ABPR) and applies across Europe,including the UK. After 31 October 2004,anyone using waste cooking oil from catering premises as an animal-feed,as an ingredient in animal-feed,or who consigns their waste cooking oil to such animal feed operations commits an **offence**.

If you produce waste cooking oil as part of your catering business,then you must ensure that it is stored properly,that none is allowed to spill and that it is collected by an authorised collector who will take your waste to an authorised site for recovery or disposal. Waste cooking oil **must not** be poured down drains or sewers because this inevitably leads to blockages and odour or vermin problems and may also pollute watercourses leading to problems for wildlife. Such action could also result in potential prosecution. Nor should waste cooking oil be disposed of with the rest of the catering or kitchen waste because it may cause spillages leading to odour or pollution problems or waste contractors may refuse to remove it. Waste cooking oil should not be taken to civic amenity sites for disposal in engine oil banks. Civic amenity sites are not for commercial waste and placing cooking oil into an oil bank will render the entire contents of the drums unsuitable for recycling.

Best practice Engage a licensed and authorised operator to take away waste cooking oil,they can also provide the following services:
- They can provide you with a barrel to store your waste oil or alternatively,you can reuse the containers,your fresh oil comes in and they will take these away and recycle them for you.
- Most collections are free,some will even pay you,for your waste oil.
- They must supply you with Waste Transfer Notes – to prove that you have disposed of your oil legally.
- And if required,your waste cooking oil can be delivered back to you as biodiesel.

Further advice on disposal of waste oils will be available from your local authority.
Type "**waste cooking oil collection**" into Google for a selection of companies,who are licenced to remove your waste oil.

Training for food handlers

'Starbucks is not an advertiser; people think we are a great marketing company, but in fact we spend very little money on marketing and more money on training our people than advertising'

Howard Schultz-founder of Starbucks

Training for food handlers A food handler is defined as any person involved in a food business that handles or prepares food whether open or packaged. Food also includes ice and drink. Food business operators are **required by law,** to ensure that food handlers receive appropriate supervision, instruction and training in food hygiene in line with their work activity and this training should enable them to handle food safely. The person responsible for developing and maintaining the business's food safety management procedures must have received adequate training to enable them to do this. In the UK food handlers do not have to hold a food hygiene certificate to prepare or sell food, although many food businesses will prefer that they do. The necessary skills may be obtained through on-the-job training, self-study or relevant prior experience.

Training Training does not have to be delivered by an accredited body but it must be of an adequate standard. It is acceptable to deliver in-house training but it is useful to demonstrate the content of such courses to Environmental Health Officers. During food hygiene inspections by council inspectors, their comments and questioning of food handlers will verify that they have received adequate training and are therefore competent in their role. All training given must be commensurate with their work activities, this means that training must relate to the actual job of the individual. Check with your local authority if they provide a formal training course. Alternatively, you can find out more about suitable courses and awarding organisations on the internet, just type **food safety training** into google.

Food hygiene refresher training UK food hygiene certificates **do not have an expiry date**. It is left to the discretion of the food business operator or environmental health officer to decide whether a refresher course is needed. This may be a result of changes to legislation, technological developments in food hygiene or even as a poor showing during a visit by the EHO. All food handlers will require basic training, before they start work which must include personal hygiene expectations and telling them what to do if they are unfit for work. See chapter 5 on fitness to work.

What level of training do we need? The degree of training needed by staff depends on what they do. For example, people involved in preparing and touching food (e.g. chefs, cooks, catering assistants, people who make sandwiches, etc.) need a higher level of training than waiters or kitchen porters.

Food hygiene training There are three levels of food hygiene training, use these explanations as a suggested guide to the level your staff should be trained:

- **Basic awareness** - for washing up staff, porters -The Essentials of Food Hygiene - the very basics of food hygiene - aimed at everyone employed in a food business.
- **Hygiene Awareness Training** - for waiting staff, counter staff, cellar men, bar staff, retail staff etc. - detailed food hygiene information aimed at food handlers involved with on-site support and front-of-house activities but **not directly involved** in the preparation of open foods.
- **Formal Training** - for food handlers who prepare and handle open food e.g. chefs, cooks, kitchen assistants, home caterers and/or mobile catering businesses. The course for this is called **Level 2 Award in Food Safety in Catering.**
-

Formal training should cover the following:
- Food poisoning micro-organisms types and sources including simple microbiology, toxins, spores, growth and death
- Premises and equipment
- Common food hazards - physical, chemical and microbiological
- Personal hygiene - basic rules and responsibilities
- Preventing food contamination and cross contamination
- Allergies
- Cleaning and disinfection
- Legal obligations
- Pest control
- Effective temperature control of food, for example storage, thawing, reheating and cooking.

It is also good practice, if managers, head chefs and food business owners take more advanced training which covers food hygiene management systems and HACCP principles in more detail. You get to practice, what you preach.

Health and safety training
Staff training is essential for the efficient and effective running of your business. Your training programme for existing and new staff should cover induction, fire safety, electrical safety, first aid arrangements and accident reporting, manual handling and chemical (e.g. cleaning products) safety. Under Health and Safety legislation staff should be trained so that they work as safely as possible without risk to themselves, colleagues or others.

Where can I go to get the training?
Check with your local authority if they provide a formal training course. Alternatively, you can find out more about suitable courses from your local authority, local library, further education college or contact one of the awarding bodies for food safety, such as the Chartered Institute of Environmental Health(CIEH). You can also get more information on google by typing *food safety courses* in the search box.

How often do we have to go on the course?
It is recommended that all staff attend a refresher course every 3 years. Keep a record of the training you and your staff have completed.

Dig deeper:
The Chartered Institute of Environmental Health-www.cieh.org
The Nationwide Caterers Association-www.ncass.org.uk

Setting up a food business from home

"Early to bed, early to rise, work like hell, and advertise"

Ted Turner

Setting up a food business from home What do you what to do? Decide what kind of food you want to sell and how. A variety of food related business options are listed below:

Cake making, decorating, wedding cakes If you enjoy baking and have an artistic touch, making and decorating cakes can be a really satisfying way of earning extra money.

Biscuit, sweet making Home made biscuits, cookies and confectionery can be a great seller, make sure that you present and package your products like the professionals. Ensure buzz words like **'Proudly handmade'**, **'Proudly home made'**, **'I made this'** or **'Made in Essex''** (or wherever you live) are prominently displayed on all your packaging and advertising.

Personal chef service Go to someone's house and prepare a home made meal for their family, or get hired to cook a romantic meal, do all the dishes and cleaning up, but be prepared to put some effort into finding your customers, you will live or die by word of mouth.

Cooking classes Offer to teach the can't cook,won't cooks but willing to pay, how to shop,prepare and cook delicious meals. You can teach people how to:
- Cook vegetarian and vegan meals
- Cook meals for diabetics
- Prepare meals for five people for under £5
- Teach good old fashioned home economics
- Make pasta
- Make cakes and desserts
- Healthly cooking
- Prepare Indian,Asian and Oriental meals

Pop up or home restaurant Feed hungry diners – in your front room?

Making and selling pre-packaged meals for special dietary needs Dairy free,vegetarian,cholesterol friendly,egg free,gluten free,iron rich vegetarian,low gi,low fat,low salt,diabetes friendly,irritable bowel syndrome,vegan,nut free.

Sandwich Delivery Route Cater to busy office workers with a sandwich,subs,snacks,healthy salads and drinks on a delivery route.

Speciality sauces Create your own sauce or one based on your grandmothers recipe: once prepared, the sauces can be sold in bulk to restaurants or packaged into smaller quantities and sold to grocery stores, supermarkets,speciality food retailers on a wholesale basis. You can even sell your products through your own website.

Packing school lunches Packaging,selling and delivering lunch boxes to schools for children whose parents are cash rich but time poor.

Muffins and cupcakes From the usual to the exotic such as Chocolate,Cheese & Chorizo,Gin&Tonic,Baked Bean,Tomato,Peanut Butter to Chunky Marmalade, the creative possibilities are endless.

Cooking lessons for children 
Start them young in making their own food, the best gift any child could have. Freeing them from relying on high calorie processed foods in the future.

The law All food businesses whether run from commercial premises or the home have to comply with the same regulations. You are still expected to maintain the same high standards of food safety and hygiene as any commercial kitchen. For details of these please refer to chapter 1,**Starting a food business,what everyone needs to know.** Seek advice from environmental health officers who will visit and inspect your kitchen and see if it is fit for purpose. They will discuss with you, what you are allowed to do at home and what you cannot, what you can use and what you are not allowed to use. They will also make sure you understand the principles of good food hygiene, product labelling and that you have considered health and safety and fire arrangements.

Training Formal catering qualifications are not strictly required for catering, which is more about producing and delivering consistently good food. However, you should undertake some form of formal food hygiene training, such as level 1 food safety awareness and level 2 food safety & hygiene for catering.

Gather your ideas Write a business plan that provides the specifics about your business, including the items you intend to sell, and how and the market you intend to sell to. In the financial section include your start up costs for equipment, supplies and food ingredients, as well as business expenses such as marketing. Include information about your projected sales and income over the next year. You may not have any intention to borrow any money, when you start up but completing the business plan will help you think about your business proposal carefully, is your product commercially viable? a pipe dream? or back to the drawing board.

Business Structure To protect your personal assets such as your home, consider creating a business entity such as a private limited company. You can register a private limited company online at www.gov.uk/register-a-company-online, It usually takes 24 hours and costs £15 (paid by debit or credit card or PayPal account).
You will need:
- The company's name and registered address
- Names and addresses of directors (and company secretary if you have one)
- Details of shareholders and share capital

Equipment Your equipment and supplies, will be dictated by the type of food you will be making but can include items such as bowls, baking dishes mixers, spoons, a computer and a printer to create ingredient labels to stick to your packaging. These should be stored separately from your personal items as should the food ingredients as well.

Obtaining skills and research Do your research, google is your friend, bing is your buddy, visit your local library, your local council may offer free workshops, The Guardian offers varied master classes such as "Launching a food and drink start up", "How to start your own street food business", "How to run a profitable food business". Leave no stone unturned in your research.

Branding What makes your product special? Why should anybody buy your product instead of the competitions?
"Most new businesses do something pretty similar to many others – they provide familiar services or products, fulfilling a definite demand – with perhaps an incremental improvement. You do not need an earth-shattering invention to achieve success. Those triumphs are rare and usually happen after immense heartache. What you want is a solid proposition that generates sales and cash quickly, using the skills you already possess, with economics you understand, and serving a known market". **Luke Johnson**

Market research Use your neighbours, friends and family as guinea pigs for tasting, testing and providing constructive feedback on your product or services. Get some strangers to carry out market research for you, as family and friends may not want to hurt your feelings by giving you blunt feedback about your product.

Team up It may help to join forces and combining skill sets with a business partner. Having a sounding board and being accountable to someone else can contribute to the business's growth.
Remember nobody is great at everything.

Marketing Market your food business. Send out samples of your food products and use high resolution pictures to use on your marketing materials, such as a blog, press release, website or brochures. Remember, online people are buying images, make sure your pictures are of top quality. You can get professionals to take your pictures or learn to take suitable ones yourself, if you are bootstrapping your start up. Always project a proffesional image. Promote your food items to seasonal events. For example, if you make cupcakes and cookies have promotional events for Valentine's Day or Mother's Day.

Keep business and home separate If you work from home it may be very difficult to separate one part of your house to be purely for business and the rest as your home. Try to find a space and keep that area for work and not let it spread because it can quite easily happen. On the other, if your home is full of stock, due to massive demand for your products, that is a good problem to have.

Walls, floors, ceilings and kitchen units You must be able to easily clean, disinfect and maintain your kitchen to avoid the risk of contaminating foodstuffs and harbouring pests.

Surfaces and equipment Your work tops and equipment must be in good condition, easy to clean and disinfect. You must also have adequate working space in the food preparation area, this will help prevent cross contamination.

Storage and refrigeration You must ensure that you have enough separate storage and refrigeration for products prepared for the business from those that you normally have for home use. If you can afford it and have the space, you should have separate units.

Utensils You must also have dedicated utensils for business purposes. These should be separate from those that you would normally have for home use to prevent cross contamination.

Refuse Food waste must not be allowed to accumulate in the food preparation area. Waste stored in the kitchen must be in a clean bin.

Cleaning Effective cleaning gets rid of bacteria. It is therefore important to clean your kitchen prior to commencing food production for business purposes. Make sure all surfaces, equipment and utensils are clean and suitably disinfected. Remember to always clean as you go.

Laundry facilities Ideally washing machines should be sited away from food preparation and storage areas. However if there is no alternative you must not do your laundry during food preparation for business purposes.

Toilet facilities
You should not have a toilet or bathroom that opens directly on to the kitchen.

Hand washing facilities
A separate facility must be provided for hand washing purposes.

Personal hygiene
A high standard of personal hygiene is important when handling and preparing food for public consumption. Good standards of hygiene help to eliminate the risk of contaminating the food and causing food poisoning. Hands should be washed regularly using warm water, soap and a nail brush especially before handling food and after visiting the toilet, smoking, eating, handling refuse and touching pets. Clean clothing must be worn by food handlers during food preparation to protect the food from the risk of contamination.

Illness
You should not handle or prepare food, if you are suffering from an illness that you could pass on to others like vomiting, diarrhoea and viral infections. For more information read chapter 5 on fitness to work.

The Family
Separating family and business use of the kitchen can be awkward but it is essential for good food hygiene. When preparing food as part of your business, you must not prepare food for your family. This will help minimise the risk of cross contamination.

Children
You must limit access to the kitchen to children, visitors during food preparation for business purposes. Keep them out.

Pets
Pets must not be allowed in the kitchen during food preparation and pet food should be kept well away from all food production and storage areas.

Plants and other decorative items
You must make sure that any plants and decorative items that you would normally have in your kitchen are out of the way during food preparation and production for business purposes. This will prevent anything falling into the food and causing contamination.

Who ever said this was easy?

Remember! Do not take chances with people's health, if food safety procedures fail then cross contamination and most likely food poisoning can quickly follow. Bad worth of mouth can give you a bad reputation and kill your business. Please note how fast and furious, bad publicity can spread on social media such as twitter, facebook and the blogosphere.

Keep the passion
There are a million reasons to start a business,never forget yours. Never forget why you started the business,passion for your product must shine through all you do and this will get you through difficult times.

Who to tell ?
If you are an employee by day and are building a business after work hours or at the weekends,there are some people you may need to keep in the loop.

- **Your boss:** do you tell your current employer? is any of their business,what you do outside office hours? You decide.
- **The insurance/mortgage people:** When starting a business at home,upgrade the insurance policy to include business cover and tell your mortgage provider. You only have to inform the local council if the use of the house is going to change from a home to business premises, which is unlikely.
- **The tax man:** You must inform HMRC of activities within three months of trading. Registration is straightforward, with forms depending on whether you set up as a sole trader, partnership or limited company. Keep the tax bill as low as possible by claiming business and home working expenses.
- **Friends and family:** so they can all start buying from you and help spread word of mouth on social media and everywhere else.

True life stories
Food businesses that started from home
Whole Foods Market. John Mackey and Rene Lawson Hardy within a year of opening their first store,the couple were evicted from their home for using their apartment storage for the store. Homeless and with no place to go,they decided to save costs by moving and living at their store full time.

The Northern Dough Company. Amy and Chris Cheadle started out making pizzas at their kitchen table. In 2011,the couple invested some savings in brand design and packaging,and took their product to a local food festival. They had enough to sell one box every two minutes – and sold out in 90 minutes. Now their "make your own pizza" products can be found on the shelves of Waitrose.

Claudi and Fin. Co-founders Lucy Woodhouse and Meriel Kehoe are makers of Greek style frozen yoghurt lollies,after struggling to find any natural ice lollies with wholesome ingredients,they set about making their own at the kitchen table. You can find their products in Sainsburys,Waitrose,Ocado,Budgen's and Supervalu and Centra in the Republic of Ireland.

Mr Singhs Sauce Mr Singh's Sauce was a labour of love for home cook Hardev Sahota,the first batch was made in his kitchen. 'With all seven of us in there,it got pretty hot,' says his son Kuldip,the company's CEO. 'We'd start work at 7pm,when we got back from our day jobs,and continue until after midnight. It was hard graft,but worth it.' The company has grown to supply the likes of Harvey Nichols,Selfridges,Ocado,Tesco,Sainsbury's and over 450 independent retailers,export to New York,South Africa and Ireland.

Pataks L.G. Pathak arrived in Britain on a freezing November with just £5 in his pocket. The only job he could get was cleaning sewers. At this point Mrs Pathak started making Indian sweets and snacks in the tiny family kitchen. Soon word spread and the queues built up. The business blossomed. And now it employs over 700 people worldwide.

The Pocket Bakery Beginning as an idea to get her children to earn their pocket money and gain a lifelong skill,Rose Prince,along with daughter Lara and son Jack,began opening up their Battersea home every Saturday morning, to sell freshly made bread. The home bakery has grown from two children selling a few loaves from the kitchen door, in south London to a blossoming business,that within three years of starting the Pocket Bakery,their bread found its way into Fortnum & Mason.

Starting a street food business

"I think of street food as the antidote to fast food; it's the clear alternative to the king, the clown and the colonel"- Anthony Bourdain

Starting a street food business You can sell food from your ethnic background, or maybe your mothers favourite recipes, even your own unique creations or a new twist on old favourites. Some of the most successful street food traders only sell one dish. Food wise, the thing that makes street food great, is when you have one dish, done really well by someone who knows what they are doing. If you find your food is popular and you can cope with the hard gruelling work on a regular basis, you may wish to consider a full-time career in street food. You will need to be in good health (the hours are long), punctual (you will have to set up your stall early), reliable (turn up for work when you have a cold, its your business, there is no calling in sick) and be ready to think on your feet when obstacles crop up or disasters happen. (and they will). You can also supplement your income with private functions and corporate events, you can even sell a product online linked to the food you sell on the streets, like the Rib man, who sells the hot sauce, he serves with his ribs, online. Running a street food business can be an intense experience, with fantastic days where you sell out and there will be days when you have brought your A game but the bin is the recipient of your hard work,(raining day anyone ?), staff do not turn up or you run out of gas at the busiest period. The competition is tough so get ready to bring your best-every time you hit the streets. Your food must be consistently good. Your competition is cooking amazing food, better be on top of your game.

What you need You will need to register your food business with the local authority in the area where you plan to trade, at least 28 days before you start trading. You are required to hold food hygiene certificates and you must also keep and maintain accurate records of your food production and storage. Safe food handling must be observed at all times.
Requirements
- Public Liability Insurance policy- It provides protection should an employee or a member of the public bring a claim against you for injury or property damage as a result of you business activities
- Food van insurance (if you use a van) insure your food van from loss, theft or damage.
- LPG (liquid petroleum gas) equipment needs to be passed by a gas safe engineer.
- Electrical equipment must be PAT (Portable Appliance Testing) tested by a qualified electrician.
- You must have adequate fire-fighting equipment .
- You must also have hot water hand-washing facilities.

Set up Types of set up:
- **Pop up gazebo/market stall**-assembly required ideal for low cost start ups.
- **Food Van**- drive up, set up, start selling, very convenient, not cheap, you can use an old van but they may just refuse to start on your biggest trading day. Make sure that it is kept locked up in safe place or you may find it vandalised or even worse stolen, on the day before you were due at Glastonbury.
- **Trailer-** drive up, set up start selling.

Money Rents for street food markets tend to be between £30 - £100 per day. Equipment, produce, tools, fuel, promotion – the costs of running a street food business all add up. Second hand equipment can be found on eBay.

Where to trade Music festivals, weekly markets, farmers markets, food festivals, street food collectives, disused car parks at night, privately owned estates, car boot sales: there is a lot of choice, visit as a punter, look around, ask questions, buy food from the competition, carry out plenty of research before you pitch up any where.

Festivals According to the Association of Independent Music Festivals in 2014, festival attendees spent more than £466 (including tickets) on average at music festivals. Paul Reed, general manager at AIF said: "A presence at festivals can greatly enhance your brand". It can be tough to get into bigger festivals as you can find yourself, competing with thousands of other enterprises for pitches, as in the case of Glastonbury. Festivals like Latitude can charge up to £10000 for a pitch, which must be paid months in advance. At some festivals, having a pitch at a popular site means that the festival organisers will also take a percentage cut of the profits, which can typically range from 25-30%.

Location, location, location You may probably not have any choice in choosing your pitch at a location, but hope to God, that you get a good one, not near the entrance (people are thinking is there something more exciting further on?), exit (people have made their purchases already) or toilets (Hell no!)

Labelling Make sure you are compliant with all labelling requirements to inform your customers about ingredients, especially in the case of any contents that may cause allergic reactions in some people. Please read chapter 6, Advice on new food allergen rules for further information. It is best practice to have display labels for your products including the name, ingredients, allergens and nutritional information.

Looking good You, your stall and food on display needs to look good all day long, stir food frequently, wipe up spills, make sure your apron is spotless, people eat with their eyes first. Your food must smell good, look good and taste good. It must be awesome, so your customers come back for more and spread the word about your fantastic food.

Never let the public touch the food on display. Ever.

Social media Join Twitter, facebook, create a blog, let your customers, suppliers and friends know where you will be trading, so they can come down and try your latest mouth watering creation.

Help You can join the Nationwide Caterers' Association, for a small annual fee, they can help you to ensure that you are fully compliant with all rules and regulations. They also provide online food hygiene training and their website has advice on all aspects of the business. You can also complete your food hygiene training with them online and they can advise you on all aspects of the business.
Dig deeper:
www.streetfood.org.uk
www.thejabberwocky.co.uk
www.marketstartup.co.uk
www.ncass.org.uk
www.streetfoodnews.co.uk
www.londonstreetfoodie co uk
www.britishstreetfood.co.uk

True life story
Katie & Kim's Kitchen
Winners of the 2013 British Street food awards, Katie and Kim could not afford to buy a food van. So they bought a horsebox instead on eBay for £300 and installed a bread oven in it, to bake their award wining cheese scones. They have now opened their own cafe in Bristol.

Ben Davy. Founder of Dough Boys Pizza, Patty Smith's and Fu-Schnikens
Frustrated with shift patterns in restaurant work, Ben started Dough Boys Pizza. Shortlist.com put them in their UK's best pizza list and they went from selling one thousand slices a week to selling the same amount on busy days. In 2014, Ben won the British Street Food Awards with Fu-Schnikens, which serves steamed buns, ramen, and dumplings. Their Patty Smith juicy burgers have gained critical acclaim mentioned in The Guardian as being 'hands down the best burger in town'.

Pop ups

A pop up restaurant location can be almost anywhere, so long as it's safe for cooking and serving food, all the usual food safety and hygiene issues apply. It is advisable to contact your local district council environmental health team for general advice. Starting and running a pop-up shop can allow you to test your skills as a business owner. They are a great outlet for innovation, freedom and creativity, and can be a good first step, if you are looking to establish a permanent business, besides it costs much less than traditional restaurant to open. It is a great way to test the waters of the catering industry to see if you can stand the heat. You can open a pop up restaurant to test out a particular 'out there" concept, using it as an method to interest investors as well as the public to try it out.

Style of outlet

When opening a pop-up, consideration needs to be given to the style of food you will be serving. Many pop-up restaurants concentrate on providing good freshly made, locally sourced produce to attract customers. Alternatively, you may wish to exploit a gap in the local market – is there a lack of restaurants serving food of a particular country, continent or style? It is important to consider at least some basic market research to see if a gap exists e.g. for a vegetarian restaurant, or food of a particular ethnic origin. On the other hand you may just want to chase a crazy idea like Fry Hard.

Fry Hard by Messhead

Fryhard held at Boxpark Shoreditch, during Easter 2015 was a pop up food event where every single item on the menu was deep fried, items for sale included crème eggs, doughnuts, jaffa cakes, babybel cheese, snickers, cupcakes and pickled eggs. Also on offer was a fully fried Easter lunch consisting of a whole fried lamb joint, roast potatoes, carrots and sprouts, All deep fried. Most people who go to a pop up restaurant are looking for a food adventure- something new, unique, and creative.

Finding the right location

A major challenge of a starting a pop-up restaurant is finding appropriate premises. When looking for a site, you will need to consider its size and the logistics of setting up a mobile kitchen or temporary dining room. Will it have access to electricity, sewer and running water? you may be lucky to find a vacant former restaurant or you can rent a cafe that serves only breakfast and lunch. The owners of the cafe may negotiate to receive a percent of the profits to cover water, sewer, electricity gas and any other associated expenses.

Safe catering, workplace health and safety

Your new pop-up restaurant may only plan to trade for a set period, and you will want to open as soon as possible to begin trading. However there are no shortcuts when it comes to food safety standards. Food businesses must ensure food is stored correctly and prepared safely to comply with food hygiene requirements. This involves providing clean storage areas, the correct equipment for refrigeration and effective monitoring and control of temperatures, combined with competent training for your staff.

Business planning, research and advertising

Businesses succeed when they spot a market opportunity and exploit it fully. This requires careful research of the local market, to find out if there is enough demand for your product. Producing a business plan can help you assess if your idea is viable, and is absolutely necessary, if you require finance to set up your pop-up shop. The short term nature of the pop up business model can help to better calculate, variable costs such as stock, but you should be prepared for high fixed costs – speedy connection of services and utilities at start up is essential.

An important consideration when planning your business idea is VAT thresholds and rates. If your business is trading for a short time you may not meet the thresholds, but voluntary registration may be beneficial. Planning your marketing campaign is an important part of your overall business strategy. The short term nature of a pop-up shop means your marketing should be innovative and targeted to provide the greatest impact. Pop-up shops rely heavily on word of mouth to drive interest and footfall.

Planning your marketing campaign is an important part of your overall business strategy. The short term nature of a pop-up shop means your marketing should be innovative and targeted to provide the greatest impact. Pop-up shops rely heavily on word of mouth to drive interest and footfall. Your aim should be to access as many social and local networks as possible. Use social media to advertise and generate interest for your pop up. Post details of your special events and specials on Facebook and twitter. If you have the time, you can create a website or a blog. Blogs are easier to set up and are free. Use blog.com, blogger.com and wordpress.com amongst many to host your blog.

Depending on the expected operating period of your pop-up shop, some forms of traditional advertising may be useful to drive sales. A leaflet campaign is quick and cheap, also posters can generate interest for your business, see if local shop owners would be willing to put them in their windows. Press releases are a way of generating interest in your pop-up business. Local newspapers and magazines may take an interest in your business, and give you some valuable free publicity.

"You can't do enough homework on your competitors and what consumers need, and this learning never ends. Week in, week out, every brand is trying to do something new or better so it's vital you keep watching. As a startup, you need a strong brand and USP to survive. Without a heap of cash to throw at marketing it's vital you have something to talk about and very strong reasons for consumers to buy your product over the more established bigger brands"- **Lucy Woodhouse co-founder of Claudi & Fin**

True life story

Mark Gevaux operates a Sunday only food stall in Brick lane, serving wraps, rolls stuffed with barbeque pork meat with and racks of baby-back ribs topped with his home made hot sauces. He can also be found outside the Boleyn tavern pub for every West Ham home game. 'You will find me on the market from about 3am cooking and getting ready to serve by 9am, I close when I sell out, but if the weather is nice, I will be gone early so if you come at 3pm and I am not there, you will have to wait another week for the best ribs in London baby'-Mark Gevaux aka 'The Rib Man.
theribman.co.uk

Further information.
www.londonpopups.com
www.boxpark.co.uk
https://business.twitter.com/
http://thenudge.com/
https://vimeo.com/album/1631962 :A series of videos profiling street food vendors

Setting up a mail order food business

UK consumers bought £8.2 billion of goods from websites in 2005
-Verdictretail.com

UK consumers bought £44.97 billion of goods from websites in 2014
Uk customers are expected to spend £52.25 billion in 2015
-Retailmenot and the Centre for Retail Research.

Get with the Program

Setting up a mail order or distance selling food business

What is distance selling? distance selling means any selling carried out,without face-to-face contact with the consumer,e.g. via the internet,text messaging,phone calls,interactive TV or mail order. Mail-order food businesses provide customers with a variety of foods and food-related items at prices,at significant discount to bricks and mortar shops. You can reach more customers by creating a website or mailing a out a catalogue,both of which allow customers to place orders online,by phone or mail. To run a profitable mail-order food business,offer a variety of food items to entice customers to make purchases and create a marketing strategy to reach as many potential customers as possible.

What do I need to do when setting up a distance selling food business? When you start a mail order or internet based food business you must,like any other food business,register with the environmental health department of your local council at least 28 days before opening. You should also take advice on legal requirements from them and the trading standards department.

E-Commerce Regulations 2002 These regulations govern the provision of information that must be on a website where a customer can enter into contract. The intention of the regulations is to enhance the quality of information given to customers to improve confidence when buying over the internet. The regulations will apply,if you sell goods or services over the internet, by email or text message.

You need to provide the following information:

- Full contact details for your business
- Details of any relevant trade body you may belong to along with your registration number (if applicable)
- Your VAT number (if applicable)
- Clear pricing information, inclusive of taxes and setting out what delivery charges may apply

Commercial Communications

You need to provide:

- Clear information on any electronic communication which relates to your advertising goods or services (e.g. promotional email)
- If you are sending a promotional email, the criteria of such promotion and how to qualify must be clear
- If you are sending an unsolicited electronic communications (e.g. text message or email), you must make it immediately clear that the message is unsolicited (e.g. in the subject line) so that the recipient can quickly identify that it is unsolicited.

More importantly, draft a business plan as a road map to guide you during each stage of your business development. Consider the types of food products to sell and then list all your start up costs such as equipment, marketing, website design, inventory, staff and delivery costs. Create a marketing strategy that includes ways to reach customers via social media or by email. Make space for a home office or lease commercial office space, better still you can even rent space from a self storage unit and run your business from there.(that is if you are not cooking what you sell).

Advantages of operating out of a storage unit are:
- Short-notice periods and low overheads
- Firms also do not have to pay business rates on any storage space they use.
- You get to switch off, not allowing working from home encroaching on your personal life, hence avoiding temptation to work endlessly.(which at the start up phase of your business, may be a necessity).
- The stock of your expanding business will take over your living space, obstructing communal living areas and your home begins to feel cluttered and cramped.
- If the business is not performing as you wanted, you can give one month's notice and move out, or you can reduce your space so it gives you nice flexibility during quiet times, reducing your overhead costs. On the other hand, you can easily expand and take on more space if needed.(a good position to be in)
- Many storage centres also provide a front-of-house reception area to take deliveries.

Website Register a domain name for your mail-order food business website, which is also your website's address. Research available domain names through a domain name registration database such as:

- www.domaincheck.co.uk
- www.123-reg.co.uk
- www.1and1.co.uk
- www.nominet.org.uk
- https://domains.google.com

Web-hosting companies provide the internet space for websites and you will need to research various web-hosting companies to determine their reliability, overall cost and available options before purchasing their services. Check out the competition's websites, see who designed them and research their services. Design a website for your mail order food business, include high resolution images, great descriptions and cost of each food item. Include contact information, methods of payment, shipping options and return/exchange policies.

Delivery How quickly should food be delivered if it's sent by post or courier? If foods that need refrigerating (such as fish, meat products, cooked foods, many dairy products and ready-prepared salads) are sent by post or courier, they should be delivered as quickly as possible, ideally next working day, and they should be kept cool until delivery. All foods must be delivered to consumers in a way that ensures that they do not become injurious to human health or unfit for human consumption. Type **'chilled food delivery'** into google for a list of companies who can deliver chilled products. When the consumer places an order, make sure the consumer knows when they can expect delivery. If the products are chilled, inform customers, how long the food would stay fresh in the insulated packaging without refrigeration, also let them know with refrigeration how long the ingredients are good for.

How should food be packaged if it is sent through the post?
You should send food to consumers in packaging that is strong enough to remain intact. Foods that need refrigerating (such as fish, meat products, cooked foods, many dairy products and ready-prepared salads) must be kept cool while they are being transported. Sometimes they will need to be packed in an insulated box with a coolant gel pack, or in a cool bag. Any packaging should be capable of protecting the food while it is in transit. For example you can use wool cool boxes which are lined with wool from British sheep, the wool is sealed within recyclable food-grade wrap to create a liner in a cardboard delivery box, which will keep chilled contents cool, below 5°c for at least 24 hours, even more effectively than polystyrene. Any packaging should be capable of protecting the food against mechanical damage and sources of contamination while it is in transit.

What laws will apply to my distance selling food business? When you sell food by mail order or via the internet, the food you sell is subject to the full body of UK food law and also any laws specific to the type of food which you are selling. **Sale of Goods Act 1979 (as amended) by the Sale & Supply of Goods to Consumers Regulations 2002:** This Act sets out what are known as Implied Terms covering contracts relating to the sale and supply of goods.

The Implied Terms are:

- Of Satisfactory Quality
- Fit for their Purpose
- As Described

The Act also covers issues to do with ownership of goods, namely they must be yours to sell, performance, delivery of goods, statements made by manufacturers which could be binding on the retailer; and finally guarantees – where one is given. A breach of the implied terms could give rise to a claim for compensation (damages). What effect this has upon your business will depend on a number of factors:

- How long the consumer has had the goods prior to realising there is a problem
- Whether the consumer has done something inconsistent with the sellers title: e.g. if a customer has begun to use the product

Does anything else indicate acceptance of the goods e.g. if they have eaten the whole dish, before complaining. Generally the above may limit a customer's right to cancel the contract and claim a refund. They may however be entitled to other remedies such as:

- Repair
- Replacement
- Damages (compensation or partial refund)

You should bear in mind in particular when considering the safety aspects of selling food by distance selling the condition which the food is likely to be in when it reaches the purchaser. The main law on distance selling is the Consumer Protection (Distance Selling) Regulations 2000, which applies to all goods sold by distance selling, not just food. This lays down important requirements such as:

- the information which the seller needs to provide to the purchase before making the sale
- right to cancel the contract
- recovery of sums paid on cancellation
- restoration of goods by the consumer after cancellation.

What information should be on my website? General rules regarding websites-The Electronic Commerce (EC Directive) Regulations 2002 require the **provision of certain mandatory general information in respect of all internet sales**, for example; where any food businesses sell, advertise goods or services to businesses or consumers on the internet or by email, they must make the same level of information available, for example on their website or in their catalogue, as when the food is bought from a retail environment.

Mandatory food labelling information (Article 9 of the EU Food Information for Consumers Regulation No.1169/11) – the **same mandatory particulars required for pre packed foods in the retail environment will also be required on any website** i.e. the true name of the food, the list of ingredients, processing aids, country of origin, instructions for use etc. Nutrition and Health Claims EU Regulation (EC) No 1924/2006 and The Nutrition and Health Claims Regulations (England) 2007 **impose restrictions on the nutrition and health claims that can be made in relation to foods including vitamin and food supplements.** These restrictions also apply to foods sold and/or advertised on websites. Only EU authorised claims, or those already submitted and awaiting approval, can be made in relation to food. For the allergens Information please read chapter 6 advice on new food allergen rules. Once again environmental health officers at your local council will be able to offer basic advice regarding your business.

True life story

Patrick Drake, bored with his career choice to become a lawyer, led a double life while working at Clifford Chance, dealing with his various briefs during office hours but sneaking into the kitchen of the fine dining room on the 30th floor during lunchtime to learn as much as he could. Eventually Drake quit the law – colleagues thought he had "lost his marbles" – and became a founding member of Hello Fresh, which delivers recipes and fresh ingredients to customers homes weekly.

Food labelling and packaging

"The devil is in the details."
Source unknown

Labels To sell food and drink products, the label must be:

- Clear and easy to read-where food is offered for retail sale, the selling price must be displayed to consumers.
- Not misleading, when selling to the general public, all pricing information must be clearly legible, unambiguous, easily identifiable and inclusive of VAT and any additional taxes.
- You must show certain basic information and list the ingredients. You might also have to show certain warnings.

Prices can be shown:

- On goods themselves
- On a ticket or notice near to the goods.
- Grouped together with other prices on a list.

Products sold loose or in catering businesses

If you run a catering business and you sell food loose or package it for sale in your shop, you only need to show:
- The name of the food
- If any of the ingredients have been irradiated, or have come from genetically modified sources
- Certain warnings
- Any food additive you have added
- Allergen information

Products sold loose or in catering businesses

If you run a catering business and you sell food loose or package it for sale in your shop, you only need to show:
- The name of the food
- If any of the ingredients have been irradiated, or have come from genetically modified sources
- Certain warnings
- Any food additive you have added
- Allergen information

Sale by Weight Many food products have to be sold by weight, where this is the case, the law requires that the customer knows the weight before paying for or receiving the goods. This can best be done by weighing in front of the customer (not out of sight!), or by marking the weight on the wrapper, or on a separate ticket. You cannot always sell by price only!

Food labelling - what you must show You must show the following information on the front of packaged food:

- The name of the food
- A 'best before' or 'use by' date (or instructions on where to find it)
- Any necessary warnings **(see table below)**
- Quantity information
- A list of ingredients (if there are more than 2) you must list them all. Ingredients must be listed in order of

weight, with the main ingredient first.
- The name and address of the manufacturer, packer or seller
- The lot number or use-by date.
- Any special storage conditions
- Instructions for use or cooking, if necessary

Food warnings
You must show an appropriate warning on the label if your food contains certain ingredients.

Ingredient	Warning
Allura red (E129)	'May have an adverse effect on activity and attention in children'
Aspartame	'Contains a source of phenylalanine'
Caffeine over 150 mg/l	'Not suitable for children, pregnant women and persons sensitive to caffeine'
Carmoisine (E122)	'May have an adverse effect on activity and attention in children'
Liquorice	'Contains liquorice'(you may need extra wording for confectionery or alcohol containing liquorice)
Polyols	'Excessive consumption may cause a laxative effect'
Ponceau 4R (E124)	'May have an adverse effect on activity and attention in children'
Quinoline yellow (E104)	'May have an adverse effect on activity and attention in children'
Raw milk	'This milk has not been heat-treated and may therefore contain organisms harmful to health'
Skimmed milk with non-milk fat	There's no fixed wording, but you must show a warning that the product is unfit or not to be used for babies.
Sulphur dioxide over 10mg/l	'Contains sulphur dioxide (or sulphites/sulfites)'
Sunset yellow (E110)	'May have an adverse effect on activity and attention in children'
Sweeteners	'With sweetener(s)'
Sweeteners and sugar	'With sugar and sweetener(s)'
Tartrazine (E102)	'May have an adverse effect on activity and attention in children'

Quantity information
You must put the net quantity in grams, kilograms, millilitres or litres on the label of:
- Packaged food over 5g or 5ml
- Packaged herbs and spices
- Solid foods packed in a liquid must show the drained net weight.
- You must be able to see the quantity information when you read the name of the food on the label and, for alcohol, the alcoholic strength.
- You do not have to show the weight or volume on foods sold by number, e.g. 2 bread rolls, provided that you can clearly see the number of items inside the packaging.

Information you may have to show
You must also show these if they apply to your product:
- Warning for drinks with an alcohol content above 1.2%
- If the product contains GM ingredients, unless their presence is accidental and 0.9% or less of the total contents.
- If the product has been radiated
- The words 'packaged in a protective atmosphere' if the food is packaged using a packaging gas

Country of origin
The label for beef, veal, fish and shellfish, honey, olive oil, wine, most fruit and vegetables and poultry imported from outside the EU must show the country of origin.

Allergens (see chapter 6 on allergens)
If your product contains any of the 14 allergens you must say so clearly on the label, and list them in the ingredients.

Nutrition labelling
You must follow the European Union (EU) rules for nutrition labelling if you want to show nutrition information on pre-packed products.
You must have nutrition labelling if:
- You make a nutrition or health claim
- You have added vitamins or minerals to the food

Nutrition and health claims
You have to follow certain rules if you want to make a nutrition claim (e.g. low fat) or a health claim (e.g. calcium helps maintain normal bones). For instance, you cannot claim or imply that food can treat, prevent or cure any disease or medical condition.

Organic food
If you are a retailer, you can label products 'organic' as long as:
- At least 95% of the farm-grown ingredients are organic.
- You sell direct to customers in your shop.

Organic certification

You must be certified by one of the organic control bodies like the Organic Food Federation or the Soil Association, if you produce or prepare organic food and you want to sell or label it as organic. You can decide which body to register with based on your location and needs. Once registered you will have to:
- Follow a strict set of guidelines laid down by national and international law
- Keep thorough and accurate records of production processes
- Allow annual and random inspections

Labelling for packaged goods
What labelling is required?

Here are the basic requirements for all food labels:
- Food name: This should be the one that is required by law, or a customary name. If neither of these applies, the name must be sufficiently precise to inform a purchaser of the food's true nature, and distinguish it from products with which it could be confused. (Note: a brand name or fancy name can still be used provided it is not substituted for the proper name.)

- List of ingredients: in descending order by weight with allergenic ingredients clearly **emphasised** within the ingredients list and a percentage by weight indication for certain ingredients or categories of ingredients appearing in the name, or given emphasis on the label.

- Shelf life: which will be a "**use by**", "**best before**" or "**best before end**" date, and possibly a **lot** or **batch** number.

- Storage or use instructions

- The name and address of manufacturer, packer or seller or importer into the EU.

- Place of origin.

- An indication of the products ABV(Alcohol by volume) if over 1.2% of volume.

- All information must be in English. Foods that only have foreign language labels cannot be sold.

- An indication of the net weight of the food, for most foods. Some foods can be sold by Number, i.e. Pack of 4.

- All information must be clear, accurate and easy to read.

Drink descriptions
If you advertise a particular brand of drink on your menus, price lists. etc, then you must sell that brand and not a cheaper substitute. If a customer asks for Coca-cola and it is out of stock, tell the customer and offer an alternative. Ensure that any leaflets, mats, posters etc, in your business, is consistent with the brands you are currently selling.

Food descriptions
Descriptions of food on menu's, blackboards and displays must be accurate, below are descriptions, you are likely to use in your business.
- Home made: should only be used for food made on the premises
- Suitable for vegetarians: must not contain any animal products
- Fresh: must not have been previously frozen, canned etc.
- Meat products: including sausages, burgers and pies must contain a certain amount of meat
- Scampi: must be whole tail scampi. Reformed scampi must be described as "reformed".
- Steak/burger weights: should be stated as the approximate uncooked weight.
- Local produce: this should either be produced/reared within county or if not in county, ideally within 20 miles of your premises

Colours in restaurant and take-away foods
Excess artificial colours in food pose a potential long term health hazard to consumers who may, as a result, suffer a skin rash, gastric problems, vomiting or a worsening of asthma etc. Foods sold from restaurants and takeaways are **not required to be marked with lists of ingredients** or to declare the presence of additives. Rules apply to commonly sold food include the following: Meat, Fish and Shellfish may not be directly coloured (however, accompanying sauces and seasoning's may contain colour). Tandoori chicken is **not permitted** to contain colour - except by virtue of the Tandoori/curry spice mixes used which themselves may contain no more than 500mg/kg of artificial colours. Rice is only able to contain colour introduced by ingredients added to it, such as seasoning's. Raita may contain colour no more than 500mg/kg of which may be artificial colours.

Prices Price labels should not mislead customers, it could be an offence to charge customers more than the indicated price.
- Is the display easy to read and visible from the customer's side of the counter?
- Your price list should be clear and prominently displayed
- Are your prices up to date and correct? they may have been adjusted on the computer system but the prices displayed on the shop floor may not have been changed.
- All additional costs, such as service and minimum charges must be clearly displayed

Please note: a customer cannot insist that you sell anything at a marked price, even if you have made a mistake and put the incorrect lower price on the item.

Employing staff for the first time

"Time spent on hiring is time well spent."
–Robert Half

Employing people - a guide for new employers

Employing people seems straightforward,hire them,they start,but is it so easy? Many employers find the list of legal rights and responsibilities of hiring staff intimidating,but complying with the law and looking after your staff will make your business efficient and profitable. Getting the 'people' part of your new business wrong could cost you time and money through:
- Recruiting undesirable employees
- Incompetent training-many new recruits leave in the first few weeks because they do not feel made welcome or receive a proper induction programme.
- Low morale and motivation
- High absence levels and turnover of employees
- Ineffective management and supervision
- Too many dismissals
- Employment tribunal claims.

There are **5** things you need to do when employing staff for the first time.
- Decide how much to pay someone - you must pay your employee at least the national minimum wage which at the time of writing is £6.50 and from Thursday 1st October 2015 will rise to £6.70. See what others are paying staff in roles,similar to what you are looking for.
- Check if someone has the legal right to work in the UK. You **must** obtain references from previous employers. Do not forget to check their **immigration status**. See the chapter 6 on immigration.
- Apply for a Disclosure and Barring Service check (DBS) (formerly known as a CRB check) if you work in a field that requires one, e.g. with vulnerable people,children or security. A standard check costs £26,whilst a more detailed enhanced check costs £44. www.gov.uk/government/organisations/disclosure-and-barring-service
- Get employment insurance,you need **employers liability insurance** as soon as you become an employer.
- Send details of the job (including terms and conditions) in writing to your new employee. You need to give your employee,a written statement of employment if you are employing someone for more than 1 month.

Visit www.gov.uk/employment-contracts-and-conditions on how to help you write an employment contract or ACAS (Advisory, Conciliation and Arbitration Service) website for templates (in tools and resources section) for job descriptions,person specification,job application form,equal opportunities form,statement of employment and induction checklist,all free for you to download,print and use.

Register as an employer with HM revenue and customs - you can do this up to 4 weeks before you pay your new staff. www.gov.uk/register-employer.

Get to know the law,for further information on the legal rights of employees visit: www.gov.uk/browse/employing-people

Essential Health & Safety Information

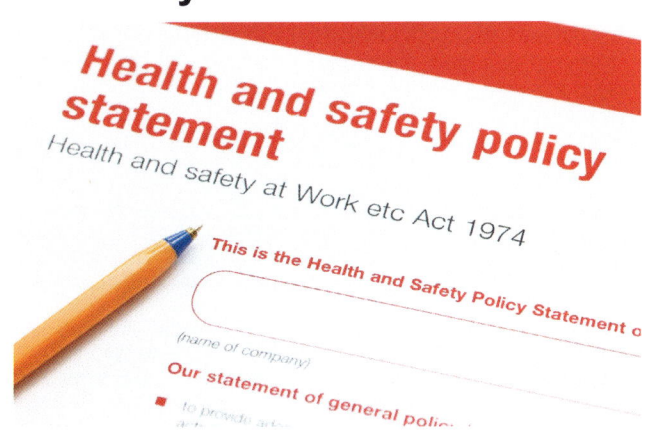

'Safety doesn't happen by accident.'
Author Unknown

Essential Health & Safety Information As a business proprietor you are required by law to carry out a risk assessment of your business. Simply, this means that you need to look at the hazards – those things in your business that could cause harm to people. See the 2016 yearbook or 1 year diary for hazard assesment forms.

The Importance of Risk Assessment After looking at the hazards,you then need to assess the likelihood of harm occurring, and finally decide whether more could be done to prevent harm. If you employ five or more people,your findings must be documented,although it is recommended that you record all risk assessments. Your assessment should be reviewed regularly. The main risks you need to consider include fire,electrical safety,slips,trips,falls,safe handling of chemicals,scalding and manual handling. Depending on your business, you may have additional,more specific hazards to consider. Your local environmental health department will be able to offer further advice.

Fire You will find advice on fire safety issues in Chapter 1, Starting a food business,what every one needs to know. The fire risk assessment form can be found in the 2016 yearbook and the 1 year diary.

Electrical Safety Electrical equipment must be maintained so as to prevent danger. 95% of electrical faults or damage can be identified by a visual inspection,such as spotting frayed wiring. Earthed equipment,such as kettles or cookers,needs to under go **portable appliance testing (PAT)every 1-2 years by a qualified electrician. New equipment should be supplied in a safe condition and do not require a formal portable appliance inspection or test. However, a simple visual check is recommended to verify the item is not damaged.**

Slips,Trips and Falls Accidents like this are a major cause of injury. To reduce the risk, floor surfaces must be of suitable material,be in good condition and free from obstructions. Check regularly for worn carpets,lifted lino,trailing cables,loose rugs and slippery surfaces. Keep the premises tidy and the lighting adequate. Stairs and steps must be free from obstruction,handrails and banisters must be in good condition and securely fixed.

Hazardous Substances It is your duty to minimise your employees' exposure to hazardous substances. Cleaning chemicals for example are generally safe but may be hazardous if used incorrectly. They must always be used according to the manufacturers' instructions. Care should be taken not to mix chemicals,and chemicals should be stored in their original containers. Staff should be clearly instructed and must be provided with protective clothing (e.g. rubber gloves,safety googles) as specified by the manufacturer's instructions. Hazardous chemical data sheets aka COSHH sheets should be available from your supplier of cleaning chemicals and must be made easily available to your staff in the event of an accident.

Gas Safety "The law places duties on the business owner or employer to ensure that any gas appliance,installation pipe work or flue under their control, is maintained in a safe condition to prevent risk of injury". - **Gas Safety (Installation & Use) Regulations 1998 - Regulation 35**. Defective gas fired appliances can emit carbon monoxide which is highly toxic. Also a gas explosion can cause enormous damage,injuring and even killing people. All gas fittings and flues must be maintained in a safe condition. An annual safety check must be carried out on each gas appliance (boiler, gas fires etc.) and flue by a "**Gas Safe**" registered fitter. Get the right engineer for the appropriate job,for example in the case of mobile catering vans,street food set ups,the engineer must be qualified to work on commercial mobile catering and LPG. A record of each safety check in the form of a detailed inspection report must be kept for two years. Any other gas equipment such as gas cookers should be serviced as recommended by the manufacturer.

Manual Handling Repeated or incorrect lifting by staff of heavy or awkward loads (such as bulk sacks or boxes of foodstuffs) can cause back injury. Manual handling should be minimised and you should ensure that staff know how to lift properly. Catering operations need to take extra care, as staff are likely to be lifting hot items such as large pots, roasting trays.

First Aid and Accidents

Adequate first aid provision for employees is essential. Provide a properly equipped first aid box and nominate an appointed person to take charge, when someone is injured and to keep the first aid box fully stocked. You should be familiar with the local medical facilities, such as your nearest accident and emergency unit. All accidents at work must be recorded in an accident book. (Where 10 or more staff are employed, you need to use the official accident book which complies with data protection requirements). The record should include the name of the injured person, date, time and circumstance of the accident, details of the injury sustained and any treatment given. Serious accidents, whether they are to staff, visitors or members of the public, must be reported to the enforcing authority via the HSE incident contact centre (Tel: 0845 3009923, e-mail: riddor@connaught.plc.uk on line at: www.hse.gov.uk/riddor/report.htm). These include accidents resulting in major injury, hospitalisation, death or where staff are off for more than 7 days as a result of an accident at work. You should have **Public Liability Insurance**, which covers the business owner's liability to guests and others for injury, loss and damage. If you employ staff you must also have **Employer's Liability Insurance**.

Information for Employees If you employ staff, the poster entitled **'Health and Safety Law, what you should know'**, must be displayed. It provides information on the basics of health and safety management. You can obtain it from HSE Books Tel: 01787 881165 and from good book sellers.

Health and Safety Policy If you employ 5 or more people, you must have a written policy document which sets out how you manage health and safety policy. It shows who does what, and when and how they do it. The policy should describe the systems and procedures you have in place to ensure employees' health and safety. It may refer to other health and safety documentation and should be reviewed regularly. The policy must be shown to all staff.

Further Sources of Information:

The Environmental Health Department of your local Council

More information is available from the Health and Safety Executive at www.hse.gov.uk

www.hse.gov.uk/riddor/reportable-incidents.htm

Starting a food import business

**It has been said that arguing against globalization is like arguing against the laws of gravity.
Kofi Annan, the seventh Secretary-General of the United Nations**

Starting a food import business If you are starting a business importing food, you need to know about the regulations and comply with them. Failure to do so could cause delay in allowing your goods into the country or cause the enforcement authorities to take action against you. All food intended for human consumption must meet the general food safety requirements of European Union law.

Importing food All food imports intended for human consumption must meet the general food safety requirements of European Union law. Most food and drink products imported from the EU have **no restrictions,** as food from the EU is not considered as imported but in 'free circulation' as food hygiene standards are the same across Europe. There may be national controls where there are risks to public health. Traders importing food from outside the EU need to ensure that they comply with EU and UK regulations on hygiene, safety, labelling and food composition regulations.
Most regulations tend to apply to food and drink that are imported from countries outside the EU. In this case you may need:
- Health certificates
- Import licences

Point of entry controls Some products can only come into the European Union (EU) through specific ports. For example, **P**roducts **O**f **A**nimal **O**rigin (POAO) such as meat, dairy foods and fish can only enter through a port with a **B**order **I**nspection **P**ost (BIP). Most BIPs are operated by port health and local authorities. All your POAO consignments must be pre-notified to the BIP and presented with the correct documentation, including the health certificates that relate to the specific consignment you are importing. Inspectors at the BIP will check your consignment to ensure that it meets EU import conditions. There is a fee payable for this work. If your goods fail the inspection, the consignment will have to be either destroyed, or transported outside the EU.
Examples of animal products imported for human consumption that must be checked include:
- Meat, including fresh meat, meat products, minced meat, meat preparations, poultry meat, rabbit, farmed game meat and wild game meat
- Eggs and egg products
- Fish and fishery products
- Milk and milk products
- Honey
- Gelatine and gelatine products

Importers of POAO from a non-EU country have certain responsibilities at the point of entry into the UK.
In particular they are required to:
- Notify the BIP in advance of arrival of any POAO goods.
- Submit the relevant documentation to the BIP, including an original health certificate. The type of certification required is dependent on the product type and country of origin
- Present the consignment to the BIP for veterinary checks to take place
- Pay for all charges for the inspection of the goods
- Retain the Common Veterinary Entry Document (CVED), issued upon clearance, for one year at the first point of destination of goods in the EU

Once a consignment has passed veterinary checks, the CVED is issued and the POAO is permitted free circulation within the EU. Free circulation is where food products can freely move within the EU without customs checks Consignments failing veterinary checks must be re-exported outside of the European Community or destroyed, you could incur additional costs if this happens.

Border inspections posts in the UK are Belfast Port, Belfast Airport, Bristol Port, East Midlands Airport, Edinburgh Airport, Falmouth, Felixstowe, Gatwick Airport, Grimsby, Heathrow Airport,Hull, Invergordon, Liverpool, London Gateway, Manchester Airport, Manston Airport, Peterhead ,Prestwick Airport, Southampton, Stansted Airport, Thamesport, Tilbury.

Banned or restricted products
Some products are not allowed to be imported or sold in the UK and the rest of the EU. For some other products there are restrictions, or in other cases, the Food Standards Agency has issued advice that they should not be eaten.

Details of some banned or restricted products
Contaminated spices and palm oils-There have been some problems with certain spices being contaminated.

Okra and curry leaves from India-Specific conditions are applicable to the import of okra and curry leaves from India for the presence pesticide residues.

Pine nuts from China-a long lasting bitter taste ('pine-mouth') that can occur after eating pine nuts originating from China, rules are being applied in China prior to export to the EU.

Rice products from China- specific rice products from China due to unauthorised genetically modified organisms (GMOs)

Sunflower oil from Ukraine- sunflower oil and products containing sunflower oil, intended for the manufacture of foodstuffs for human consumption,originating in or consigned from Ukraine can only enter the EU,if accompanied by a valid certificate certifying the absence of unacceptable levels of mineral paraffin together with the results of sampling and analysis for mineral paraffin.

Food handling and safety,things to consider
You are **responsible** for ensuring that all the food products,you import are fit for human consumption and not harmful to human or animal health. The following checklist will help you ensure that any food products you plan to import or source from within the European Union (EU) meet the required standards.
- Do you have the names,addresses and other contact details of your suppliers?
- Have you ensured that food handling and hygiene procedures at the place of origin,comply with EU standards?
- Can you ensure traceability of your products in the event of any problems? Is there a robust audit trail documenting the movement and handling of your goods?
- Do you need to have any food samples **tested**,chemically or microbiologically,to make sure they comply with food safety requirements? Although this is not a legal requirement,it can provide reassurance that it is safe to import a specific food product. List of food testing laboratories can be found at www.food.gov.uk/enforcement/monitoring/foodlabs/foodcontrollabs
- Is your chosen outer packaging robust enough to protect your food products against damage,contamination and other problems for the full length of their transit journey?
- Does your outer packaging carry all the information necessary to identify your goods,including the name and address of the supplier,the nature of the consignment and the country of origin?
- Does the manufacturer or freight forwarder transporting your goods comply with food handling and safety procedures? For instance,you may want to check that they are not over-fumigating the goods or that refrigerated vehicles keeps,food at the recommended temperature constantly.
- Does the information given on the sales packaging comply with the relevant EU legislation?
- Does it include an **ingredients list** and,where applicable,additional information such as Quantitative Ingredient Declarations (QUIDs are the quantity, in percentage terms, of an ingredient or category of ingredients used in the manufacture or preparation of a foodstuff.) and best-before or use-by dates and/or warning information? You can have this checked by a public analyst to ensure that it complies.
- Does your type of food require any extra checks? Foods such as bivalve molluscs like oysters, mussels,clams,cockles and scallops have strict rules regarding their importation. See here for more information: www.food.gov.uk/business-industry/imports/want_to_import/fisheryproducts
- Composite products -contains both processed products of animal origin and products of plant origin such as cakes, biscuits soup stocks and flavourings. See here for further details:*www.food.gov.uk/business-industry/imports*
- Do you need an import licence? Some foods are banned, restricted or subject to quota. Such licences in the UK are issued by the Rural Payments Agency (RPA).*www.gov.uk/government/collections/import-and-export-common-agricultural-policy-cap-goods*

- Have you allowed for paying import duty and VAT, as well as CAP levies and tariff quotas for your goods on entry into the UK? See here: *www.gov.uk/trade-tariff*

Can I bring in personal imports of food from a Third country?

You **cannot**, under any circumstances, bring in personal imports of POAO into the UK. All POAO, however small, must be imported through a BIP and have the appropriate documentation. Personal imports when cleared for entry are for your own consumption and cannot be sold on.

Imports from the EU

You can import organic produce from the EU as long as your supplier is registered with an EU organic certification body.

Imports from outside the EU

You can import certain organic products from countries that are covered under 'equivalence agreements' - this means they have no import restrictions. The countries that have equivalence agreements with the UK are: Argentina, Australia, Costa Rica, India, Israel, Japan, New Zealand and Switzerland. Not all products will be covered by equivalence agreements. Call the Department for Environment, Food and Rural Affairs (Defra) helpline (03459 33 55 77) if you are unsure whether a product is covered by an agreement.

Dig deeper:
www.food.gov.uk/business-industry/imports
www.gov.uk/bringing-food-animals-plants-into-uk/food
www.gov.uk/government/collections/guidance-on-importing-and-exporting-live-animals-or-animal-products
www.gov.uk/government/organisations/animal-and-plant-health-agency
www.food.gov.uk/business-industry/imports/want_to_import
ec.europa.eu/food/safety/international_affairs/trade/index_en.htm

Regarding additives such as colourings, sweeteners, flavourings and preservatives, please contact The food standards agency's additives team on on 020 7276 8570 or by email at *foodadditives@foodstandards.gsi.gov.uk*.

True life story

Food importer fined over horse meat

A food import company was fined **£5,000** after a pork sausage product was found to contain almost 50% horse meat. A test purchase was carried out at a shop in Dartford, Kent, by Kent County Council's trading standards department in October 2014. Tests by Kent Scientific Services on the vacuum-packed Lukanka Chumerna product, which was on sale labelled as containing pork sausage meat, found it was 46% horse meat. It emerged that the Bulgarian-manufactured product had not been tested, despite widespread media coverage about undeclared horse meat in various food products. At Dartford Magistrates' Court the company pleaded guilty to a charge under the Food Safety Act, the spokesman said. As well as being fined **£5,000,** an award of **£2,500** was made towards the council's costs, plus a **£120** surcharge.
Source:www.dailymail.co.uk

Fake honey lands food importer $30,000 fine

A food importer in Australia was fined **$30,600** for selling syrup derived from corn and sugar cane from Turkey as Victorian honey. The company has also been forced to remove all the "misleading" products off supermarket shelves after concerns were raised by the local honey bee industry to the consumer watchdog. Federal agriculture minister Barnaby Joyce said the finding was a win for consumers and local honey producers, which would no longer be forced to compete with the illegally

sold products. Not only did the company mislead consumers about the content of the honey, but also about where it was from, he said on Tuesday. The Australian Competition and Consumer Commission has also put other fake honey suppliers on notice.
Source: The Guardian

Food Dye

A YORKSHIRE food importer was fined **£12,000** after a spice mix containing an illegal cancer-causing food dye was found on sale in Bradford. The discovery of the dye, known as Sudan 1, sparked a nationwide alert to track down which businesses had been supplied with packs of the "mixed bisar" product. The business owner said importing food had been a new venture but the company had no knowledge of the regulatory framework in which it should have been operating. The Recorder said "In my judgement this is a very serious catalogue of offending which put at risk the health of the people of this area and indeed further afield and that calls for significant punishment," said the judge. The firm was also ordered to pay a further **£3,801.40** in costs.
Source:www.yorkshirepost.co.uk

Fake Rice

An investigation into a Southall-based importer that passed off cheaper quality rice as the more expensive Basmati

variety was fined **£11,000**. The concerns led to Ealing Council and Reading Borough Council together to carry out sample testing on rice supplied by the company,to shops and wholesalers in the two boroughs. In one sample there was not a single grain of Basmati rice – which is usually a much more expensive variety than other long grain rice – despite it being labelled so on the packet. The company, plead guilty to four charges of falsely labelling cheaper quality rice and misleading customers. Ealing Magistrate's Court fined the company **£2,000** for each offence and ordered it to pay the council's costs of **£3,630,** plus a victim surcharge of **£120** amounting to a total fine of **£11,750.**
www.indianewsbulletin.com

Leeds supermarket fined for illegally dyed chilli powder
On the 26th of November 2013, officers from Trading Standards visited the premises of a Leeds supermarket to find a number of non-compliances: **22** items of food were found on display for sale past their **use by date.** This totalled **547** days; the Food Labelling Regulations 1996 made it an offence to sell food beyond the marked use by date.
A number of items were found not **labelled in English** which was also a requirement under the Food Labelling Regulations 1996. At the time of their visit, in addition to these findings, officers took samples of chilli powder, which was subsequently analysed by the Public Analyst, who found that it contained both Sudan I and Sudan IV; illegal dyes. On 13th January 2014, officers returned to procure 'formal' samples of chilli products from the same source,to confirm the presence of Sudan dyes and to prevent any further product reaching the market place by seizing any potentially offending stock,which had been imported from Turkey. To place a food on the market which contains a non-approved additive is an offence under the Food Additives, Flavourings, Enzymes and Extraction Solvents (England) Regulations 2013. Expert toxicological opinion is that it is prudent to assume that Sudan 1 is a genotoxic carcinogen and, at the level it was detected in the samples, renders the food injurious to health. In April 2014, one of the company directors, was interviewed by officers in relation to the chilli products containing Sudan dyes, the director informed officers that they had been imported from Turkey from a company,they dealt with on a regular basis and that she was not aware of the dangers of Sudan dyes or the potential for contamination. The business did not test any of their imported products to ensure that they were safe and legal to be sold in the UK. The magistrates recognised the severity of the case and they were fined **£3000** and ordered to pay **£2188** and **£120** victim surcharge. David Lodge, Head of West Yorkshire Trading Standards, said, "Consumers trust that the food they buy is safe to eat. Products past their use by date, containing illegal dyes and not labelled in a language easily understood by consumers is putting the general public's health and well being at danger. This is a great concern to West Trading Standards and it is a success story that these products have been removed from the market."

Shark Fin Soup
A stock of illegally imported shark fins was been confiscated from one of Britain's most exclusive Chinese restaurants and destroyed by Trading Standards. The restaurant in London's West End – where lunch costs around **£70** a head – is celebrated by critics for serving some of the best Chinese food in the capital.
The upmarket restaurant came under investigation by Westminster City Council trading standards after the venue's marketing manager, admitted it was selling shark fin soup – alongside other exotic items not listed on the menu,during an interview with the Independent newspaper. The Manager said many of the ingredients were brought through airport customs in suitcases because "if they were sent over,they'd get confiscated". The comments led to complaints to the local council by the marine conservation charity Bite-Back. Subsequent inquiries found the shark fins were being sent by post from Hong Kong in contravention of UK import law.
He also had boasted of a range of rare off-menu items – including abalone and sea cucumber – and an increasing demand for them fuelled by wealthy Chinese tourists. A set menu could cost diners **£2,800** a head, he said. The restaurant did not remove the soup from its menu but now must import it through legal channels. Shark fin and all the other ingredients are legal if imported properly, according to the Department for Environment, Food and Rural Affairs. However, there is growing pressure for restaurants in the UK to remove the ingredient from their menus. In recent years, a third of restaurants who previously offered shark fins have removed it from menus. A council officer said: "The council undertook an investigation and discovered that they imported the produce through an unapproved channel and as such we have taken appropriate action against the restaurant."

Source The Independent

Why Businesses Fail

'Let me tell you something you already know. The world ain't all sunshine and rainbows. It's a very mean and nasty place, and I don't care how tough you are, it will beat you to your knees and keep you there permanently if you let it. You, me, or nobody is gonna hit as hard as life. But it ain't about how hard you hit. It's about how hard you can get hit and keep moving forward; how much you can take and keep moving forward. That's how winning is done! Now, if you know what you're worth, then go out and get what you're worth. But you gotta be willing to take the hits, and not pointing fingers saying you ain't where you wanna be because of him, or her, or anybody. Cowards do that and that ain't you.' Rocky Balboa

Why businesses fail It's no secret that many small businesses fail in the first five years. The question is: Why do they fail and what can I do to prevent my own business suffering a similar fate. Here are a few reasons,which might help you to determine why your business is not growing and things to avoid if you are about to start.

Business plan Create a solid business plan and back up plan b, in case things go sideways which they will. Your business plan? it can be a simple three-page plan or a huge 100 page bible. The point is that,you will have looked at all the aspects of your business and are prepared to handle problems when they arise. Your business plan also helps you to focus on your goals and vision, as well as setting out plans for accomplishing them. Once your business starts you will comparing reality with the figures in the plan.

"Any plan won't survive its first encounter with reality. The reality will always be different. It will never be the plan." Jeff Bezos. Amazon.

And do not get complacent and lazy– revisit ,revise and adapt your business plan to reality regularly. Make sure you price your products at a level that gives you a competitive return for your long hours worked and investment.

Poor customer service Poor customer service will drive customers away and sink your business. Once you have a customer, you have to keep them coming back,make sure you pay attention to what the customer wants and make sure you provide quick return of calls,text,feedback and emails. Resolve complaints speedily. The kitchen should not rule your business, in the form of a chef who thinks that their creations are more important than consistently reliable, quick and friendly customer service.

Location,location,location An unsuitable location can be the single biggest reason why food shops fail. Low traffic equals few customers through the door,which will most likely lead to the business failing. Wrong location: If your business has a physical location, you need to make sure that you are convenient to your customers, suppliers and employees. Even traffic patterns and ease of parking can make or break your business.
Location: You have to be careful in choosing where your café/shop/restaurant should be located. Is this place lucrative? accessible? safe? Is you rent too high? are you paying unrealistically high rent for a prime location?

Poor pricing strategy Charging an average price for products or basing the selling price on costs rather than on market expectation. Be brave and charge what you think your product is worth. You can be a provider of value products or services, hover in the crowded middle or be reassuringly expensive as a provider of premium niche products.

Fantasy People often fall in love with the idea of being their own boss and not the hard daily grind that running a successful business requires. It will be a hard slog, with you working 60 hour weeks or longer. Maybe you even hold down a full time job and spend all your evenings and weekends on your business, unable to spend time with family and friends. Some new business's close down simply because the owner decides to get a life, running your own business requires a huge investment of time, money, energy and selfishness (an absolute necessity at the start)

Mr Singhs sauce
Mr Singh's Sauce was a labour of love for home cook Hardev Sahota, the first batch was made in his kitchen. 'With all seven of us in there, it got pretty hot,' says his son Kuldip, the company's CEO. 'We'd start work at 7pm, when we got back from our day jobs, and continue until after midnight. It was hard graft, but worth it.'

Putting all your eggs in one basket Small business owners sometimes will have just **one** product, **one** income stream, **one** service or **one** big client. They cling tightly to this one thing because it brings in significant predictable revenue stream, But how will the business survive, if this key contributor disappears? Variety and diversification will cushion you against the ups and downs of business life. Have a plan b, for when that one thing disappears it could be your financial backer, biggest client or bank finance.

Poor record keeping and financial controls You have to keep financial and business records, you have to review your income and expenses regularly and you have to calculate and pay taxes and deal with other business-related paper work which never seems to end. **If it was supposed to be easy, everybody would be doing it.** If you do not know how to manage paper work, or do not want to, get a professional in. You **can** open a business without understanding the fundamentals of business, accounting, branding, marketing, customer service, food & beverage, staff recruitment and management? But in order to survive, you will have to learn very quickly and put what you have learnt into action. In the words of the founder of Subway Fred DeLuca; **Ready Fire Aim** which means you open a business, then make constant course adjustments along the way to get it running successfully.

Arm yourself Talk to other people who are successfully running their own businesses, read about industry leaders, find a relevant book, find a website about business start-ups, get a coach, do your homework. Never stop increasing your business and industry skills by attending classes, seminars and networking. There is nothing new under the sun, someone somewhere, has been down the path you are currently on and have gone onto success. You job is to learn from them. Whatever information, you need to be successful, it is out there written down by those with experience. That nugget is in the pages of a book or floating on the internet.

Find it. Read it. Use it.

"You want weapons? We're in a library! Books! The best weapons in the world! This room's the greatest arsenal we could have - arm yourselves!"- Dr Who

Competition Customers will go where they can find the best products and services. It's important for you to know who your competition is, what they have to offer, and what makes your own products or services better or worse than theirs. Offer something that the competition, does not.

Most new business, do something similar to others with an incremental improvement-Luke Johnson

Ineffective marketing Learn the basics of marketing and make sure that you track the success or failure of each marketing technique you use, dump those that are not working. See what successful people in your situation have done, learn from them and copy, success leaves clues, follow them.

Money You need to be able to live for one to two years without income when getting started as often businesses are very slow to get off the ground. Also, you have to create and use a realistic business budget, and not constantly drain the business income on personal spending.

Poor cash flow aka Cash is king
"Cash flow is everything-know it, understand it, learn it, and live by it-it's your bible-Caprice Bourret
Having enough cash in the bank, to pay your bills is crucial. And having enough cash on hand, or access to capital via a loan, to launch the next stage of your business growth is mandatory. Too many small business owners stall because they simply do not have access to sources of cash to continue to trade or expand in order to accommodate new business opportunities. Without an adequate supply of cash flowing through your business, your days are numbered.

"Cash flow is your bible-you have to know what's going in and going out for the next nine months. If there's a problem, you have the time to find solutions now"- Caprice Bourret
You need to get paid – bad debts often become a major issue, accounts receivable is your biggest contributor to liquidity. It is imperative therefore that you devise a strategy that will facilitate you being paid promptly, whether your clients are small businesses, multinationals, or public sector entities. Once you have facilities in place, it will help you to survive some

companies long payment terms,which can be anything from 30 days(if you are lucky) to 90 plus days,upon that some companies may even ask for a supplier invoice discount.

Getting paid on time

- You are never to busy to send your invoices out on time. Use cloud accounting software such as Fresh books, Quick books and Sage One, to send out your invoices and reminders.
- Account reconciliation: make sure your clients include your invoice numbers as references for every payment they make, to help you work out which invoices have been paid.
- Make sure that when you send invoices out ,they are accurate, as time correcting mistakes will lengthen payment times.
- All completed work **must be invoiced**,otherwise your business will be throwing away money by working for nothing.
- Build up a good working relationship with your client's accounts department.

Saturated market Are there simply too many food outlets in the area in relation to the supply of customers? Are there too many sellers chasing the same number of customers. Too many people doing the same thing,following the latest popular business trend? A bubble that may soon burst.

General Business Incompetence 46% of businesses fail not because of lack of knowledge of their line of goods and services (e.g. food and drink), but a lack of knowledge of business, e.g. pricing, bad planning, bad financial management etc.....make sure you understand the financial drivers in your business, in particular your gross and net margins and your break even point. Some entrepreneurs attempt to start-up their venture with low capital, just enough to open the doors,but not enough to sustain life during the first few lean months.

Poor financial controls Most restaurants that have failed,had prime costs,(labour costs and food costs),that exceeded 65% of revenues which indicated a greater potential for failure. Prime costs are the most important measure of profitability,they should be around 60% to 65% of turnover in total. If you can get that percentage figure even lower then even better for your business. Checking your prime cost percentage should be done on a weekly basis. When prime costs are figured out on a weekly basis, you can correct emerging problems early, whether they are food, drink or payroll oriented.

Finally:

'The greatest failure in life is to stop trying'
Napoleon Hill

For Your Information

1. Paper work matters,recording temperatures,keeping all invoices,filling forms,bureaucratic red tape etc.,it never ends but it has to be done. Record and keep all relevant information.

2. You must always contact the environmental health service in your local council for advice,their word is final.

3. Laziness is the food business proprietors greatest enemy.

4. **Never** let the public touch the food on display. **Ever.** They must not be able to sneeze,spit or cough over displayed food.

5. Personal hygiene: nothing matters more than hand-washing and good clean habits.

6. Lukewarm food does not belong in a professionally well run kitchen.

7. Immigration: **Check. Obtain. Copy.**

8. Repetition is the mother of skill.

9. The customer is always right. Unless you can prove otherwise conclusively.

10. Temperature checks,temperature checks,its all about the temperature checks.

11. Always do your homework. Google is your friend,you can never carry out too much research. **Find the information. Read the information. Use the information.**

12. Location,Location,Location.

13. Wanna be starting something,do not follow,start the trend,create a niche and work it.

14. Self employed? No sick days.

15. The buck stops with you.

16. "Know every integral part of your business,have passion for what you do,live it and breathe it and have pride in your product,as customers aren't impulsive like they used to be. They want quality and a good price and if you don't give it to them,a competitor will."- Caprice Bourret

17. There should not be any mysteries in your business. The phrase "i don't know' must never pass your lips. You must know everything about your business.

18. **Once more with feeling: Wash your hands,wash your hands,wash your hands,wash your hands,wash your hands.**

19. **Turnover is vanity,profit is sanity but cash is reality.**

Improvise
Adapt
Overcome

1 Year week to view diary

FOOD SAFETY MANAGEMENT SYSTEM

Contents

Your details

Food business registration form

Return to work form

Hazard spotting checklist

Monthly probe thermometer check

Fire safety checklist

Contact list

Supplier list

Staff training record

Recording sheets

Chef's allergen menu matrix sheets

Name of business:	Address:
Phone number:	Mobile:
Email:	Facebook:
Twitter:	
Name of record keeper(s):	Start date of this diary:
Unit Manager(s):	Finish date of this diary:

What to do:

- The manager must either record the information required or nominate and train a member of staff to carry out the duty and sign as required.
- You **must record** all your opening and closing checks **daily**. Do not do them at the end of the week in one go.
- Use a thermometer to double check your fridge temperature as the numbers on the fridge may not be accurate.
- Tick to show that all the safe methods have been followed.
- Record all problems encountered and actions taken in the notes sections.
- Keep this record until your local authority enforcement officer says that you do not have to.

Daily duties:

Opening Checks: must be done at the start of the day

- Check that all fridges, chilled display equipment and freezers are working properly.
- Fridges and chillers **5°C** or below
- Freezers should operate at **-18°C** or below.
- All other equipment is clean and in working order.
- All members of staff are clean, wearing fresh uniforms and fit for work.
- The entire kitchen is clean
- Make sure there are plenty of hand washing and cleaning materials.

Closing checks: must be done at the end of the day.

- The entire kitchen is clean and spotless.
- All fridges, chilled display equipment and freezers are working fine.
- No food is left out.
- All food past use by date is thrown away.
- All bins emptied.

Safe Methods

- Cooking and reheating; make sure the food reaches a core temperature of **75°C**. The food is safe, if it has reached a high enough temperature for a long enough period.

- Hot holding; ensure that the temperature of the hot plate/cabinet is above **63°C**.
- Chilled storage; It is a legal requirement in England, Wales and Northern Ireland that certain chilled foods must be kept at **8°C** or below.
- Cross-contamination; it is important for staff to follow good personal hygiene practices to help prevent bacteria from spreading to food.
- Cleaning; effective cleaning is essential to get rid of harmful bacteria and stop them spreading. Clear and clean your kitchen as you go.

Notes:

APPLICATION FOR THE REGISTRATION OF A FOOD BUSINESS ESTABLISHMENT

(Regulation (EC) No. 852/2004 on the hygiene of foodstuffs, Article 6(2))

This form should be completed by food business operators in respect of new food business establishments and received by the relevant Food Authority 28 days before commencing food operations. On the basis of the activities carried out, certain food business establishments are required to be approved rather than registered. If you are unsure whether any aspect of your food operations would require your establishment to be approved, please contact your local council for guidance.

Address of establishment _____

(or address at which moveable establishment is kept) _____

_____

Post code _____

Trading name of food business _____ Telephone/Mobile no _____

Full Name of food business operator(s) _____
(or Limited company where relevant)

Head Office address of food business operator _____
(where different from address of establishment)
_____ Post code _____

Telephone no. _____ E-mail _____

Type of food activity (Please tick ALL the boxes that apply):

Staff restaurant/canteen/Kitchen ☐	Hospital/Residential Home/School ☐
Retailer (including farm shop) ☐	Distribution/Warehousing ☐
Restaurant/Café/Snack bar ☐	Food manufacturing/Processing ☐
Market/Market stall ☐	Importer ☐
Takeaway ☐	Catering ☐
Hotel/Pub/Guest house ☐	Packer ☐
Private house used for a food business ☐	Moveable establishment e.g ice cream/Burger van ☐
Wholesaler/ Cash and Carry ☐	Primary producer-livestock ☐
Food Broker ☐	Primary producer-arable ☐

Other (please give details) _____

_____

If this is a new business, the date you intend to open _____

Signature of food business operator _____

Date _____

Name (BLOCK CAPITALS) _____

AFTER THIS FORM HAS BEEN SUBMITTED, FOOD BUSINESS OPERATORS MUST NOTIFY ANY SIGNIFICANT CHANGE IN ACTIVITIES TO THE ACTIVITIES STATED ABOVE (INCLUDING CLOSURE) TO THE FOOD AUTHORITY AND SHOULD DO SO WITHIN 28 DAYS OF THE CHANGE(S)

Return to Work Form

Return to work interviews must be conducted after every period of absence and on the day an individual returns to work.

Part 1: Self-Certification *(to be completed by employee)*

Name:	Job Title:
1st Day of Absence:	Date Returned to Work:
Number of working days absent:	Are you: full time / part time * *Delete as appropriate
State briefly why you were unfit for work (specify nature of illness or injury. Words like "illness" or "unwell" are not enough)	
I reported my absence to:	on (date):

Signed (employee): Date:

Part 2: Return To Work Discussion *(to be completed by manager)*

Method of discussion   Face to Face ☐   Telephone ☐

Manager's Name:	Date of RTW Discussion:
Has the necessary medical certification been presented? (e.g., where required, a fit note/s)	Yes/No
Summary of discussion:	
Any other comments or issues raised, and any further action agreed:	

Signed (employee): Date:

Signed (manager): Date

92

Return to Work Form

Return to work interviews must be conducted after every period of absence and on the day an individual returns to work.

Part 1: Self-Certification (*to be completed by employee*)

Name:	Job Title:
1st Day of Absence:	Date Returned to Work:
Number of working days absent:	Are you: full time / part time * *Delete as appropriate
State briefly why you were unfit for work (specify nature of illness or injury. Words like "illness" or "unwell" are not enough)	
I reported my absence to:	on (date):

Signed (employee): Date:

Part 2: Return To Work Discussion (*to be completed by manager*)

Method of discussion   Face to Face ☐   Telephone ☐

Manager's Name:	Date of RTW Discussion:
Has the necessary medical certification been presented? (e.g., where required, a fit note/s)	Yes/No
Summary of discussion:	
Any other comments or issues raised, and any further action agreed:	

Signed (employee): Date:

Signed (manager): Date

Return to Work Form

Return to work interviews must be conducted after every period of absence and on the day   an individual returns to work.

Part 1: Self-Certification *(to be completed by employee)*

Name:	Job Title:
1st Day of Absence:	Date Returned to Work:
Number of working days absent:	Are you: full time / part time * *Delete as appropriate
State briefly why you were unfit for work (specify nature of illness or injury. Words like "illness" or "unwell" are not enough)	
I reported my absence to:	on (date):

Signed (employee): Date:

Part 2: Return To Work Discussion *(to be completed by manager)*

Method of discussion   Face to Face ☐   Telephone ☐

Manager's Name:	Date of RTW Discussion:
Has the necessary medical certification been presented? (e.g., where required, a fit note/s)	Yes/No
Summary of discussion:	
Any other comments or issues raised, and any further action agreed:	

Signed (employee): Date:

Signed (manager): Date

Return to Work Form

Return to work interviews must be conducted after every period of absence and on the day an individual returns to work.

Part 1: Self-Certification (*to be completed by employee*)

Name:	Job Title:
1st Day of Absence:	Date Returned to Work:
Number of working days absent:	Are you: full time / part time * *Delete as appropriate
State briefly why you were unfit for work (specify nature of illness or injury. Words like "illness" or "unwell" are not enough)	
I reported my absence to:	on (date):

Signed (employee): Date:

Part 2: Return To Work Discussion (*to be completed by manager*)

Method of discussion   Face to Face ☐   Telephone ☐

Manager's Name:	Date of RTW Discussion:
Has the necessary medical certification been presented? (e.g., where required, a fit note/s)	Yes/No
Summary of discussion:	
Any other comments or issues raised, and any further action agreed:	

Signed (employee): Date:

Signed (manager): Date

Slips and trips Hazard spotting checklist

This checklist will help you identify slip and trip hazards in your workplace and decide what action to take. It will be of benefit to anyone who assesses and manages slips and trips at work. The checklist provides examples of hazards that can be found in and around workplaces, and suggests actions that you can take to resolve them.

The list tries to cover as many slip and trip hazards as possible. Some may not apply to you, while you may come across others not mentioned here, but which you will need to consider. Room has been left on the checklist for you to add any hazards that are specific to your workplace. To get the most from the checklist, you will need to walk through your workplace, including the outside grounds as appropriate, speak to union and employee safety representatives, workers and others to get their views of hazards and risks in the workplace, and then together decide what you could practically do to put them right. It is important to take action once a hazard has been identified.

Potential issue	Tick if 'yes'	Suggested action
Outdoor areas		
Can anything be found on the paths, steps and fire escapes that could cause slips, eg build-up of leaves, wet grass, moss, mud etc?		Set up a regular work schedule for clearing paths, tackle busy routes first. Consider cutting back plants and trees that overlap paths.
Are paths prone to ice build-up during winter months?		Consider alternative, safer routes. Monitor weather conditions and put a winter procedures in place, eg gritting.
Are fire escapes slippery when wet?		Improve grip – consider applying slip-resistant coating/strips or bolt-on slip-resistant material (caution – do not create a trip hazard).
Doorway		
Is the floor between the building threshold (entrance) and the entrance matting slippery when wet?		Improve grip – consider extending mat or exterior paving, applying slip-resistant coating/strips or changing to more slip-resistant material.
Entrances		
Is there water on the floor from rain etc? Is it making the floor slippery?		Stop water entering building – construct canopies over entrances, improve external drainage, keep doors closed when you can. Prevent water spreading – fit large and absorbent entrance mats to dry shoes. Remove water quickly – review cleaning system, introduce dry mopping, consider introducing heaters/underfloor heating to speed up drying time. Improve grip – consider fitting slip-resistant flooring.
Are there any trip hazards in the area, eg trailing cables, deliveries, mats with curled up edges, or other objects?		Housekeeping needed – tidy away cables, provide safe delivery storage area, clear away boxes and equipment, fix down mat edges or replace if necessary.
Corridors and offices		
Are there any subtle changes in floor		Highlight hazard – improve lighting, use eye-

level,eg slopes,small steps,abrupt changes from one flooring material to another?		catching colour on slope/step, clearly highlight change from one flooring material to another.
Are the floors smooth in areas where contamination can be found on the floor (eg liquids, food and food wrappers, dusts, polythene, condensation etc?)		Stop contamination from getting onto floor – provide bins for litter, fix leaks, fit lids on containers, close doors leading from working areas. Prevent spreading – drip trays beneath plants/ machines/water coolers. Remove contamination quickly – review cleaning system, spot clean spills, dry mop large wet areas, vacuum/brush up dry materials.
Are the tiles or flooring becoming unstuck or curling at the edges? Are there holes?		Maintenance required – fix down tiles and carpet edges, replace if necessary, fill in holes, replace cracked tiles
Is the anti-slip floor coating or grip tape worn smooth or damaged?		Maintenance required – replace damaged and worn coatings. Consider changing flooring
Are there any trip hazards around workstations or in corridors and walkways, eg trailing cables, boxes, deliveries, equipment or other objects?		Housekeeping needed – keep walkways clear, tidy away or use cable covers, provide additional storage, clear away boxes and equipment.
Are light levels too low to see the floor surface clearly?		Improve lighting – new bulbs, additional lights.
Is light reflecting on the smooth flooring creating glare?		Is light reflecting on the smooth flooring creating glare? Consider removing floor surface shine.
Stairs and ramps		
Are step nosings (edge of step) hard to see, rounded, damaged or slippery?		Check lighting is sufficient to see step edges clearly. Highlight the very edge of the step with a nosing that has a high visibility, square edge and non-slip finish. For difficult to replace round-edged nosing, ensure non-slip edging wraps right around the edge of the nosing.
Are handrails available? Are they easy to reach and useable		Provide a handrail on at least one side of the stairs; if flight of stairs is wider than 1 m, provide handrails on both sides and a third, middle handrail if 2 m or wider. Handrail heights should be between 900 mm and 1000 mm and be parallel to the pitch line (slope) of the flight of stairs. On landings where the handrail provides guarding the height should be 1100 mm.

		Recommendations for handrail shape, diameter and distance from wall can be found in the Building Regulations and British Standards.
Is the height (rise) of the steps or depth of tread (going) inconsistent throughout the flight?		Highlight the problem, eg with warning notice. Correct the rise/going of the stairs so they are all of equal height.
Are the stair treads slippery?		Thoroughly clean on a regular basis to remove contaminants. Replace stair covering with one with better slip resistance
Are any ramps or slopes in or around the workplace difficult to see?		Highlight ramp with contrasting colour and check lighting levels. Improve grip – consider fitting slip-resistant flooring. As with flights of stairs, consider providing handrails
Work areas and work platforms (eg kitchens, warehouses, storerooms)		
As part of the work process, is contamination (fluids, solids, dust, debris etc) getting onto the floor? Is the floor slippery? People – spillages, overfilling containers, clearing waste off work surfaces onto the floor, discarding debris onto the floor. Machines – leaks, overspray, spills, by-product. Process – overspills, leaks, by-product.		Stop contamination from getting onto floor – change system of work, improve work area layout, provide bins, dust extraction, lids on containers, reduce quantity of product in containers, fix leaking machinery. Prevent contamination spreading – use drip trays, screens to stop splashes, good floor drainage, highlipped sinks, bunding around machines. Remove contamination quickly – spot clean spills, dry mop large wet areas, vacuum/brush up dry materials. Improve grip – consider slip-resistant flooring; provide slip-resistant footwear.
Is condensation forming on the floor? Is condensation forming on overhead pipework and dripping onto the floor. Is the floor slippery?		Improve ventilation – use extraction. Insulate overhead pipework. Improve grip – consider slip-resistant flooring; provide slip-resistant footwear.
Is poor drainage causing a pooling of fluids on the floor?		Improve floor drainage.
Cold store – is there ice build-up on the floor? Is the floor slippery?		Remove ice. Door maintenance – check door closes and seals properly – replace seals, fix door and frame. Prevent humidity, eg fit automatic doors,

98

		curtains, humidity controls. Consider supplying slip-resistant footwear
Are designated walkways unusable or partially blocked?		Create a clear and even walkway through the workplace. Housekeeping needed – tidy away cables, provide additional storage, clear away clutter, boxes and equipment, safely store pallets.
Are walkways uneven, do they have holes or missing tiles?		Barrier off area as a temporary solution, ensure barriers cannot be easily moved. Highlight hazard, eg improve lighting, use eye-catching colour on defective area as a temporary solution. Maintenance required – fill in holes, relay/replace defective flooring.
Are there any raised carpet edges or holes?		Firmly stick down raised or loose edges. Maintenance required – replace all or damaged section of carpet.
Are the tiles or flooring becoming unstuck or curling at the edges?		Firmly stick down loose tiles and raised edges. Maintenance required – replace all or damaged section of flooring.
Are there any trip hazards around workstations, eg trailing cables, boxes, deliveries or other objects?		Encourage a 'see it, sort it' mentality among staff. Housekeeping needed – keep walkways clear, tidy away or use cable covers, provide additional storage, clear away boxes and equipment.
Are light levels too low to see clearly? Is light bouncing off the flooring creating glare?		Improve lighting – new bulbs, re-angle, additional lights, install antiglare grills. Stop glare – consider removing floor surface shine.
Toilets, bath and shower rooms		
Is water getting onto the floor? Is the floor slippery when wet?		Stop water getting onto the floor – improve shower curtains/screens, position sufficient hand dryers close to sinks. Remove water quickly – regular monitoring, spot clean, dry mop wet areas. Improve floor drainage where possible. Improve grip – consider fitting slip-resistant flooring.
Are taps or pipes leaking?		Prevent contamination spreading – provide drip trays as a temporary solution. Maintenance required – fix leaks and taps.

Cleaning

Are spillages left on the floor for some time before they are cleaned up? Food or cooking spills are one of the main causes of slips in kitchens.		Encourage a 'see it, sort it' mentality among staff. Ensure spills cleaning equipment is readily available for use. Review/improve cleaning regime and timings of cleaning schedule. Consider introducing a roving cleaner.
Are small spills wet mopped?		Spot clean small spills using absorbent cloth/paper towel. Provide training and then supervise. Ensure spills cleaning equipment is readily available for use.
Can people walk through areas during wet mopping or when floors are still wet? Is the floor smooth or slippery when wet?		Keep people off smooth wet floors – Barrier off/close off areas, wet mop out of hours when no-one is around. Reduce drying time – dry mop the floors with a clean, proprietary dry mop.
Are warning signs left out long after the spill has gone and floor has dried?		Remove cones and signs as soon as cleaning is completed and floor is dry. Provide training and then supervise.
Does the floor look dirty even though it has just been cleaned?		Check manufacturers/suppliers cleaning instructions are being followed. Review floor cleaning method, alter to suit floor type. Provide training on new method and then supervise.
Are people slipping on the floor even though it has been cleaned and is dry?		Thoroughly clean to remove build-up of polish, grease etc. Review and alter floor cleaning method. Provide training on new method and then supervise.
Can cleaning equipment leads be seen crossing or blocking walkways, creating a trip hazard?		Coil up unused equipment cable. Change power source – provide additional power sockets; use socket nearest area being cleaned. Consider change to battery-powered equipment. Provide training on new method and then supervise.

Do bin bags/cleaning equipment in walkways create trip hazards?		Provide training on awareness of trip hazards and how to avoid them and then supervise.
Tasks		
Do tasks stop people seeing slip or trip hazards, eg carrying items that restrict view, upset people's balance, rushing?		Review and improve manual handling and moving procedures. Review work activity.

MONTHLY PROBE THERMOMETER CHECK

Probe thermometer recording details

Month											
Ice water reading											
Boiling water reading											
Checked by											

- The readings in iced water should be **-1°C** to **+1°C**, if outside this range the unit should be replaced or returned to the manufacturer to be recalibrated.
- The reading in boiling water should be between **99°C** and **101°C**, if outside this range the unit should be replaced or returned to the manufacturer to be recalibrated.

Date and Details of Yearly Calibration		Date of next Yearly Calibration			

N.B. The electronic display unit should be checked at least once per year. Manufacturers may offer a calibration service.

Fire Safety & Risk Assessment for Catering Establishments

Fire Safety law has undergone a change with the introduction of the Regulatory Reform (Fire Safety) Order 2005 that came into force on 1st October 2006. Premises such as food businesses are affected however the fundamental principles are still the same:

- Controlling fire risks, preventing fire in the first place.

- Early warning in case of fire.

- Adequate escape routes.

- Adequate training and information for staff.

This legislation does not just affect employers as was previously the case, but all premises to which the public have access. Responsibility for complying with the Fire Safety Order rests with the "responsible person". In a workplace, this is the employer and any other person who may have control of any part of the premises, e.g. the occupier or owner.

The responsible person must carry out a fire risk assessment that must focus on the safety in case of fire of all relevant persons. It should pay particular attention to those at special risk, such as the disabled and those with special needs, and must include consideration of any dangerous substances liable to be on the premises. The fire risk assessment will help identify risks that can be removed or reduced and to decide the nature and extent of the general fire precautions needed to be taken to protect people against the fire risks that remain.

If five or more people are employed, or the premises are licensed, the significant findings of the assessment **must** be recorded.

Fire Risk Assessment

Performing a risk assessment is easy. It must also be remembered that it must be regularly reviewed to ensure that it is current.

Here are the five steps:

- Identify potential fire hazards e.g. ignition sources and fuel

- Identify people at risk e.g. staff, visitors etc.

- Evaluate, remove or reduce hazards, and protect. Identify what could be done to control the hazard if not controlled by existing arrangements.

- Record, plan, inform, instruct and train. Although this is not mandatory if you employ less than five employees, recording your risk assessment regardless of the size of your premises is considered "Best Practice" and is strongly recommended by the Fire Service.

Keep the assessment under review and revise as and when necessary.

Expanding on the five steps above, the following needs to be taken into account with respect to food businesses:

- Fire hazards should be identified and controlled e.g. smoking materials, cooking areas, heating, electrical apparatus and wiring, gas, flammable materials, hot work.

- People need to be alerted to the outbreak of fire, so there must be a means for raising the alarm. Examples of this may range from shouting or using whistles, to very sophisticated alarm systems incorporating automatic detectors throughout the premises. Most food businesses would probably fall somewhere in the middle, where a manually operated electrical alarm system would be the most reliable. Whatever system is chosen, it is vital that it can be heard throughout the building.

- Once people are alerted, they need a good escape route that is protected from risk areas by closed doors, well lit and free from obstruction. They will need a door to escape through which is not locked from the inside.

- Should it be necessary to tackle a very small fire, to enable others to escape, then suitable fire fighting equipment should be provided. Ordinarily this would include at least one fire extinguisher at each level and a fire blanket in any kitchen area.

- Importantly, you will need a means of summoning assistance from the fire service –typically a telephone box, mobile phone or an agreement with a neighbour.

- It is imperative that the staff are aware of the fire safety measures. This requires regular staff training sessions to cover all aspects of fire safety within the premises, including their responsibility for others who may be on the premises. Training based on written instructions should be carried out on induction and at least annually thereafter.

- To ensure that fire safety management of the premises is effective it is necessary to keep records of; weekly fire alarm tests, monthly emergency lighting tests, monthly fire fighting equipment inspections and six monthly staff training sessions.

Fire safety need not be expensive but you must think the issues through and control the hazards. If you require specific advice, please feel free to contact a fire safety officer and discuss it.

Fire Safety Checklist
Complete the tick boxes for all the questions. If you answer "No" to any of the questions, this would indicate that you need to take further action.

Risk Assessment	Yes	No	N/A
Has the risk assessment been carried out?			
Are the hazards clearly identified (e.g. smoking, cooking, heating, electrics, gas, flammable materials, hot work)?			
Are the hazards adequately controlled?			
Fire alarms			
Is there a means for raising the alarm?			
Can the alarm be heard in all occupied areas?			
In the alarm tested weekly?			
Is the premises fitted with an electrical alarm system incorporating manual call points?			

If not describe the alarm system:			

Escape Routes

Are there clearly identifiable escape routes with correct signage where necessary?			
Are there doors separating the escape routes from the risk rooms (kitchen, store, process area etc.)?			
Can all doors on escape routes be easily opened from the inside without the use of a key, card or digital lock?			

Emergency Lighting

Is emergency lighting installed on the escape routes?			
If yes, is it tested on a monthly basis?			
If there is no emergency lighting, is there enough borrowed light (from street lighting or other) to safely negotiate the escape routes if they are used during the hours of darkness?			

Fire Fighting Equipment

Is there an adequate provision of fire fighting equipment (water extinguishers; at least one per floor, other extinguishers appropriate to risk, fire blanket) in the Kitchen?			
Describe any deficiencies:			
Is the fire fighting equipment inspected regularly by the occupier and annually by a qualified engineer?			

Fire Safety Management			
Is there a method for summoning the fire service without placing anyone at risk?			
Do the staff receive regular fire safety training regarding all of the above items including their actions in the event of a fire?			
Are records kept of the following:			
Fire alarm tests?			
Emergency Lighting tests?			
Fire fighting equipment inspections?			
Staff training?			
Please provide details of any other installations present or any other positive or negative comments:			

Contacts list
Please record the contacts details of different services or people you may need to contact.
Such as:

Environmental health	Police
Electrician	Head office
Plumber	Area manager
Fridge repairs	Unit manager
Refuse collector/recycling service	Payroll
Human resources	Security

Contact name:	Contact name:
Telephone: Mobile:	Telephone: Mobile:
Address:	Address:
Role:	Role:

Contact name:	Contact name:
Telephone: Mobile:	Telephone: Mobile:
Address:	Address:
Role:	Role:

Contact name:	Contact name:
Telephone: Mobile:	Telephone: Mobile:
Address:	Address:
Role:	Role:

Contact name:	Contact name:
Telephone: Mobile:	Telephone: Mobile:
Address:	Address:
Role:	Role:

Contact name:	Contact name:
Telephone: Mobile:	Telephone: Mobile:
Address:	Address:
Role:	Role:

Contact name:	Contact name:
Telephone: Mobile:	Telephone: Mobile:
Address:	Address:
Role:	Role:

Contact name:	Contact name:
Telephone: Mobile:	Telephone: Mobile:
Address:	Address:
Role:	Role:

Contact name:	Contact name:
Telephone: Mobile:	Telephone: Mobile:
Address:	Address:
Role:	Role:

Contact name:	Contact name:
Telephone: Mobile:	Telephone: Mobile:
Address:	Address:
Role:	Role:

Contact name:	Contact name:
Telephone: Mobile:	Telephone: Mobile:
Address:	Address:
Role:	Role:

Contact name:	Contact name:
Telephone: Mobile:	Telephone: Mobile:
Address:	Address:
Role:	Role:

Contact name:	Contact name:
Telephone: Mobile:	Telephone: Mobile:
Address:	Address:
Role:	Role:

Contact name:	Contact name:
Telephone: Mobile:	Telephone: Mobile:
Address:	Address:
Role:	Role:

Contact name:	Contact name:
Telephone: Mobile:	Telephone: Mobile:
Address:	Address:
Role:	Role:

Contact name:	Contact name:
Telephone: Mobile:	Telephone: Mobile:
Address:	Address:
Role:	Role:

Contact name:	Contact name:
Telephone: Mobile:	Telephone: Mobile:
Address:	Address:
Role:	Role:

Contact name:	Contact name:
Telephone: Mobile:	Telephone: Mobile:
Address:	Address:
Role:	Role:

Contact name:	Contact name:
Telephone: Mobile:	Telephone: Mobile:
Address:	Address:
Role:	Role:

Contact name:	Contact name:
Telephone: Mobile:	Telephone: Mobile:
Address:	Address:
Role:	Role:

Supplier List

Supplier name:	Supplier name:
Type of goods:	Type of goods:
Telephone: Mobile:	Telephone: Mobile:
Account number:	Account number:
Delivery days:	Delivery days:
Lead time for order:	Lead time for order:
Minimum order amount:	Minimum order amount:
Address:	Address:

Supplier name:	Supplier name:
Type of goods:	Type of goods:
Telephone: Mobile:	Telephone: Mobile:
Account number:	Account number:
Delivery days:	Delivery days:
Lead time for order:	Lead time for order:
Minimum order amount:	Minimum order amount:
Address:	Address:

Supplier name:	Supplier name:
Type of goods:	Type of goods:
Telephone: Mobile:	Telephone: Mobile:
Account number:	Account number:
Delivery days:	Delivery days:
Lead time for order:	Lead time for order:
Minimum order amount:	Minimum order amount:
Address:	Address:

Notes:

Supplier name:	Supplier name:
Type of goods:	Type of goods:
Telephone: Mobile:	Telephone: Mobile:
Account number:	Account number:
Delivery days:	Delivery days:
Lead time for order:	Lead time for order:
Minimum order amount:	Minimum order amount:
Address:	Address:

Supplier name:	Supplier name:
Type of goods:	Type of goods:
Telephone: Mobile:	Telephone: Mobile:
Account number:	Account number:
Delivery days:	Delivery days:
Lead time for order:	Lead time for order:
Minimum order amount:	Minimum order amount:
Address:	Address:

Supplier name:	Supplier name:
Type of goods:	Type of goods:
Telephone: Mobile:	Telephone: Mobile:
Account number:	Account number:
Delivery days:	Delivery days:
Lead time for order:	Lead time for order:
Minimum order amount:	Minimum order amount:
Address:	Address:

Notes:

Supplier name:	Supplier name:
Type of goods:	Type of goods:
Telephone: Mobile:	Telephone: Mobile:
Account number:	Account number:
Delivery days:	Delivery days:
Lead time for order:	Lead time for order:
Minimum order amount:	Minimum order amount:
Address:	Address:

Supplier name:	Supplier name:
Type of goods:	Type of goods:
Telephone: Mobile:	Telephone: Mobile:
Account number:	Account number:
Delivery days:	Delivery days:
Lead time for order:	Lead time for order:
Minimum order amount:	Minimum order amount:
Address:	Address:

Supplier name:	Supplier name:
Type of goods:	Type of goods:
Telephone: Mobile:	Telephone: Mobile:
Account number:	Account number:
Delivery days:	Delivery days:
Lead time for order:	Lead time for order:
Minimum order amount:	Minimum order amount:
Address:	Address:

Notes:

Staff training record	Employee name:		Trainer:	
Nature of Training		**Dates**	**Employee Signature**	**Trainer**
Basic hygiene rules				
Accepting deliveries				
Food preparation and handling				
Defrosting				
Cooking				
Cooling/Freezing				
Reheating				
Hot holding/Chilled food display				
Transport and delivery				
Physical/Chemical/Cross contamination				
Food allergies				
Using a thermometer				
Cleaning				
Pest control				
Personal hygiene				
Other training:				

Staff training record	Employee name:		Trainer:	
Nature of Training		**Dates**	**Employee Signature**	**Trainer**
Basic hygiene rules				
Accepting deliveries				
Food preparation and handling				
Defrosting				
Cooking				
Cooling/Freezing				
Reheating				
Hot holding/Chilled food display				
Transport and delivery				
Physical/Chemical/Cross contamination				
Food allergies				
Using a thermometer				
Cleaning				
Pest control				
Personal hygiene				
Other training:				

Staff training record	Employee name:		Trainer:	
Nature of Training	**Dates**	**Employee Signature**		**Trainer**
Basic hygiene rules				
Accepting deliveries				
Food preparation and handling				
Defrosting				
Cooking				
Cooling/Freezing				
Reheating				
Hot holding/Chilled food display				
Transport and delivery				
Physical/Chemical/Cross contamination				
Food allergies				
Using a thermometer				
Cleaning				
Pest control				
Personal hygiene				
Other training:				

Staff training record	Employee name:		Trainer:	
Nature of Training	**Dates**	**Employee Signature**		**Trainer**
Basic hygiene rules				
Accepting deliveries				
Food preparation and handling				
Defrosting				
Cooking				
Cooling/Freezing				
Reheating				
Hot holding/Chilled food display				
Transport and delivery				
Physical/Chemical/Cross contamination				
Food allergies				
Using a thermometer				
Cleaning				
Pest control				
Personal hygiene				
Other training:				

Staff training record	Employee name:		Trainer:	
Nature of Training	**Dates**	**Employee Signature**	**Trainer**	
Basic hygiene rules				
Accepting deliveries				
Food preparation and handling				
Defrosting				
Cooking				
Cooling/Freezing				
Reheating				
Hot holding/Chilled food display				
Transport and delivery				
Physical/Chemical/Cross contamination				
Food allergies				
Using a thermometer				
Cleaning				
Pest control				
Personal hygiene				
Other training:				

Staff training record	Employee name:		Trainer:	
Nature of Training	**Dates**	**Employee Signature**	**Trainer**	
Basic hygiene rules				
Accepting deliveries				
Food preparation and handling				
Defrosting				
Cooking				
Cooling/Freezing				
Reheating				
Hot holding/Chilled food display				
Transport and delivery				
Physical/Chemical/Cross contamination				
Food allergies				
Using a thermometer				
Cleaning				
Pest control				
Personal hygiene				
Other training:				

Staff training record   Employee name: Trainer:

Nature of Training	Dates	Employee Signature	Trainer
Basic hygiene rules			
Accepting deliveries			
Food preparation and handling			
Defrosting			
Cooking			
Cooling/Freezing			
Reheating			
Hot holding/Chilled food display			
Transport and delivery			
Physical/Chemical/Cross contamination			
Food allergies			
Using a thermometer			
Cleaning			
Pest control			
Personal hygiene			
Other training:			

Staff training record   Employee name: Trainer:

Nature of Training	Dates	Employee Signature	Trainer
Basic hygiene rules			
Accepting deliveries			
Food preparation and handling			
Defrosting			
Cooking			
Cooling/Freezing			
Reheating			
Hot holding/Chilled food display			
Transport and delivery			
Physical/Chemical/Cross contamination			
Food allergies			
Using a thermometer			
Cleaning			
Pest control			
Personal hygiene			
Other training:			

Staff training record Employee name:		Trainer:	
Nature of Training	**Dates**	**Employee Signature**	**Trainer**
Basic hygiene rules			
Accepting deliveries			
Food preparation and handling			
Defrosting			
Cooking			
Cooling/Freezing			
Reheating			
Hot holding/Chilled food display			
Transport and delivery			
Physical/Chemical/Cross contamination			
Food allergies			
Using a thermometer			
Cleaning			
Pest control			
Personal hygiene			
Other training:			

Staff training record Employee name:		Trainer:	
Nature of Training	**Dates**	**Employee Signature**	**Trainer**
Basic hygiene rules			
Accepting deliveries			
Food preparation and handling			
Defrosting			
Cooking			
Cooling/Freezing			
Reheating			
Hot holding/Chilled food display			
Transport and delivery			
Physical/Chemical/Cross contamination			
Food allergies			
Using a thermometer			
Cleaning			
Pest control			
Personal hygiene			
Other training:			

Staff training record	Employee name:		Trainer:	
Nature of Training	**Dates**	**Employee Signature**	**Trainer**	
Basic hygiene rules				
Accepting deliveries				
Food preparation and handling				
Defrosting				
Cooking				
Cooling/Freezing				
Reheating				
Hot holding/Chilled food display				
Transport and delivery				
Physical/Chemical/Cross contamination				
Food allergies				
Using a thermometer				
Cleaning				
Pest control				
Personal hygiene				
Other training:				

Staff training record	Employee name:		Trainer:	
Nature of Training	**Dates**	**Employee Signature**	**Trainer**	
Basic hygiene rules				
Accepting deliveries				
Food preparation and handling				
Defrosting				
Cooking				
Cooling/Freezing				
Reheating				
Hot holding/Chilled food display				
Transport and delivery				
Physical/Chemical/Cross contamination				
Food allergies				
Using a thermometer				
Cleaning				
Pest control				
Personal hygiene				
Other training:				

Staff training record	Employee name:		Trainer:	
Nature of Training		**Dates**	**Employee Signature**	**Trainer**
Basic hygiene rules				
Accepting deliveries				
Food preparation and handling				
Defrosting				
Cooking				
Cooling/Freezing				
Reheating				
Hot holding/Chilled food display				
Transport and delivery				
Physical/Chemical/Cross contamination				
Food allergies				
Using a thermometer				
Cleaning				
Pest control				
Personal hygiene				
Other training:				

Staff training record	Employee name:		Trainer:	
Nature of Training		**Dates**	**Employee Signature**	**Trainer**
Basic hygiene rules				
Accepting deliveries				
Food preparation and handling				
Defrosting				
Cooking				
Cooling/Freezing				
Reheating				
Hot holding/Chilled food display				
Transport and delivery				
Physical/Chemical/Cross contamination				
Food allergies				
Using a thermometer				
Cleaning				
Pest control				
Personal hygiene				
Other training:				

Staff training record	Employee name:		Trainer:	
Nature of Training	**Dates**	**Employee Signature**		**Trainer**
Basic hygiene rules				
Accepting deliveries				
Food preparation and handling				
Defrosting				
Cooking				
Cooling/Freezing				
Reheating				
Hot holding/Chilled food display				
Transport and delivery				
Physical/Chemical/Cross contamination				
Food allergies				
Using a thermometer				
Cleaning				
Pest control				
Personal hygiene				
Other training:				

Staff training record	Employee name:		Trainer:	
Nature of Training	**Dates**	**Employee Signature**		**Trainer**
Basic hygiene rules				
Accepting deliveries				
Food preparation and handling				
Defrosting				
Cooking				
Cooling/Freezing				
Reheating				
Hot holding/Chilled food display				
Transport and delivery				
Physical/Chemical/Cross contamination				
Food allergies				
Using a thermometer				
Cleaning				
Pest control				
Personal hygiene				
Other training:				

Staff training record	Employee name:		Trainer:	
Nature of Training		**Dates**	**Employee Signature**	**Trainer**
Basic hygiene rules				
Accepting deliveries				
Food preparation and handling				
Defrosting				
Cooking				
Cooling/Freezing				
Reheating				
Hot holding/Chilled food display				
Transport and delivery				
Physical/Chemical/Cross contamination				
Food allergies				
Using a thermometer				
Cleaning				
Pest control				
Personal hygiene				
Other training:				

Staff training record	Employee name:		Trainer:	
Nature of Training		**Dates**	**Employee Signature**	**Trainer**
Basic hygiene rules				
Accepting deliveries				
Food preparation and handling				
Defrosting				
Cooking				
Cooling/Freezing				
Reheating				
Hot holding/Chilled food display				
Transport and delivery				
Physical/Chemical/Cross contamination				
Food allergies				
Using a thermometer				
Cleaning				
Pest control				
Personal hygiene				
Other training:				

Staff training record	Employee name:		Trainer:	
Nature of Training	**Dates**	**Employee Signature**	**Trainer**	
Basic hygiene rules				
Accepting deliveries				
Food preparation and handling				
Defrosting				
Cooking				
Cooling/Freezing				
Reheating				
Hot holding/Chilled food display				
Transport and delivery				
Physical/Chemical/Cross contamination				
Food allergies				
Using a thermometer				
Cleaning				
Pest control				
Personal hygiene				
Other training:				

Staff training record	Employee name:		Trainer:	
Nature of Training	**Dates**	**Employee Signature**	**Trainer**	
Basic hygiene rules				
Accepting deliveries				
Food preparation and handling				
Defrosting				
Cooking				
Cooling/Freezing				
Reheating				
Hot holding/Chilled food display				
Transport and delivery				
Physical/Chemical/Cross contamination				
Food allergies				
Using a thermometer				
Cleaning				
Pest control				
Personal hygiene				
Other training:				

Staff training record	Employee name:		Trainer:	
Nature of Training	**Dates**	**Employee Signature**	**Trainer**	
Basic hygiene rules				
Accepting deliveries				
Food preparation and handling				
Defrosting				
Cooking				
Cooling/Freezing				
Reheating				
Hot holding/Chilled food display				
Transport and delivery				
Physical/Chemical/Cross contamination				
Food allergies				
Using a thermometer				
Cleaning				
Pest control				
Personal hygiene				
Other training:				

Staff training record	Employee name:		Trainer:	
Nature of Training	**Dates**	**Employee Signature**	**Trainer**	
Basic hygiene rules				
Accepting deliveries				
Food preparation and handling				
Defrosting				
Cooking				
Cooling/Freezing				
Reheating				
Hot holding/Chilled food display				
Transport and delivery				
Physical/Chemical/Cross contamination				
Food allergies				
Using a thermometer				
Cleaning				
Pest control				
Personal hygiene				
Other training:				

Staff training record	Employee name:		Trainer:	
Nature of Training	**Dates**	**Employee Signature**		**Trainer**
Basic hygiene rules				
Accepting deliveries				
Food preparation and handling				
Defrosting				
Cooking				
Cooling/Freezing				
Reheating				
Hot holding/Chilled food display				
Transport and delivery				
Physical/Chemical/Cross contamination				
Food allergies				
Using a thermometer				
Cleaning				
Pest control				
Personal hygiene				
Other training:				

Staff training record	Employee name:		Trainer:	
Nature of Training	**Dates**	**Employee Signature**		**Trainer**
Basic hygiene rules				
Accepting deliveries				
Food preparation and handling				
Defrosting				
Cooking				
Cooling/Freezing				
Reheating				
Hot holding/Chilled food display				
Transport and delivery				
Physical/Chemical/Cross contamination				
Food allergies				
Using a thermometer				
Cleaning				
Pest control				
Personal hygiene				
Other training:				

Week Starting: Date/Month/Year	Temperature recordings		Please tick boxes √		Week 1				
Monday	Time	Dish	Temp	Time	Dish	Temp	Time	Dish	Temp
Opening checks done ☐									
Issues: Yes ☐ No ☐									
Closing checks ☐									
Safe methods followed ☐									
Name:									
Signature:									
Tuesday	Time	Dish	Temp	Time	Dish	Temp	Time	Dish	Temp
Opening checks done ☐									
Issues: Yes ☐ No ☐									
Closing checks ☐									
Safe methods followed ☐									
Name:									
Signature:									
Wednesday	Time	Dish	Temp	Time	Dish	Temp	Time	Dish	Temp
Opening checks done ☐									
Issues: Yes ☐ No ☐									
Closing checks ☐									
Safe methods followed ☐									
Name:									
Signature:									
Thursday	Time	Dish	Temp	Time	Dish	Temp	Time	Dish	Temp
Opening checks done ☐									
Issues: Yes ☐ No ☐									
Closing checks ☐									
Safe methods followed ☐									
Name:									
Signature:									

Temperature recordings   Please tick boxes √

Friday	Time	Dish	Temp	Time	Dish	Temp	Time	Dish	Temp
Opening checks done ☐									
Issues: Yes ☐ No ☐									
Closing checks ☐									
Safe methods followed ☐									
Name:									
Signature:									

Saturday	Time	Dish	Temp	Time	Dish	Temp	Time	Dish	Temp
Opening checks done ☐									
Issues: Yes ☐ No ☐									
Closing checks ☐									
Safe methods followed ☐									
Name:									
Signature:									

Sunday	Time	Dish	Temp	Time	Dish	Temp	Time	Dish	Temp
Opening checks done ☐									
Issues: Yes ☐ No ☐									
Closing checks ☐									
Safe methods followed ☐									
Name:									
Signature:									

Fridge/Freezer/Chiller Temperature records

Day	Frid/Frz/Chil 1	Frid/Frz/Chil 2	Frid/Frz/Chil 3	Frid/Frz/Chil 4	Frid/Frz/Chil 6	Frid/Frz/Chil 7
Monday	Opening: Closing:	Opening: Closing:	Opening: Closing:	Opening: Closing:	Opening: Closing:	Opening: Closing:
Tuesday	Opening: Closing:	Opening: Closing:	Opening: Closing:	Opening: Closing:	Opening: Closing:	Opening: Closing:
Wednesday	Opening: Closing:	Opening: Closing:	Opening: Closing:	Opening: Closing:	Opening: Closing:	Opening: Closing:
Thursday	Opening: Closing:	Opening: Closing:	Opening: Closing:	Opening: Closing:	Opening: Closing:	Opening: Closing:

Friday	Opening: Closing:	Opening: Closing:	Opening: Closing:	Opening: Closing:	Opening: Closing:	Opening: Closing:
Saturday	Opening: Closing:	Opening: Closing:	Opening: Closing:	Opening: Closing:	Opening: Closing:	Opening: Closing:
Sunday	Opening: Closing:	Opening: Closing:	Opening: Closing:	Opening: Closing:	Opening: Closing:	Opening: Closing:

Cleaning schedule

Task	Please tick boxes √	Mon	Tues	Wed	Thurs	Fri	Sat	Sun
Clean and sanitise refrigerators and freezers								
Clean and sanitise the sinks and taps								
Empty and clean the coffee machine								
Clean the grills,ovens,hobs,griddles and stoves								
Clean the fryers								
Brush the grill and clean out grease traps								
Clean and sanitise all kitchen preparation surfaces								
Clean and sanitise all cutting boards								
Clean the meat and cheese slicer,if used								
Sanitise the telephone and all surfaces								
Clean behind fridges,ovens and fryers								
Empty bins and clean the kitchen floor								
Any other Step(s):								
Supervisor signature:	Date:							

Weekly review-The Good,The Bad,The Ugly,Hirings and Firings

What went right:	**What went wrong:**

Notes:

Week Starting: Date/Month/Year	Temperature recordings			Please tick boxes √			Week 2		
Monday	Time	Dish	Temp	Time	Dish	Temp	Time	Dish	Temp
Opening checks done ☐									
Issues: Yes ☐ No ☐									
Closing checks ☐									
Safe methods followed ☐									
Name:									
Signature:									
Tuesday	Time	Dish	Temp	Time	Dish	Temp	Time	Dish	Temp
Opening checks done ☐									
Issues: Yes ☐ No ☐									
Closing checks ☐									
Safe methods followed ☐									
Name:									
Signature:									
Wednesday	Time	Dish	Temp	Time	Dish	Temp	Time	Dish	Temp
Opening checks done ☐									
Issues: Yes ☐ No ☐									
Closing checks ☐									
Safe methods followed ☐									
Name:									
Signature:									
Thursday	Time	Dish	Temp	Time	Dish	Temp	Time	Dish	Temp
Opening checks done ☐									
Issues: Yes ☐ No ☐									
Closing checks ☐									
Safe methods followed ☐									
Name:									
Signature:									

Temperature recordings   Please tick boxes √

Friday	Time	Dish	Temp	Time	Dish	Temp	Time	Dish	Temp
Opening checks done ☐									
Issues: Yes ☐ No ☐									
Closing checks ☐									
Safe methods followed ☐									
Name:									
Signature:									

Saturday	Time	Dish	Temp	Time	Dish	Temp	Time	Dish	Temp
Opening checks done ☐									
Issues: Yes ☐ No ☐									
Closing checks ☐									
Safe methods followed ☐									
Name:									
Signature:									

Sunday	Time	Dish	Temp	Time	Dish	Temp	Time	Dish	Temp
Opening checks done ☐									
Issues: Yes ☐ No ☐									
Closing checks ☐									
Safe methods followed ☐									
Name:									
Signature:									

Fridge/Freezer/Chiller Temperature records

Day	Frid/Frz/Chil 1	Frid/Frz/Chil 2	Frid/Frz/Chil 3	Frid/Frz/Chil 4	Frid/Frz/Chil 6	Frid/Frz/Chil 7
Monday	Opening: Closing:	Opening: Closing:	Opening: Closing:	Opening: Closing:	Opening: Closing:	Opening: Closing:
Tuesday	Opening: Closing:	Opening: Closing:	Opening: Closing:	Opening: Closing:	Opening: Closing:	Opening: Closing:
Wednesday	Opening: Closing:	Opening: Closing:	Opening: Closing:	Opening: Closing:	Opening: Closing:	Opening: Closing:
Thursday	Opening: Closing:	Opening: Closing:	Opening: Closing:	Opening: Closing:	Opening: Closing:	Opening: Closing:

Friday	Opening: Closing:	Opening: Closing:	Opening: Closing:	Opening: Closing:	Opening: Closing:	Opening: Closing:
Saturday	Opening: Closing:	Opening: Closing:	Opening: Closing:	Opening: Closing:	Opening: Closing:	Opening: Closing:
Sunday	Opening: Closing:	Opening: Closing:	Opening: Closing:	Opening: Closing:	Opening: Closing:	Opening: Closing:

Cleaning schedule

Task	Please tick boxes √	Mon	Tues	Wed	Thurs	Fri	Sat	Sun
Clean and sanitise refrigerators and freezers								
Clean and sanitise the sinks and taps								
Empty and clean the coffee machine								
Clean the grills,ovens,hobs,griddles and stoves								
Clean the fryers								
Brush the grill and clean out grease traps								
Clean and sanitise all kitchen preparation surfaces								
Clean and sanitise all cutting boards								
Clean the meat and cheese slicer,if used								
Sanitise the telephone and all surfaces								
Clean behind fridges,ovens and fryers								
Empty bins and clean the kitchen floor								
Any other Step(s):								

Supervisor signature: Date:

Weekly review-The Good,The Bad,The Ugly,Hirings and Firings

What went right:	What went wrong:

Notes:

Week Starting: Date/Month/Year	Temperature recordings			Please tick boxes √			Week 3		
Monday	Time	Dish	Temp	Time	Dish	Temp	Time	Dish	Temp
Opening checks done ☐									
Issues: Yes ☐ No ☐									
Closing checks ☐									
Safe methods followed ☐									
Name:									
Signature:									
Tuesday	Time	Dish	Temp	Time	Dish	Temp	Time	Dish	Temp
Opening checks done ☐									
Issues: Yes ☐ No ☐									
Closing checks ☐									
Safe methods followed ☐									
Name:									
Signature:									
Wednesday	Time	Dish	Temp	Time	Dish	Temp	Time	Dish	Temp
Opening checks done ☐									
Issues: Yes ☐ No ☐									
Closing checks ☐									
Safe methods followed ☐									
Name:									
Signature:									
Thursday	Time	Dish	Temp	Time	Dish	Temp	Time	Dish	Temp
Opening checks done ☐									
Issues: Yes ☐ No ☐									
Closing checks ☐									
Safe methods followed ☐									
Name:									
Signature:									

Temperature recordings			Please tick boxes √								
Friday	Time	Dish		Temp	Time	Dish		Temp	Time	Dish	Temp
Opening checks done ☐											
Issues: Yes ☐ No ☐											
Closing checks ☐											
Safe methods followed ☐											
Name:											
Signature:											
Saturday	Time	Dish		Temp	Time	Dish		Temp	Time	Dish	Temp
Opening checks done ☐											
Issues: Yes ☐ No ☐											
Closing checks ☐											
Safe methods followed ☐											
Name:											
Signature:											
Sunday	Time	Dish		Temp	Time	Dish		Temp	Time	Dish	Temp
Opening checks done ☐											
Issues: Yes ☐ No ☐											
Closing checks ☐											
Safe methods followed ☐											
Name:											
Signature:											

Fridge/Freezer/Chiller Temperature records

Day	Frid/Frz/Chil 1	Frid/Frz/Chil 2	Frid/Frz/Chil 3	Frid/Frz/Chil 4	Frid/Frz/Chil 6	Frid/Frz/Chil 7
Monday	Opening: Closing:	Opening: Closing:	Opening: Closing:	Opening: Closing:	Opening: Closing:	Opening: Closing:
Tuesday	Opening: Closing:	Opening: Closing:	Opening: Closing:	Opening: Closing:	Opening: Closing:	Opening: Closing:
Wednesday	Opening: Closing:	Opening: Closing:	Opening: Closing:	Opening: Closing:	Opening: Closing:	Opening: Closing:
Thursday	Opening: Closing:	Opening: Closing:	Opening: Closing:	Opening: Closing:	Opening: Closing:	Opening: Closing:

Friday	Opening: Closing:	Opening: Closing:	Opening: Closing:	Opening: Closing:	Opening: Closing:	Opening: Closing:
Saturday	Opening: Closing:	Opening: Closing:	Opening: Closing:	Opening: Closing:	Opening: Closing:	Opening: Closing:
Sunday	Opening: Closing:	Opening: Closing:	Opening: Closing:	Opening: Closing:	Opening: Closing:	Opening: Closing:

Cleaning schedule

Task	Please tick boxes √	Mon	Tues	Wed	Thurs	Fri	Sat	Sun
Clean and sanitise refrigerators and freezers								
Clean and sanitise the sinks and taps								
Empty and clean the coffee machine								
Clean the grills,ovens,hobs,griddles and stoves								
Clean the fryers								
Brush the grill and clean out grease traps								
Clean and sanitise all kitchen preparation surfaces								
Clean and sanitise all cutting boards								
Clean the meat and cheese slicer,if used								
Sanitise the telephone and all surfaces								
Clean behind fridges,ovens and fryers								
Empty bins and clean the kitchen floor								
Any other Step(s):								

Supervisor signature: Date:

Weekly review-The Good,The Bad,The Ugly,Hirings and Firings

What went right:	What went wrong:

Notes:

Week Starting: Date/Month/Year	Temperature recordings			Please tick boxes √ Week 4					
Monday	Time	Dish	Temp	Time	Dish	Temp	Time	Dish	Temp
Opening checks done ☐									
Issues: Yes ☐ No ☐									
Closing checks ☐									
Safe methods followed ☐									
Name:									
Signature:									
Tuesday	Time	Dish	Temp	Time	Dish	Temp	Time	Dish	Temp
Opening checks done ☐									
Issues: Yes ☐ No ☐									
Closing checks ☐									
Safe methods followed ☐									
Name:									
Signature:									
Wednesday	Time	Dish	Temp	Time	Dish	Temp	Time	Dish	Temp
Opening checks done ☐									
Issues: Yes ☐ No ☐									
Closing checks ☐									
Safe methods followed ☐									
Name:									
Signature:									
Thursday	Time	Dish	Temp	Time	Dish	Temp	Time	Dish	Temp
Opening checks done ☐									
Issues: Yes ☐ No ☐									
Closing checks ☐									
Safe methods followed ☐									
Name:									
Signature:									

Temperature recordings			Please tick boxes √							
Friday	Time	Dish		Temp	Time	Dish	Temp	Time	Dish	Temp
Opening checks done ☐										
Issues: Yes ☐ No ☐										
Closing checks ☐										
Safe methods followed ☐										
Name:										
Signature:										
Saturday	Time	Dish		Temp	Time	Dish	Temp	Time	Dish	Temp
Opening checks done ☐										
Issues: Yes ☐ No ☐										
Closing checks ☐										
Safe methods followed ☐										
Name:										
Signature:										
Sunday	Time	Dish		Temp	Time	Dish	Temp	Time	Dish	Temp
Opening checks done ☐										
Issues: Yes ☐ No ☐										
Closing checks ☐										
Safe methods followed ☐										
Name:										
Signature:										

Fridge/Freezer/Chiller Temperature records

Day	Frid/Frz/Chil 1	Frid/Frz/Chil 2	Frid/Frz/Chil 3	Frid/Frz/Chil 4	Frid/Frz/Chil 6	Frid/Frz/Chil 7
Monday	Opening: Closing:	Opening: Closing:	Opening: Closing:	Opening: Closing:	Opening: Closing:	Opening: Closing:
Tuesday	Opening: Closing:	Opening: Closing:	Opening: Closing:	Opening: Closing:	Opening: Closing:	Opening: Closing:
Wednesday	Opening: Closing:	Opening: Closing:	Opening: Closing:	Opening: Closing:	Opening: Closing:	Opening: Closing:
Thursday	Opening: Closing:	Opening: Closing:	Opening: Closing:	Opening: Closing:	Opening: Closing:	Opening: Closing:

Friday	Opening: Closing:	Opening: Closing:	Opening: Closing:	Opening: Closing:	Opening: Closing:	Opening: Closing:
Saturday	Opening: Closing:	Opening: Closing:	Opening: Closing:	Opening: Closing:	Opening: Closing:	Opening: Closing:
Sunday	Opening: Closing:	Opening: Closing:	Opening: Closing:	Opening: Closing:	Opening: Closing:	Opening: Closing:

Cleaning schedule

Task	Please tick boxes √	Mon	Tues	Wed	Thurs	Fri	Sat	Sun
Clean and sanitise refrigerators and freezers								
Clean and sanitise the sinks and taps								
Empty and clean the coffee machine								
Clean the grills,ovens,hobs,griddles and stoves								
Clean the fryers								
Brush the grill and clean out grease traps								
Clean and sanitise all kitchen preparation surfaces								
Clean and sanitise all cutting boards								
Clean the meat and cheese slicer,if used								
Sanitise the telephone and all surfaces								
Clean behind fridges,ovens and fryers								
Empty bins and clean the kitchen floor								
Any other Step(s):								
Supervisor signature:		Date:						

Kitchen hygiene: monthly cleaning

Task	Please tick boxes √	When	Who	Comment
Wash kitchen walls and storage areas				
Clean and sanitise refrigerators and freezers				
Clean cooker hood and filters				
Supervisor signature:		**Date:**		

Always use appropriate personal protective equipment (PPE) when undertaking any cleaning task and follow the manufacturer's product use and, where relevant, dilution guidance.

138

4-weekly review

You should regularly review the methods used in your business to check that they are up to date, and still being followed by you and your staff.

You can use the checklist below to help you.
Look back over the past 4 weeks' diary entries. If you had a serious problem, or the same thing went wrong three times or more, make a note of it here, find out why and do something about it. Did you have a serious problem or did the same thing go wrong three times or more?
Yes ☐ No ☐
Details:

What did you do about it?

Did you get a new member of staff in the past 4 weeks? Yes ☐ No ☐

Were they trained in your methods? Yes ☐ No ☐

Have you changed your menu?

Have you reviewed your safe methods?

Any changes/new methods? Yes ☐ No ☐

Have you changed supplier/bought new ingredients? Yes ☐ No ☐

Do these affect any of your safe methods?

Other changes:

Notes:

Week Starting: Date/Month/Year	Temperature recordings			Please tick boxes √			Week 1		
Monday	Time	Dish	Temp	Time	Dish	Temp	Time	Dish	Temp
Opening checks done ☐									
Issues: Yes ☐ No ☐									
Closing checks ☐									
Safe methods followed ☐									
Name:									
Signature:									
Tuesday	Time	Dish	Temp	Time	Dish	Temp	Time	Dish	Temp
Opening checks done ☐									
Issues: Yes ☐ No ☐									
Closing checks ☐									
Safe methods followed ☐									
Name:									
Signature:									
Wednesday	Time	Dish	Temp	Time	Dish	Temp	Time	Dish	Temp
Opening checks done ☐									
Issues: Yes ☐ No ☐									
Closing checks ☐									
Safe methods followed ☐									
Name:									
Signature:									
Thursday	Time	Dish	Temp	Time	Dish	Temp	Time	Dish	Temp
Opening checks done ☐									
Issues: Yes ☐ No ☐									
Closing checks ☐									
Safe methods followed ☐									
Name:									
Signature:									

Temperature recordings   Please tick boxes √

Friday	Time	Dish	Temp	Time	Dish	Temp	Time	Dish	Temp
Opening checks done ☐									
Issues: Yes ☐ No ☐									
Closing checks ☐									
Safe methods followed ☐									
Name:									
Signature:									
Saturday	Time	Dish	Temp	Time	Dish	Temp	Time	Dish	Temp
Opening checks done ☐									
Issues: Yes ☐ No ☐									
Closing checks ☐									
Safe methods followed ☐									
Name:									
Signature:									
Sunday	Time	Dish	Temp	Time	Dish	Temp	Time	Dish	Temp
Opening checks done ☐									
Issues: Yes ☐ No ☐									
Closing checks ☐									
Safe methods followed ☐									
Name:									
Signature:									

Fridge/Freezer/Chiller Temperature records

Day	Frid/Frz/Chil 1	Frid/Frz/Chil 2	Frid/Frz/Chil 3	Frid/Frz/Chil 4	Frid/Frz/Chil 6	Frid/Frz/Chil 7
Monday	Opening: Closing:	Opening: Closing:	Opening: Closing:	Opening: Closing:	Opening: Closing:	Opening: Closing:
Tuesday	Opening: Closing:	Opening: Closing:	Opening: Closing:	Opening: Closing:	Opening: Closing:	Opening: Closing:
Wednesday	Opening: Closing:	Opening: Closing:	Opening: Closing:	Opening: Closing:	Opening: Closing:	Opening: Closing:
Thursday	Opening: Closing:	Opening: Closing:	Opening: Closing:	Opening: Closing:	Opening: Closing:	Opening: Closing:

Friday	Opening: Closing:	Opening: Closing:	Opening: Closing:	Opening: Closing:	Opening: Closing:	Opening: Closing:
Saturday	Opening: Closing:	Opening: Closing:	Opening: Closing:	Opening: Closing:	Opening: Closing:	Opening: Closing:
Sunday	Opening: Closing:	Opening: Closing:	Opening: Closing:	Opening: Closing:	Opening: Closing:	Opening: Closing:

Cleaning schedule

Task	Please tick boxes √	Mon	Tues	Wed	Thurs	Fri	Sat	Sun
Clean and sanitise refrigerators and freezers								
Clean and sanitise the sinks and taps								
Empty and clean the coffee machine								
Clean the grills,ovens,hobs,griddles and stoves								
Clean the fryers								
Brush the grill and clean out grease traps								
Clean and sanitise all kitchen preparation surfaces								
Clean and sanitise all cutting boards								
Clean the meat and cheese slicer,if used								
Sanitise the telephone and all surfaces								
Clean behind fridges,ovens and fryers								
Empty bins and clean the kitchen floor								
Any other Step(s):								
Supervisor signature:		Date:						

Weekly review-The Good,The Bad,The Ugly,Hirings and Firings

What went right:

What went wrong:

Notes:

Week Starting: Date/Month/Year	Temperature recordings			Please tick boxes √			Week 2		
Monday	Time	Dish	Temp	Time	Dish	Temp	Time	Dish	Temp
Opening checks done ☐									
Issues: Yes ☐ No ☐									
Closing checks ☐									
Safe methods followed ☐									
Name:									
Signature:									
Tuesday	Time	Dish	Temp	Time	Dish	Temp	Time	Dish	Temp
Opening checks done ☐									
Issues: Yes ☐ No ☐									
Closing checks ☐									
Safe methods followed ☐									
Name:									
Signature:									
Wednesday	Time	Dish	Temp	Time	Dish	Temp	Time	Dish	Temp
Opening checks done ☐									
Issues: Yes ☐ No ☐									
Closing checks ☐									
Safe methods followed ☐									
Name:									
Signature:									
Thursday	Time	Dish	Temp	Time	Dish	Temp	Time	Dish	Temp
Opening checks done ☐									
Issues: Yes ☐ No ☐									
Closing checks ☐									
Safe methods followed ☐									
Name:									
Signature:									

Temperature recordings			Please tick boxes √							
Friday	Time	Dish		Temp	Time	Dish	Temp	Time	Dish	Temp
Opening checks done ☐										
Issues: Yes ☐ No ☐										
Closing checks ☐										
Safe methods followed ☐										
Name:										
Signature:										
Saturday	Time	Dish		Temp	Time	Dish	Temp	Time	Dish	Temp
Opening checks done ☐										
Issues: Yes ☐ No ☐										
Closing checks ☐										
Safe methods followed ☐										
Name:										
Signature:										
Sunday	Time	Dish		Temp	Time	Dish	Temp	Time	Dish	Temp
Opening checks done ☐										
Issues: Yes ☐ No ☐										
Closing checks ☐										
Safe methods followed ☐										
Name:										
Signature:										

Fridge/Freezer/Chiller Temperature records

Day	Frid/Frz/Chil 1	Frid/Frz/Chil 2	Frid/Frz/Chil 3	Frid/Frz/Chil 4	Frid/Frz/Chil 6	Frid/Frz/Chil 7
Monday	Opening: Closing:	Opening: Closing:	Opening: Closing:	Opening: Closing:	Opening: Closing:	Opening: Closing:
Tuesday	Opening: Closing:	Opening: Closing:	Opening: Closing:	Opening: Closing:	Opening: Closing:	Opening: Closing:
Wednesday	Opening: Closing:	Opening: Closing:	Opening: Closing:	Opening: Closing:	Opening: Closing:	Opening: Closing:
Thursday	Opening: Closing:	Opening: Closing:	Opening: Closing:	Opening: Closing:	Opening: Closing:	Opening: Closing:

Friday	Opening: Closing:	Opening: Closing:	Opening: Closing:	Opening: Closing:	Opening: Closing:	Opening: Closing:
Saturday	Opening: Closing:	Opening: Closing:	Opening: Closing:	Opening: Closing:	Opening: Closing:	Opening: Closing:
Sunday	Opening: Closing:	Opening: Closing:	Opening: Closing:	Opening: Closing:	Opening: Closing:	Opening: Closing:

Cleaning schedule

Task Please tick boxes √	Mon	Tues	Wed	Thurs	Fri	Sat	Sun
Clean and sanitise refrigerators and freezers							
Clean and sanitise the sinks and taps							
Empty and clean the coffee machine							
Clean the grills,ovens,hobs,griddles and stoves							
Clean the fryers							
Brush the grill and clean out grease traps							
Clean and sanitise all kitchen preparation surfaces							
Clean and sanitise all cutting boards							
Clean the meat and cheese slicer,if used							
Sanitise the telephone and all surfaces							
Clean behind fridges,ovens and fryers							
Empty bins and clean the kitchen floor							
Any other Step(s):							

Supervisor signature:　　　　　　　　　　　Date:

Weekly review-The Good,The Bad,The Ugly,Hirings and Firings

What went right:	What went wrong:

Notes:

Week Starting: Date/Month/Year	Temperature recordings			Please tick boxes √ Week 3					
Monday	Time	Dish	Temp	Time	Dish	Temp	Time	Dish	Temp
Opening checks done ☐									
Issues: Yes ☐ No ☐									
Closing checks ☐									
Safe methods followed ☐									
Name:									
Signature:									
Tuesday	Time	Dish	Temp	Time	Dish	Temp	Time	Dish	Temp
Opening checks done ☐									
Issues: Yes ☐ No ☐									
Closing checks ☐									
Safe methods followed ☐									
Name:									
Signature:									
Wednesday	Time	Dish	Temp	Time	Dish	Temp	Time	Dish	Temp
Opening checks done ☐									
Issues: Yes ☐ No ☐									
Closing checks ☐									
Safe methods followed ☐									
Name:									
Signature:									
Thursday	Time	Dish	Temp	Time	Dish	Temp	Time	Dish	Temp
Opening checks done ☐									
Issues: Yes ☐ No ☐									
Closing checks ☐									
Safe methods followed ☐									
Name:									
Signature:									

Temperature recordings   Please tick boxes √

Friday	Time	Dish	Temp	Time	Dish	Temp	Time	Dish	Temp
Opening checks done ☐									
Issues: Yes ☐ No ☐									
Closing checks ☐									
Safe methods followed ☐									
Name:									
Signature:									
Saturday	Time	Dish	Temp	Time	Dish	Temp	Time	Dish	Temp
Opening checks done ☐									
Issues: Yes ☐ No ☐									
Closing checks ☐									
Safe methods followed ☐									
Name:									
Signature:									
Sunday	Time	Dish	Temp	Time	Dish	Temp	Time	Dish	Temp
Opening checks done ☐									
Issues: Yes ☐ No ☐									
Closing checks ☐									
Safe methods followed ☐									
Name:									
Signature:									

Fridge/Freezer/Chiller Temperature records

Day	Frid/Frz/Chil 1	Frid/Frz/Chil 2	Frid/Frz/Chil 3	Frid/Frz/Chil 4	Frid/Frz/Chil 6	Frid/Frz/Chil 7
Monday	Opening: Closing:	Opening: Closing:	Opening: Closing:	Opening: Closing:	Opening: Closing:	Opening: Closing:
Tuesday	Opening: Closing:	Opening: Closing:	Opening: Closing:	Opening: Closing:	Opening: Closing:	Opening: Closing:
Wednesday	Opening: Closing:	Opening: Closing:	Opening: Closing:	Opening: Closing:	Opening: Closing:	Opening: Closing:
Thursday	Opening: Closing:	Opening: Closing:	Opening: Closing:	Opening: Closing:	Opening: Closing:	Opening: Closing:

Friday	Opening: Closing:	Opening: Closing:	Opening: Closing:	Opening: Closing:	Opening: Closing:	Opening: Closing:
Saturday	Opening: Closing:	Opening: Closing:	Opening: Closing:	Opening: Closing:	Opening: Closing:	Opening: Closing:
Sunday	Opening: Closing:	Opening: Closing:	Opening: Closing:	Opening: Closing:	Opening: Closing:	Opening: Closing:

Cleaning schedule

Task	Please tick boxes √	Mon	Tues	Wed	Thurs	Fri	Sat	Sun
Clean and sanitise refrigerators and freezers								
Clean and sanitise the sinks and taps								
Empty and clean the coffee machine								
Clean the grills, ovens, hobs, griddles and stoves								
Clean the fryers								
Brush the grill and clean out grease traps								
Clean and sanitise all kitchen preparation surfaces								
Clean and sanitise all cutting boards								
Clean the meat and cheese slicer, if used								
Sanitise the telephone and all surfaces								
Clean behind fridges, ovens and fryers								
Empty bins and clean the kitchen floor								
Any other Step(s):								
Supervisor signature:	Date:							

Weekly review-The Good, The Bad, The Ugly, Hirings and Firings

What went right:	What went wrong:

Notes:

148

Week Starting: Date/Month/Year	Temperature recordings								Please tick boxes √ Week 4	
Monday	Time	Dish	Temp	Time	Dish	Temp	Time	Dish		Temp
Opening checks done ☐										
Issues: Yes ☐ No ☐										
Closing checks ☐										
Safe methods followed ☐										
Name:										
Signature:										
Tuesday	Time	Dish	Temp	Time	Dish	Temp	Time	Dish		Temp
Opening checks done ☐										
Issues: Yes ☐ No ☐										
Closing checks ☐										
Safe methods followed ☐										
Name:										
Signature:										
Wednesday	Time	Dish	Temp	Time	Dish	Temp	Time	Dish		Temp
Opening checks done ☐										
Issues: Yes ☐ No ☐										
Closing checks ☐										
Safe methods followed ☐										
Name:										
Signature:										
Thursday	Time	Dish	Temp	Time	Dish	Temp	Time	Dish		Temp
Opening checks done ☐										
Issues: Yes ☐ No ☐										
Closing checks ☐										
Safe methods followed ☐										
Name:										
Signature:										

Temperature recordings			Please tick boxes √						
Friday	Time	Dish		Temp	Time	Dish	Temp	Time	Dish	Temp
Opening checks done ☐										
Issues: Yes ☐ No ☐										
Closing checks ☐										
Safe methods followed ☐										
Name:										
Signature:										
Saturday	Time	Dish		Temp	Time	Dish	Temp	Time	Dish	Temp
Opening checks done ☐										
Issues: Yes ☐ No ☐										
Closing checks ☐										
Safe methods followed ☐										
Name:										
Signature:										
Sunday	Time	Dish		Temp	Time	Dish	Temp	Time	Dish	Temp
Opening checks done ☐										
Issues: Yes ☐ No ☐										
Closing checks ☐										
Safe methods followed ☐										
Name:										
Signature:										

Fridge/Freezer/Chiller Temperature records

Day	Frid/Frz/Chil 1	Frid/Frz/Chil 2	Frid/Frz/Chil 3	Frid/Frz/Chil 4	Frid/Frz/Chil 6	Frid/Frz/Chil 7
Monday	Opening: Closing:	Opening: Closing:	Opening: Closing:	Opening: Closing:	Opening: Closing:	Opening: Closing:
Tuesday	Opening: Closing:	Opening: Closing:	Opening: Closing:	Opening: Closing:	Opening: Closing:	Opening: Closing:
Wednesday	Opening: Closing:	Opening: Closing:	Opening: Closing:	Opening: Closing:	Opening: Closing:	Opening: Closing:
Thursday	Opening: Closing:	Opening: Closing:	Opening: Closing:	Opening: Closing:	Opening: Closing:	Opening: Closing:

Friday	Opening: Closing:	Opening: Closing:	Opening: Closing:	Opening: Closing:	Opening: Closing:	Opening: Closing:
Saturday	Opening: Closing:	Opening: Closing:	Opening: Closing:	Opening: Closing:	Opening: Closing:	Opening: Closing:
Sunday	Opening: Closing:	Opening: Closing:	Opening: Closing:	Opening: Closing:	Opening: Closing:	Opening: Closing:

Cleaning schedule

Task Please tick boxes √	Mon	Tues	Wed	Thurs	Fri	Sat	Sun
Clean and sanitise refrigerators and freezers							
Clean and sanitise the sinks and taps							
Empty and clean the coffee machine							
Clean the grills,ovens,hobs,griddles and stoves							
Clean the fryers							
Brush the grill and clean out grease traps							
Clean and sanitise all kitchen preparation surfaces							
Clean and sanitise all cutting boards							
Clean the meat and cheese slicer,if used							
Sanitise the telephone and all surfaces							
Clean behind fridges,ovens and fryers							
Empty bins and clean the kitchen floor							
Any other Step(s):							
Supervisor signature:		Date:					

Kitchen hygiene: monthly cleaning

Task Please tick boxes √	When	Who	Comment
Wash kitchen walls and storage areas			
Clean and sanitise refrigerators and freezers			
Clean cooker hood and filters			
Supervisor signature:		**Date:**	

Always use appropriate personal protective equipment (PPE) when undertaking any cleaning task and follow the manufacturer's product use and, where relevant, dilution guidance.

4-weekly review

You should regularly review the methods used in your business to check that they are up to date, and still being followed by you and your staff.

You can use the checklist below to help you.
Look back over the past 4 weeks' diary entries. If you had a serious problem, or the same thing went wrong three times or more, make a note of it here, find out why and do something about it. Did you have a serious problem or did the same thing go wrong three times or more?
Yes ☐ No ☐
Details:

What did you do about it?

Did you get a new member of staff in the past 4 weeks? Yes ☐ No ☐

Were they trained in your methods? Yes ☐ No ☐

Have you changed your menu?

Have you reviewed your safe methods?

Any changes/new methods? Yes ☐ No ☐

Have you changed supplier/bought new ingredients? Yes ☐ No ☐

Do these affect any of your safe methods?

Other changes:

Notes:

Week Starting: Date/Month/Year	Temperature recordings			Please tick boxes √			Week 1		
Monday	Time	Dish	Temp	Time	Dish	Temp	Time	Dish	Temp
Opening checks done ☐									
Issues: Yes ☐ No ☐									
Closing checks ☐									
Safe methods followed ☐									
Name:									
Signature:									
Tuesday	Time	Dish	Temp	Time	Dish	Temp	Time	Dish	Temp
Opening checks done ☐									
Issues: Yes ☐ No ☐									
Closing checks ☐									
Safe methods followed ☐									
Name:									
Signature:									
Wednesday	Time	Dish	Temp	Time	Dish	Temp	Time	Dish	Temp
Opening checks done ☐									
Issues: Yes ☐ No ☐									
Closing checks ☐									
Safe methods followed ☐									
Name:									
Signature:									
Thursday	Time	Dish	Temp	Time	Dish	Temp	Time	Dish	Temp
Opening checks done ☐									
Issues: Yes ☐ No ☐									
Closing checks ☐									
Safe methods followed ☐									
Name:									
Signature:									

Temperature recordings			Please tick boxes √							
Friday	Time	Dish		Temp	Time	Dish	Temp	Time	Dish	Temp
Opening checks done ☐										
Issues: Yes ☐ No ☐										
Closing checks ☐										
Safe methods followed ☐										
Name:										
Signature:										
Saturday	Time	Dish		Temp	Time	Dish	Temp	Time	Dish	Temp
Opening checks done ☐										
Issues: Yes ☐ No ☐										
Closing checks ☐										
Safe methods followed ☐										
Name:										
Signature:										
Sunday	Time	Dish		Temp	Time	Dish	Temp	Time	Dish	Temp
Opening checks done ☐										
Issues: Yes ☐ No ☐										
Closing checks ☐										
Safe methods followed ☐										
Name:										
Signature:										

Fridge/Freezer/Chiller Temperature records

Day	Frid/Frz/Chil 1	Frid/Frz/Chil 2	Frid/Frz/Chil 3	Frid/Frz/Chil 4	Frid/Frz/Chil 6	Frid/Frz/Chil 7
Monday	Opening: Closing:	Opening: Closing:	Opening: Closing:	Opening: Closing:	Opening: Closing:	Opening: Closing:
Tuesday	Opening: Closing:	Opening: Closing:	Opening: Closing:	Opening: Closing:	Opening: Closing:	Opening: Closing:
Wednesday	Opening: Closing:	Opening: Closing:	Opening: Closing:	Opening: Closing:	Opening: Closing:	Opening: Closing:
Thursday	Opening: Closing:	Opening: Closing:	Opening: Closing:	Opening: Closing:	Opening: Closing:	Opening: Closing:

Friday	Opening: Closing:	Opening: Closing:	Opening: Closing:	Opening: Closing:	Opening: Closing:	Opening: Closing:
Saturday	Opening: Closing:	Opening: Closing:	Opening: Closing:	Opening: Closing:	Opening: Closing:	Opening: Closing:
Sunday	Opening: Closing:	Opening: Closing:	Opening: Closing:	Opening: Closing:	Opening: Closing:	Opening: Closing:

Cleaning schedule

Task — Please tick boxes √	Mon	Tues	Wed	Thurs	Fri	Sat	Sun
Clean and sanitise refrigerators and freezers							
Clean and sanitise the sinks and taps							
Empty and clean the coffee machine							
Clean the grills, ovens, hobs, griddles and stoves							
Clean the fryers							
Brush the grill and clean out grease traps							
Clean and sanitise all kitchen preparation surfaces							
Clean and sanitise all cutting boards							
Clean the meat and cheese slicer, if used							
Sanitise the telephone and all surfaces							
Clean behind fridges, ovens and fryers							
Empty bins and clean the kitchen floor							
Any other Step(s):							

Supervisor signature: Date:

Weekly review-The Good, The Bad, The Ugly, Hirings and Firings

What went right:	What went wrong:

Notes:

Week Starting: Date/Month/Year	Temperature recordings			Please tick boxes √			Week 2		
Monday	Time	Dish	Temp	Time	Dish	Temp	Time	Dish	Temp
Opening checks done ☐									
Issues: Yes ☐ No ☐									
Closing checks ☐									
Safe methods followed ☐									
Name:									
Signature:									
Tuesday	Time	Dish	Temp	Time	Dish	Temp	Time	Dish	Temp
Opening checks done ☐									
Issues: Yes ☐ No ☐									
Closing checks ☐									
Safe methods followed ☐									
Name:									
Signature:									
Wednesday	Time	Dish	Temp	Time	Dish	Temp	Time	Dish	Temp
Opening checks done ☐									
Issues: Yes ☐ No ☐									
Closing checks ☐									
Safe methods followed ☐									
Name:									
Signature:									
Thursday	Time	Dish	Temp	Time	Dish	Temp	Time	Dish	Temp
Opening checks done ☐									
Issues: Yes ☐ No ☐									
Closing checks ☐									
Safe methods followed ☐									
Name:									
Signature:									

Temperature recordings   Please tick boxes √

Friday	Time	Dish	Temp	Time	Dish	Temp	Time	Dish	Temp
Opening checks done ☐									
Issues: Yes ☐ No ☐									
Closing checks ☐									
Safe methods followed ☐									
Name:									
Signature:									

Saturday	Time	Dish	Temp	Time	Dish	Temp	Time	Dish	Temp
Opening checks done ☐									
Issues: Yes ☐ No ☐									
Closing checks ☐									
Safe methods followed ☐									
Name:									
Signature:									

Sunday	Time	Dish	Temp	Time	Dish	Temp	Time	Dish	Temp
Opening checks done ☐									
Issues: Yes ☐ No ☐									
Closing checks ☐									
Safe methods followed ☐									
Name:									
Signature:									

Fridge/Freezer/Chiller Temperature records

Day	Frid/Frz/Chil 1	Frid/Frz/Chil 2	Frid/Frz/Chil 3	Frid/Frz/Chil 4	Frid/Frz/Chil 6	Frid/Frz/Chil 7
Monday	Opening: Closing:	Opening: Closing:	Opening: Closing:	Opening: Closing:	Opening: Closing:	Opening: Closing:
Tuesday	Opening: Closing:	Opening: Closing:	Opening: Closing:	Opening: Closing:	Opening: Closing:	Opening: Closing:
Wednesday	Opening: Closing:	Opening: Closing:	Opening: Closing:	Opening: Closing:	Opening: Closing:	Opening: Closing:
Thursday	Opening: Closing:	Opening: Closing:	Opening: Closing:	Opening: Closing:	Opening: Closing:	Opening: Closing:

Friday	Opening: Closing:	Opening: Closing:	Opening: Closing:	Opening: Closing:	Opening: Closing:	Opening: Closing:
Saturday	Opening: Closing:	Opening: Closing:	Opening: Closing:	Opening: Closing:	Opening: Closing:	Opening: Closing:
Sunday	Opening: Closing:	Opening: Closing:	Opening: Closing:	Opening: Closing:	Opening: Closing:	Opening: Closing:

Cleaning schedule

Task	Please tick boxes √	Mon	Tues	Wed	Thurs	Fri	Sat	Sun
Clean and sanitise refrigerators and freezers								
Clean and sanitise the sinks and taps								
Empty and clean the coffee machine								
Clean the grills, ovens, hobs, griddles and stoves								
Clean the fryers								
Brush the grill and clean out grease traps								
Clean and sanitise all kitchen preparation surfaces								
Clean and sanitise all cutting boards								
Clean the meat and cheese slicer, if used								
Sanitise the telephone and all surfaces								
Clean behind fridges, ovens and fryers								
Empty bins and clean the kitchen floor								
Any other Step(s):								

Supervisor signature: Date:

Weekly review-The Good, The Bad, The Ugly, Hirings and Firings

What went right:	What went wrong:

Notes:

Week Starting: Date/Month/Year	Temperature recordings			Please tick boxes √			Week 3		
Monday	Time	Dish	Temp	Time	Dish	Temp	Time	Dish	Temp
Opening checks done ☐									
Issues: Yes ☐ No ☐									
Closing checks ☐									
Safe methods followed ☐									
Name:									
Signature:									
Tuesday	Time	Dish	Temp	Time	Dish	Temp	Time	Dish	Temp
Opening checks done ☐									
Issues: Yes ☐ No ☐									
Closing checks ☐									
Safe methods followed ☐									
Name:									
Signature:									
Wednesday	Time	Dish	Temp	Time	Dish	Temp	Time	Dish	Temp
Opening checks done ☐									
Issues: Yes ☐ No ☐									
Closing checks ☐									
Safe methods followed ☐									
Name:									
Signature:									
Thursday	Time	Dish	Temp	Time	Dish	Temp	Time	Dish	Temp
Opening checks done ☐									
Issues: Yes ☐ No ☐									
Closing checks ☐									
Safe methods followed ☐									
Name:									
Signature:									

Temperature recordings		Please tick boxes √								
Friday	Time	Dish		Temp	Time	Dish		Temp	Time	Dish	Temp
Opening checks done ☐											
Issues: Yes ☐ No ☐											
Closing checks ☐											
Safe methods followed ☐											
Name:											
Signature:											
Saturday	Time	Dish		Temp	Time	Dish		Temp	Time	Dish	Temp
Opening checks done ☐											
Issues: Yes ☐ No ☐											
Closing checks ☐											
Safe methods followed ☐											
Name:											
Signature:											
Sunday	Time	Dish		Temp	Time	Dish		Temp	Time	Dish	Temp
Opening checks done ☐											
Issues: Yes ☐ No ☐											
Closing checks ☐											
Safe methods followed ☐											
Name:											
Signature:											

Fridge/Freezer/Chiller Temperature records

Day	**Frid/Frz/Chil 1**	**Frid/Frz/Chil 2**	**Frid/Frz/Chil 3**	**Frid/Frz/Chil 4**	**Frid/Frz/Chil 6**	**Frid/Frz/Chil 7**
Monday	Opening: Closing:	Opening: Closing:	Opening: Closing:	Opening: Closing:	Opening: Closing:	Opening: Closing:
Tuesday	Opening: Closing:	Opening: Closing:	Opening: Closing:	Opening: Closing:	Opening: Closing:	Opening: Closing:
Wednesday	Opening: Closing:	Opening: Closing:	Opening: Closing:	Opening: Closing:	Opening: Closing:	Opening: Closing:
Thursday	Opening: Closing:	Opening: Closing:	Opening: Closing:	Opening: Closing:	Opening: Closing:	Opening: Closing:

Friday	Opening: Closing:	Opening: Closing:	Opening: Closing:	Opening: Closing:	Opening: Closing:	Opening: Closing:
Saturday	Opening: Closing:	Opening: Closing:	Opening: Closing:	Opening: Closing:	Opening: Closing:	Opening: Closing:
Sunday	Opening: Closing:	Opening: Closing:	Opening: Closing:	Opening: Closing:	Opening: Closing:	Opening: Closing:

Cleaning schedule

Task — Please tick boxes √	Mon	Tues	Wed	Thurs	Fri	Sat	Sun
Clean and sanitise refrigerators and freezers							
Clean and sanitise the sinks and taps							
Empty and clean the coffee machine							
Clean the grills,ovens,hobs,griddles and stoves							
Clean the fryers							
Brush the grill and clean out grease traps							
Clean and sanitise all kitchen preparation surfaces							
Clean and sanitise all cutting boards							
Clean the meat and cheese slicer,if used							
Sanitise the telephone and all surfaces							
Clean behind fridges,ovens and fryers							
Empty bins and clean the kitchen floor							
Any other Step(s):							

Supervisor signature: Date:

Weekly review-The Good,The Bad,The Ugly,Hirings and Firings

What went right:	What went wrong:

Notes:

Week Starting: Date/Month/Year	Temperature recordings			Please tick boxes √ Week 4					
Monday	Time	Dish	Temp	Time	Dish	Temp	Time	Dish	Temp
Opening checks done ☐									
Issues: Yes ☐ No ☐									
Closing checks ☐									
Safe methods followed ☐									
Name:									
Signature:									
Tuesday	Time	Dish	Temp	Time	Dish	Temp	Time	Dish	Temp
Opening checks done ☐									
Issues: Yes ☐ No ☐									
Closing checks ☐									
Safe methods followed ☐									
Name:									
Signature:									
Wednesday	Time	Dish	Temp	Time	Dish	Temp	Time	Dish	Temp
Opening checks done ☐									
Issues: Yes ☐ No ☐									
Closing checks ☐									
Safe methods followed ☐									
Name:									
Signature:									
Thursday	Time	Dish	Temp	Time	Dish	Temp	Time	Dish	Temp
Opening checks done ☐									
Issues: Yes ☐ No ☐									
Closing checks ☐									
Safe methods followed ☐									
Name:									
Signature:									

Temperature recordings			Please tick boxes √							
Friday	Time	Dish		Temp	Time	Dish	Temp	Time	Dish	Temp
Opening checks done ☐										
Issues: Yes ☐ No ☐										
Closing checks ☐										
Safe methods followed ☐										
Name:										
Signature:										
Saturday	Time	Dish		Temp	Time	Dish	Temp	Time	Dish	Temp
Opening checks done ☐										
Issues: Yes ☐ No ☐										
Closing checks ☐										
Safe methods followed ☐										
Name:										
Signature:										
Sunday	Time	Dish		Temp	Time	Dish	Temp	Time	Dish	Temp
Opening checks done ☐										
Issues: Yes ☐ No ☐										
Closing checks ☐										
Safe methods followed ☐										
Name:										
Signature:										

Fridge/Freezer/Chiller Temperature records

Day	Frid/Frz/Chil 1	Frid/Frz/Chil 2	Frid/Frz/Chil 3	Frid/Frz/Chil 4	Frid/Frz/Chil 6	Frid/Frz/Chil 7
Monday	Opening: Closing:	Opening: Closing:	Opening: Closing:	Opening: Closing:	Opening: Closing:	Opening: Closing:
Tuesday	Opening: Closing:	Opening: Closing:	Opening: Closing:	Opening: Closing:	Opening: Closing:	Opening: Closing:
Wednesday	Opening: Closing:	Opening: Closing:	Opening: Closing:	Opening: Closing:	Opening: Closing:	Opening: Closing:
Thursday	Opening: Closing:	Opening: Closing:	Opening: Closing:	Opening: Closing:	Opening: Closing:	Opening: Closing:

Friday	Opening: Closing:	Opening: Closing:	Opening: Closing:	Opening: Closing:	Opening: Closing:	Opening: Closing:
Saturday	Opening: Closing:	Opening: Closing:	Opening: Closing:	Opening: Closing:	Opening: Closing:	Opening: Closing:
Sunday	Opening: Closing:	Opening: Closing:	Opening: Closing:	Opening: Closing:	Opening: Closing:	Opening: Closing:

Cleaning schedule

Task	Please tick boxes √	Mon	Tues	Wed	Thurs	Fri	Sat	Sun
Clean and sanitise refrigerators and freezers								
Clean and sanitise the sinks and taps								
Empty and clean the coffee machine								
Clean the grills, ovens, hobs, griddles and stoves								
Clean the fryers								
Brush the grill and clean out grease traps								
Clean and sanitise all kitchen preparation surfaces								
Clean and sanitise all cutting boards								
Clean the meat and cheese slicer, if used								
Sanitise the telephone and all surfaces								
Clean behind fridges, ovens and fryers								
Empty bins and clean the kitchen floor								
Any other Step(s):								
Supervisor signature:		Date:						

Kitchen hygiene: monthly cleaning

Task	Please tick boxes √	When	Who	Comment
Wash kitchen walls and storage areas				
Clean and sanitise refrigerators and freezers				
Clean cooker hood and filters				
Supervisor signature:		**Date:**		

Always use appropriate personal protective equipment (PPE) when undertaking any cleaning task and follow the manufacturer's product use and, where relevant, dilution guidance.

4-weekly review

You should regularly review the methods used in your business to check that they are up to date, and still being followed by you and your staff.

You can use the checklist below to help you.
Look back over the past 4 weeks' diary entries. If you had a serious problem, or the same thing went wrong three times or more, make a note of it here, find out why and do something about it. Did you have a serious problem or did the same thing go wrong three times or more?
Yes ☐ No ☐
Details:

What did you do about it?

Did you get a new member of staff in the past 4 weeks? Yes ☐ No ☐

Were they trained in your methods? Yes ☐ No ☐

Have you changed your menu?

Have you reviewed your safe methods?

Any changes/new methods? Yes ☐ No ☐

Have you changed supplier/bought new ingredients? Yes ☐ No ☐

Do these affect any of your safe methods?

Other changes:

Notes:

Week Starting: Date/Month/Year	Temperature recordings			Please tick boxes √			Week 1		
Monday	Time	Dish	Temp	Time	Dish	Temp	Time	Dish	Temp
Opening checks done ☐									
Issues: Yes ☐ No ☐									
Closing checks ☐									
Safe methods followed ☐									
Name:									
Signature:									
Tuesday	Time	Dish	Temp	Time	Dish	Temp	Time	Dish	Temp
Opening checks done ☐									
Issues: Yes ☐ No ☐									
Closing checks ☐									
Safe methods followed ☐									
Name:									
Signature:									
Wednesday	Time	Dish	Temp	Time	Dish	Temp	Time	Dish	Temp
Opening checks done ☐									
Issues: Yes ☐ No ☐									
Closing checks ☐									
Safe methods followed ☐									
Name:									
Signature:									
Thursday	Time	Dish	Temp	Time	Dish	Temp	Time	Dish	Temp
Opening checks done ☐									
Issues: Yes ☐ No ☐									
Closing checks ☐									
Safe methods followed ☐									
Name:									
Signature:									

Temperature recordings		Please tick boxes √							
Friday	Time	Dish	Temp	Time	Dish	Temp	Time	Dish	Temp
Opening checks done ☐									
Issues: Yes ☐ No ☐									
Closing checks ☐									
Safe methods followed ☐									
Name:									
Signature:									
Saturday	Time	Dish	Temp	Time	Dish	Temp	Time	Dish	Temp
Opening checks done ☐									
Issues: Yes ☐ No ☐									
Closing checks ☐									
Safe methods followed ☐									
Name:									
Signature:									
Sunday	Time	Dish	Temp	Time	Dish	Temp	Time	Dish	Temp
Opening checks done ☐									
Issues: Yes ☐ No ☐									
Closing checks ☐									
Safe methods followed ☐									
Name:									
Signature:									

Fridge/Freezer/Chiller Temperature records

Day	Frid/Frz/Chil 1	Frid/Frz/Chil 2	Frid/Frz/Chil 3	Frid/Frz/Chil 4	Frid/Frz/Chil 6	Frid/Frz/Chil 7
Monday	Opening: Closing:	Opening: Closing:	Opening: Closing:	Opening: Closing:	Opening: Closing:	Opening: Closing:
Tuesday	Opening: Closing:	Opening: Closing:	Opening: Closing:	Opening: Closing:	Opening: Closing:	Opening: Closing:
Wednesday	Opening: Closing:	Opening: Closing:	Opening: Closing:	Opening: Closing:	Opening: Closing:	Opening: Closing:
Thursday	Opening: Closing:	Opening: Closing:	Opening: Closing:	Opening: Closing:	Opening: Closing:	Opening: Closing:

Friday	Opening: Closing:	Opening: Closing:	Opening: Closing:	Opening: Closing:	Opening: Closing:	Opening: Closing:
Saturday	Opening: Closing:	Opening: Closing:	Opening: Closing:	Opening: Closing:	Opening: Closing:	Opening: Closing:
Sunday	Opening: Closing:	Opening: Closing:	Opening: Closing:	Opening: Closing:	Opening: Closing:	Opening: Closing:

Cleaning schedule

Task	Please tick boxes √	Mon	Tues	Wed	Thurs	Fri	Sat	Sun
Clean and sanitise refrigerators and freezers								
Clean and sanitise the sinks and taps								
Empty and clean the coffee machine								
Clean the grills,ovens,hobs,griddles and stoves								
Clean the fryers								
Brush the grill and clean out grease traps								
Clean and sanitise all kitchen preparation surfaces								
Clean and sanitise all cutting boards								
Clean the meat and cheese slicer,if used								
Sanitise the telephone and all surfaces								
Clean behind fridges,ovens and fryers								
Empty bins and clean the kitchen floor								
Any other Step(s):								

Supervisor signature: Date:

Weekly review-The Good,The Bad,The Ugly,Hirings and Firings

What went right:	What went wrong:

Notes:

Week Starting: Date/Month/Year	Temperature recordings			Please tick boxes √			Week 2		
Monday	Time	Dish	Temp	Time	Dish	Temp	Time	Dish	Temp
Opening checks done ☐									
Issues: Yes ☐ No ☐									
Closing checks ☐									
Safe methods followed ☐									
Name:									
Signature:									
Tuesday	Time	Dish	Temp	Time	Dish	Temp	Time	Dish	Temp
Opening checks done ☐									
Issues: Yes ☐ No ☐									
Closing checks ☐									
Safe methods followed ☐									
Name:									
Signature:									
Wednesday	Time	Dish	Temp	Time	Dish	Temp	Time	Dish	Temp
Opening checks done ☐									
Issues: Yes ☐ No ☐									
Closing checks ☐									
Safe methods followed ☐									
Name:									
Signature:									
Thursday	Time	Dish	Temp	Time	Dish	Temp	Time	Dish	Temp
Opening checks done ☐									
Issues: Yes ☐ No ☐									
Closing checks ☐									
Safe methods followed ☐									
Name:									
Signature:									

Temperature recordings		Please tick boxes √								
Friday	Time	Dish		Temp	Time	Dish		Temp	Time	Dish	Temp
Opening checks done ☐											
Issues: Yes ☐ No ☐											
Closing checks ☐											
Safe methods followed ☐											
Name:											
Signature:											
Saturday	Time	Dish		Temp	Time	Dish		Temp	Time	Dish	Temp
Opening checks done ☐											
Issues: Yes ☐ No ☐											
Closing checks ☐											
Safe methods followed ☐											
Name:											
Signature:											
Sunday	Time	Dish		Temp	Time	Dish		Temp	Time	Dish	Temp
Opening checks done ☐											
Issues: Yes ☐ No ☐											
Closing checks ☐											
Safe methods followed ☐											
Name:											
Signature:											

Fridge/Freezer/Chiller Temperature records

Day	Frid/Frz/Chil 1	Frid/Frz/Chil 2	Frid/Frz/Chil 3	Frid/Frz/Chil 4	Frid/Frz/Chil 6	Frid/Frz/Chil 7
Monday	Opening: Closing:	Opening: Closing:	Opening: Closing:	Opening: Closing:	Opening: Closing:	Opening: Closing:
Tuesday	Opening: Closing:	Opening: Closing:	Opening: Closing:	Opening: Closing:	Opening: Closing:	Opening: Closing:
Wednesday	Opening: Closing:	Opening: Closing:	Opening: Closing:	Opening: Closing:	Opening: Closing:	Opening: Closing:
Thursday	Opening: Closing:	Opening: Closing:	Opening: Closing:	Opening: Closing:	Opening: Closing:	Opening: Closing:

Friday	Opening: Closing:	Opening: Closing:	Opening: Closing:	Opening: Closing:	Opening: Closing:	Opening: Closing:
Saturday	Opening: Closing:	Opening: Closing:	Opening: Closing:	Opening: Closing:	Opening: Closing:	Opening: Closing:
Sunday	Opening: Closing:	Opening: Closing:	Opening: Closing:	Opening: Closing:	Opening: Closing:	Opening: Closing:

Cleaning schedule

Task	Please tick boxes √	Mon	Tues	Wed	Thurs	Fri	Sat	Sun
Clean and sanitise refrigerators and freezers								
Clean and sanitise the sinks and taps								
Empty and clean the coffee machine								
Clean the grills,ovens,hobs,griddles and stoves								
Clean the fryers								
Brush the grill and clean out grease traps								
Clean and sanitise all kitchen preparation surfaces								
Clean and sanitise all cutting boards								
Clean the meat and cheese slicer,if used								
Sanitise the telephone and all surfaces								
Clean behind fridges,ovens and fryers								
Empty bins and clean the kitchen floor								
Any other Step(s):								

Supervisor signature: Date:

Weekly review-The Good,The Bad,The Ugly,Hirings and Firings

What went right:	What went wrong:

Notes:

Week Starting: Date/Month/Year	Temperature recordings			Please tick boxes √			Week 3		
Monday	Time	Dish	Temp	Time	Dish	Temp	Time	Dish	Temp
Opening checks done ☐									
Issues: Yes ☐ No ☐									
Closing checks ☐									
Safe methods followed ☐									
Name:									
Signature:									
Tuesday	Time	Dish	Temp	Time	Dish	Temp	Time	Dish	Temp
Opening checks done ☐									
Issues: Yes ☐ No ☐									
Closing checks ☐									
Safe methods followed ☐									
Name:									
Signature:									
Wednesday	Time	Dish	Temp	Time	Dish	Temp	Time	Dish	Temp
Opening checks done ☐									
Issues: Yes ☐ No ☐									
Closing checks ☐									
Safe methods followed ☐									
Name:									
Signature:									
Thursday	Time	Dish	Temp	Time	Dish	Temp	Time	Dish	Temp
Opening checks done ☐									
Issues: Yes ☐ No ☐									
Closing checks ☐									
Safe methods followed ☐									
Name:									
Signature:									

Temperature recordings   Please tick boxes √

Friday	Time	Dish	Temp	Time	Dish	Temp	Time	Dish	Temp
Opening checks done ☐									
Issues: Yes ☐ No ☐									
Closing checks ☐									
Safe methods followed ☐									
Name:									
Signature:									

Saturday	Time	Dish	Temp	Time	Dish	Temp	Time	Dish	Temp
Opening checks done ☐									
Issues: Yes ☐ No ☐									
Closing checks ☐									
Safe methods followed ☐									
Name:									
Signature:									

Sunday	Time	Dish	Temp	Time	Dish	Temp	Time	Dish	Temp
Opening checks done ☐									
Issues: Yes ☐ No ☐									
Closing checks ☐									
Safe methods followed ☐									
Name:									
Signature:									

Fridge/Freezer/Chiller Temperature records

Day	Frid/Frz/Chil 1	Frid/Frz/Chil 2	Frid/Frz/Chil 3	Frid/Frz/Chil 4	Frid/Frz/Chil 6	Frid/Frz/Chil 7
Monday	Opening: Closing:	Opening: Closing:	Opening: Closing:	Opening: Closing:	Opening: Closing:	Opening: Closing:
Tuesday	Opening: Closing:	Opening: Closing:	Opening: Closing:	Opening: Closing:	Opening: Closing:	Opening: Closing:
Wednesday	Opening: Closing:	Opening: Closing:	Opening: Closing:	Opening: Closing:	Opening: Closing:	Opening: Closing:
Thursday	Opening: Closing:	Opening: Closing:	Opening: Closing:	Opening: Closing:	Opening: Closing:	Opening: Closing:

Friday	Opening: Closing:	Opening: Closing:	Opening: Closing:	Opening: Closing:	Opening: Closing:	Opening: Closing:
Saturday	Opening: Closing:	Opening: Closing:	Opening: Closing:	Opening: Closing:	Opening: Closing:	Opening: Closing:
Sunday	Opening: Closing:	Opening: Closing:	Opening: Closing:	Opening: Closing:	Opening: Closing:	Opening: Closing:

Cleaning schedule

Task	Please tick boxes √	Mon	Tues	Wed	Thurs	Fri	Sat	Sun
Clean and sanitise refrigerators and freezers								
Clean and sanitise the sinks and taps								
Empty and clean the coffee machine								
Clean the grills,ovens,hobs,griddles and stoves								
Clean the fryers								
Brush the grill and clean out grease traps								
Clean and sanitise all kitchen preparation surfaces								
Clean and sanitise all cutting boards								
Clean the meat and cheese slicer,if used								
Sanitise the telephone and all surfaces								
Clean behind fridges,ovens and fryers								
Empty bins and clean the kitchen floor								
Any other Step(s):								
Supervisor signature:			Date:					

Weekly review-The Good,The Bad,The Ugly,Hirings and Firings

What went right:	What went wrong:

Notes:

Week Starting: | **Temperature recordings** | Please tick boxes √ | Week 4

174

Date/Month/Year									
Monday	Time	Dish	Temp	Time	Dish	Temp	Time	Dish	Temp
Opening checks done ☐									
Issues: Yes ☐ No ☐									
Closing checks ☐									
Safe methods followed ☐									
Name:									
Signature:									
Tuesday	Time	Dish	Temp	Time	Dish	Temp	Time	Dish	Temp
Opening checks done ☐									
Issues: Yes ☐ No ☐									
Closing checks ☐									
Safe methods followed ☐									
Name:									
Signature:									
Wednesday	Time	Dish	Temp	Time	Dish	Temp	Time	Dish	Temp
Opening checks done ☐									
Issues: Yes ☐ No ☐									
Closing checks ☐									
Safe methods followed ☐									
Name:									
Signature:									
Thursday	Time	Dish	Temp	Time	Dish	Temp	Time	Dish	Temp
Opening checks done ☐									
Issues: Yes ☐ No ☐									
Closing checks ☐									
Safe methods followed ☐									
Name:									
Signature:									

Temperature recordings   Please tick boxes √

Friday	Time	Dish	Temp	Time	Dish	Temp	Time	Dish	Temp
Opening checks done ☐									
Issues: Yes ☐ No ☐									
Closing checks ☐									
Safe methods followed ☐									
Name:									
Signature:									
Saturday	Time	Dish	Temp	Time	Dish	Temp	Time	Dish	Temp
Opening checks done ☐									
Issues: Yes ☐ No ☐									
Closing checks ☐									
Safe methods followed ☐									
Name:									
Signature:									
Sunday	Time	Dish	Temp	Time	Dish	Temp	Time	Dish	Temp
Opening checks done ☐									
Issues: Yes ☐ No ☐									
Closing checks ☐									
Safe methods followed ☐									
Name:									
Signature:									

Fridge/Freezer/Chiller Temperature records

Day	Frid/Frz/Chil 1	Frid/Frz/Chil 2	Frid/Frz/Chil 3	Frid/Frz/Chil 4	Frid/Frz/Chil 6	Frid/Frz/Chil 7
Monday	Opening: Closing:	Opening: Closing:	Opening: Closing:	Opening: Closing:	Opening: Closing:	Opening: Closing:
Tuesday	Opening: Closing:	Opening: Closing:	Opening: Closing:	Opening: Closing:	Opening: Closing:	Opening: Closing:
Wednesday	Opening: Closing:	Opening: Closing:	Opening: Closing:	Opening: Closing:	Opening: Closing:	Opening: Closing:
Thursday	Opening: Closing:	Opening: Closing:	Opening: Closing:	Opening: Closing:	Opening: Closing:	Opening: Closing:

Friday	Opening: Closing:	Opening: Closing:	Opening: Closing:	Opening: Closing:	Opening: Closing:	Opening: Closing:
Saturday	Opening: Closing:	Opening: Closing:	Opening: Closing:	Opening: Closing:	Opening: Closing:	Opening: Closing:
Sunday	Opening: Closing:	Opening: Closing:	Opening: Closing:	Opening: Closing:	Opening: Closing:	Opening: Closing:

Cleaning schedule

Task Please tick boxes √	Mon	Tues	Wed	Thurs	Fri	Sat	Sun
Clean and sanitise refrigerators and freezers							
Clean and sanitise the sinks and taps							
Empty and clean the coffee machine							
Clean the grills, ovens, hobs, griddles and stoves							
Clean the fryers							
Brush the grill and clean out grease traps							
Clean and sanitise all kitchen preparation surfaces							
Clean and sanitise all cutting boards							
Clean the meat and cheese slicer, if used							
Sanitise the telephone and all surfaces							
Clean behind fridges, ovens and fryers							
Empty bins and clean the kitchen floor							
Any other Step(s):							
Supervisor signature: Date:							

Kitchen hygiene: monthly cleaning

Task Please tick boxes √	When	Who	Comment
Wash kitchen walls and storage areas			
Clean and sanitise refrigerators and freezers			
Clean cooker hood and filters			
Supervisor signature:		**Date:**	

Always use appropriate personal protective equipment (PPE) when undertaking any cleaning task and follow the manufacturer's product use and, where relevant, dilution guidance.

4-weekly review

You should regularly review the methods used in your business to check that they are up to date, and still being followed by you and your staff.

You can use the checklist below to help you.
Look back over the past 4 weeks' diary entries. If you had a serious problem, or the same thing went wrong three times or more, make a note of it here, find out why and do something about it. Did you have a serious problem or did the same thing go wrong three times or more?
Yes ☐ No ☐
Details:

What did you do about it?

Did you get a new member of staff in the past 4 weeks? Yes ☐ No ☐

Were they trained in your methods? Yes ☐ No ☐

Have you changed your menu?

Have you reviewed your safe methods?

Any changes/new methods? Yes ☐ No ☐

Have you changed supplier/bought new ingredients? Yes ☐ No ☐

Do these affect any of your safe methods?

Other changes:

Notes:

Week Starting: Date/Month/Year	Temperature recordings			Please tick boxes √			Week 1		
Monday	Time	Dish	Temp	Time	Dish	Temp	Time	Dish	Temp
Opening checks done ☐									
Issues: Yes ☐ No ☐									
Closing checks ☐									
Safe methods followed ☐									
Name:									
Signature:									
Tuesday	Time	Dish	Temp	Time	Dish	Temp	Time	Dish	Temp
Opening checks done ☐									
Issues: Yes ☐ No ☐									
Closing checks ☐									
Safe methods followed ☐									
Name:									
Signature:									
Wednesday	Time	Dish	Temp	Time	Dish	Temp	Time	Dish	Temp
Opening checks done ☐									
Issues: Yes ☐ No ☐									
Closing checks ☐									
Safe methods followed ☐									
Name:									
Signature:									
Thursday	Time	Dish	Temp	Time	Dish	Temp	Time	Dish	Temp
Opening checks done ☐									
Issues: Yes ☐ No ☐									
Closing checks ☐									
Safe methods followed ☐									
Name:									
Signature:									

Temperature recordings		Please tick boxes √								
Friday	Time	Dish		Temp	Time	Dish		Temp	Time	Dish	Temp
Opening checks done ☐										
Issues: Yes ☐ No ☐										
Closing checks ☐										
Safe methods followed ☐										
Name:										
Signature:										
Saturday	Time	Dish		Temp	Time	Dish		Temp	Time	Dish	Temp
Opening checks done ☐										
Issues: Yes ☐ No ☐										
Closing checks ☐										
Safe methods followed ☐										
Name:										
Signature:										
Sunday	Time	Dish		Temp	Time	Dish		Temp	Time	Dish	Temp
Opening checks done ☐										
Issues: Yes ☐ No ☐										
Closing checks ☐										
Safe methods followed ☐										
Name:										
Signature:										

Fridge/Freezer/Chiller Temperature records

Day	Frid/Frz/Chil 1	Frid/Frz/Chil 2	Frid/Frz/Chil 3	Frid/Frz/Chil 4	Frid/Frz/Chil 6	Frid/Frz/Chil 7
Monday	Opening: Closing:	Opening: Closing:	Opening: Closing:	Opening: Closing:	Opening: Closing:	Opening: Closing:
Tuesday	Opening: Closing:	Opening: Closing:	Opening: Closing:	Opening: Closing:	Opening: Closing:	Opening: Closing:
Wednesday	Opening: Closing:	Opening: Closing:	Opening: Closing:	Opening: Closing:	Opening: Closing:	Opening: Closing:
Thursday	Opening: Closing:	Opening: Closing:	Opening: Closing:	Opening: Closing:	Opening: Closing:	Opening: Closing:

Friday	Opening: Closing:	Opening: Closing:	Opening: Closing:	Opening: Closing:	Opening: Closing:	Opening: Closing:
Saturday	Opening: Closing:	Opening: Closing:	Opening: Closing:	Opening: Closing:	Opening: Closing:	Opening: Closing:
Sunday	Opening: Closing:	Opening: Closing:	Opening: Closing:	Opening: Closing:	Opening: Closing:	Opening: Closing:

Cleaning schedule

Task Please tick boxes √	Mon	Tues	Wed	Thurs	Fri	Sat	Sun
Clean and sanitise refrigerators and freezers							
Clean and sanitise the sinks and taps							
Empty and clean the coffee machine							
Clean the grills,ovens,hobs,griddles and stoves							
Clean the fryers							
Brush the grill and clean out grease traps							
Clean and sanitise all kitchen preparation surfaces							
Clean and sanitise all cutting boards							
Clean the meat and cheese slicer,if used							
Sanitise the telephone and all surfaces							
Clean behind fridges,ovens and fryers							
Empty bins and clean the kitchen floor							
Any other Step(s):							
Supervisor signature: Date:							

Weekly review-The Good,The Bad,The Ugly,Hirings and Firings

What went right:	What went wrong:

Notes:

Week Starting: Date/Month/Year	Temperature recordings			Please tick boxes √		Week 2			
Monday	Time	Dish	Temp	Time	Dish	Temp	Time	Dish	Temp
Opening checks done ☐									
Issues: Yes ☐ No ☐									
Closing checks ☐									
Safe methods followed ☐									
Name:									
Signature:									
Tuesday	Time	Dish	Temp	Time	Dish	Temp	Time	Dish	Temp
Opening checks done ☐									
Issues: Yes ☐ No ☐									
Closing checks ☐									
Safe methods followed ☐									
Name:									
Signature:									
Wednesday	Time	Dish	Temp	Time	Dish	Temp	Time	Dish	Temp
Opening checks done ☐									
Issues: Yes ☐ No ☐									
Closing checks ☐									
Safe methods followed ☐									
Name:									
Signature:									
Thursday	Time	Dish	Temp	Time	Dish	Temp	Time	Dish	Temp
Opening checks done ☐									
Issues: Yes ☐ No ☐									
Closing checks ☐									
Safe methods followed ☐									
Name:									
Signature:									

Temperature recordings   Please tick boxes √

Friday	Time	Dish	Temp	Time	Dish	Temp	Time	Dish	Temp
Opening checks done ☐									
Issues: Yes ☐ No ☐									
Closing checks ☐									
Safe methods followed ☐									
Name:									
Signature:									

Saturday	Time	Dish	Temp	Time	Dish	Temp	Time	Dish	Temp
Opening checks done ☐									
Issues: Yes ☐ No ☐									
Closing checks ☐									
Safe methods followed ☐									
Name:									
Signature:									

Sunday	Time	Dish	Temp	Time	Dish	Temp	Time	Dish	Temp
Opening checks done ☐									
Issues: Yes ☐ No ☐									
Closing checks ☐									
Safe methods followed ☐									
Name:									
Signature:									

Fridge/Freezer/Chiller Temperature records

Day	Frid/Frz/Chil 1	Frid/Frz/Chil 2	Frid/Frz/Chil 3	Frid/Frz/Chil 4	Frid/Frz/Chil 6	Frid/Frz/Chil 7
Monday	Opening: Closing:	Opening: Closing:	Opening: Closing:	Opening: Closing:	Opening: Closing:	Opening: Closing:
Tuesday	Opening: Closing:	Opening: Closing:	Opening: Closing:	Opening: Closing:	Opening: Closing:	Opening: Closing:
Wednesday	Opening: Closing:	Opening: Closing:	Opening: Closing:	Opening: Closing:	Opening: Closing:	Opening: Closing:
Thursday	Opening: Closing:	Opening: Closing:	Opening: Closing:	Opening: Closing:	Opening: Closing:	Opening: Closing:

Friday	Opening: Closing:	Opening: Closing:	Opening: Closing:	Opening: Closing:	Opening: Closing:	Opening: Closing:
Saturday	Opening: Closing:	Opening: Closing:	Opening: Closing:	Opening: Closing:	Opening: Closing:	Opening: Closing:
Sunday	Opening: Closing:	Opening: Closing:	Opening: Closing:	Opening: Closing:	Opening: Closing:	Opening: Closing:

Cleaning schedule

Task	Please tick boxes √	Mon	Tues	Wed	Thurs	Fri	Sat	Sun
Clean and sanitise refrigerators and freezers								
Clean and sanitise the sinks and taps								
Empty and clean the coffee machine								
Clean the grills,ovens,hobs,griddles and stoves								
Clean the fryers								
Brush the grill and clean out grease traps								
Clean and sanitise all kitchen preparation surfaces								
Clean and sanitise all cutting boards								
Clean the meat and cheese slicer,if used								
Sanitise the telephone and all surfaces								
Clean behind fridges,ovens and fryers								
Empty bins and clean the kitchen floor								
Any other Step(s):								
Supervisor signature:		Date:						

Weekly review-The Good,The Bad,The Ugly,Hirings and Firings

What went right:	What went wrong:

Notes:

Week Starting: Date/Month/Year	Temperature recordings			Please tick boxes √			Week 3		
Monday	Time	Dish	Temp	Time	Dish	Temp	Time	Dish	Temp
Opening checks done ☐									
Issues: Yes ☐ No ☐									
Closing checks ☐									
Safe methods followed ☐									
Name:									
Signature:									
Tuesday	Time	Dish	Temp	Time	Dish	Temp	Time	Dish	Temp
Opening checks done ☐									
Issues: Yes ☐ No ☐									
Closing checks ☐									
Safe methods followed ☐									
Name:									
Signature:									
Wednesday	Time	Dish	Temp	Time	Dish	Temp	Time	Dish	Temp
Opening checks done ☐									
Issues: Yes ☐ No ☐									
Closing checks ☐									
Safe methods followed ☐									
Name:									
Signature:									
Thursday	Time	Dish	Temp	Time	Dish	Temp	Time	Dish	Temp
Opening checks done ☐									
Issues: Yes ☐ No ☐									
Closing checks ☐									
Safe methods followed ☐									
Name:									
Signature:									

Temperature recordings			Please tick boxes √							
Friday	Time	Dish		Temp	Time	Dish		Temp	Time	Dish	Temp
Opening checks done ☐										
Issues: Yes ☐ No ☐										
Closing checks ☐										
Safe methods followed ☐										
Name:										
Signature:										
Saturday	Time	Dish		Temp	Time	Dish		Temp	Time	Dish	Temp
Opening checks done ☐										
Issues: Yes ☐ No ☐										
Closing checks ☐										
Safe methods followed ☐										
Name:										
Signature:										
Sunday	Time	Dish		Temp	Time	Dish		Temp	Time	Dish	Temp
Opening checks done ☐										
Issues: Yes ☐ No ☐										
Closing checks ☐										
Safe methods followed ☐										
Name:										
Signature:										

Fridge/Freezer/Chiller Temperature records

Day	Frid/Frz/Chil 1	Frid/Frz/Chil 2	Frid/Frz/Chil 3	Frid/Frz/Chil 4	Frid/Frz/Chil 6	Frid/Frz/Chil 7
Monday	Opening: Closing:	Opening: Closing:	Opening: Closing:	Opening: Closing:	Opening: Closing:	Opening: Closing:
Tuesday	Opening: Closing:	Opening: Closing:	Opening: Closing:	Opening: Closing:	Opening: Closing:	Opening: Closing:
Wednesday	Opening: Closing:	Opening: Closing:	Opening: Closing:	Opening: Closing:	Opening: Closing:	Opening: Closing:
Thursday	Opening: Closing:	Opening: Closing:	Opening: Closing:	Opening: Closing:	Opening: Closing:	Opening: Closing:

Friday	Opening: Closing:	Opening: Closing:	Opening: Closing:	Opening: Closing:	Opening: Closing:	Opening: Closing:
Saturday	Opening: Closing:	Opening: Closing:	Opening: Closing:	Opening: Closing:	Opening: Closing:	Opening: Closing:
Sunday	Opening: Closing:	Opening: Closing:	Opening: Closing:	Opening: Closing:	Opening: Closing:	Opening: Closing:

Cleaning schedule

Task — Please tick boxes √	Mon	Tues	Wed	Thurs	Fri	Sat	Sun
Clean and sanitise refrigerators and freezers							
Clean and sanitise the sinks and taps							
Empty and clean the coffee machine							
Clean the grills,ovens,hobs,griddles and stoves							
Clean the fryers							
Brush the grill and clean out grease traps							
Clean and sanitise all kitchen preparation surfaces							
Clean and sanitise all cutting boards							
Clean the meat and cheese slicer,if used							
Sanitise the telephone and all surfaces							
Clean behind fridges,ovens and fryers							
Empty bins and clean the kitchen floor							
Any other Step(s):							

Supervisor signature: Date:

Weekly review-The Good,The Bad,The Ugly,Hirings and Firings

What went right:	What went wrong:

Notes:

Week Starting: Date/Month/Year	Temperature recordings			Please tick boxes √			Week 4		
Monday	Time	Dish	Temp	Time	Dish	Temp	Time	Dish	Temp
Opening checks done ☐									
Issues: Yes ☐ No ☐									
Closing checks ☐									
Safe methods followed ☐									
Name:									
Signature:									
Tuesday	Time	Dish	Temp	Time	Dish	Temp	Time	Dish	Temp
Opening checks done ☐									
Issues: Yes ☐ No ☐									
Closing checks ☐									
Safe methods followed ☐									
Name:									
Signature:									
Wednesday	Time	Dish	Temp	Time	Dish	Temp	Time	Dish	Temp
Opening checks done ☐									
Issues: Yes ☐ No ☐									
Closing checks ☐									
Safe methods followed ☐									
Name:									
Signature:									
Thursday	Time	Dish	Temp	Time	Dish	Temp	Time	Dish	Temp
Opening checks done ☐									
Issues: Yes ☐ No ☐									
Closing checks ☐									
Safe methods followed ☐									
Name:									
Signature:									

Temperature recordings   Please tick boxes √

Friday	Time	Dish	Temp	Time	Dish	Temp	Time	Dish	Temp
Opening checks done ☐									
Issues: Yes ☐ No ☐									
Closing checks ☐									
Safe methods followed ☐									
Name:									
Signature:									
Saturday	Time	Dish	Temp	Time	Dish	Temp	Time	Dish	Temp
Opening checks done ☐									
Issues: Yes ☐ No ☐									
Closing checks ☐									
Safe methods followed ☐									
Name:									
Signature:									
Sunday	Time	Dish	Temp	Time	Dish	Temp	Time	Dish	Temp
Opening checks done ☐									
Issues: Yes ☐ No ☐									
Closing checks ☐									
Safe methods followed ☐									
Name:									
Signature:									

Fridge/Freezer/Chiller Temperature records

Day	Frid/Frz/Chil 1	Frid/Frz/Chil 2	Frid/Frz/Chil 3	Frid/Frz/Chil 4	Frid/Frz/Chil 6	Frid/Frz/Chil 7
Monday	Opening: Closing:	Opening: Closing:	Opening: Closing:	Opening: Closing:	Opening: Closing:	Opening: Closing:
Tuesday	Opening: Closing:	Opening: Closing:	Opening: Closing:	Opening: Closing:	Opening: Closing:	Opening: Closing:
Wednesday	Opening: Closing:	Opening: Closing:	Opening: Closing:	Opening: Closing:	Opening: Closing:	Opening: Closing:
Thursday	Opening: Closing:	Opening: Closing:	Opening: Closing:	Opening: Closing:	Opening: Closing:	Opening: Closing:

Friday	Opening: Closing:	Opening: Closing:	Opening: Closing:	Opening: Closing:	Opening: Closing:	Opening: Closing:
Saturday	Opening: Closing:	Opening: Closing:	Opening: Closing:	Opening: Closing:	Opening: Closing:	Opening: Closing:
Sunday	Opening: Closing:	Opening: Closing:	Opening: Closing:	Opening: Closing:	Opening: Closing:	Opening: Closing:

Cleaning schedule

Task	Please tick boxes √	Mon	Tues	Wed	Thurs	Fri	Sat	Sun
Clean and sanitise refrigerators and freezers								
Clean and sanitise the sinks and taps								
Empty and clean the coffee machine								
Clean the grills,ovens,hobs,griddles and stoves								
Clean the fryers								
Brush the grill and clean out grease traps								
Clean and sanitise all kitchen preparation surfaces								
Clean and sanitise all cutting boards								
Clean the meat and cheese slicer,if used								
Sanitise the telephone and all surfaces								
Clean behind fridges,ovens and fryers								
Empty bins and clean the kitchen floor								
Any other Step(s):								
Supervisor signature:		Date:						

Kitchen hygiene: monthly cleaning

Task	Please tick boxes √	When	Who	Comment
Wash kitchen walls and storage areas				
Clean and sanitise refrigerators and freezers				
Clean cooker hood and filters				
Supervisor signature:		**Date:**		

Always use appropriate personal protective equipment (PPE) when undertaking any cleaning task and follow the manufacturer's product use and, where relevant, dilution guidance.

4-weekly review

You should regularly review the methods used in your business to check that they are up to date, and still being followed by you and your staff.

You can use the checklist below to help you.
Look back over the past 4 weeks' diary entries. If you had a serious problem, or the same thing went wrong three times or more, make a note of it here, find out why and do something about it. Did you have a serious problem or did the same thing go wrong three times or more?
Yes ☐   No ☐
Details:

What did you do about it?

Did you get a new member of staff in the past 4 weeks? Yes ☐   No ☐

Were they trained in your methods? Yes ☐   No ☐

Have you changed your menu?

Have you reviewed your safe methods?

Any changes/new methods?   Yes ☐   No ☐

Have you changed supplier/bought new ingredients?   Yes ☐   No ☐

Do these affect any of your safe methods?

Other changes:

Notes:

Week Starting: Date/Month/Year	Temperature recordings			Please tick boxes √		Week 1			
Monday	Time	Dish	Temp	Time	Dish	Temp	Time	Dish	Temp
Opening checks done ☐									
Issues: Yes ☐ No ☐									
Closing checks ☐									
Safe methods followed ☐									
Name:									
Signature:									
Tuesday	Time	Dish	Temp	Time	Dish	Temp	Time	Dish	Temp
Opening checks done ☐									
Issues: Yes ☐ No ☐									
Closing checks ☐									
Safe methods followed ☐									
Name:									
Signature:									
Wednesday	Time	Dish	Temp	Time	Dish	Temp	Time	Dish	Temp
Opening checks done ☐									
Issues: Yes ☐ No ☐									
Closing checks ☐									
Safe methods followed ☐									
Name:									
Signature:									
Thursday	Time	Dish	Temp	Time	Dish	Temp	Time	Dish	Temp
Opening checks done ☐									
Issues: Yes ☐ No ☐									
Closing checks ☐									
Safe methods followed ☐									
Name:									
Signature:									

Temperature recordings   Please tick boxes √

Friday	Time	Dish	Temp	Time	Dish	Temp	Time	Dish	Temp
Opening checks done ☐									
Issues: Yes ☐ No ☐									
Closing checks ☐									
Safe methods followed ☐									
Name:									
Signature:									
Saturday	Time	Dish	Temp	Time	Dish	Temp	Time	Dish	Temp
Opening checks done ☐									
Issues: Yes ☐ No ☐									
Closing checks ☐									
Safe methods followed ☐									
Name:									
Signature:									
Sunday	Time	Dish	Temp	Time	Dish	Temp	Time	Dish	Temp
Opening checks done ☐									
Issues: Yes ☐ No ☐									
Closing checks ☐									
Safe methods followed ☐									
Name:									
Signature:									

Fridge/Freezer/Chiller Temperature records

Day	Frid/Frz/Chil 1	Frid/Frz/Chil 2	Frid/Frz/Chil 3	Frid/Frz/Chil 4	Frid/Frz/Chil 6	Frid/Frz/Chil 7
Monday	Opening: Closing:	Opening: Closing:	Opening: Closing:	Opening: Closing:	Opening: Closing:	Opening: Closing:
Tuesday	Opening: Closing:	Opening: Closing:	Opening: Closing:	Opening: Closing:	Opening: Closing:	Opening: Closing:
Wednesday	Opening: Closing:	Opening: Closing:	Opening: Closing:	Opening: Closing:	Opening: Closing:	Opening: Closing:
Thursday	Opening: Closing:	Opening: Closing:	Opening: Closing:	Opening: Closing:	Opening: Closing:	Opening: Closing:

Friday	Opening: Closing:	Opening: Closing:	Opening: Closing:	Opening: Closing:	Opening: Closing:	Opening: Closing:
Saturday	Opening: Closing:	Opening: Closing:	Opening: Closing:	Opening: Closing:	Opening: Closing:	Opening: Closing:
Sunday	Opening: Closing:	Opening: Closing:	Opening: Closing:	Opening: Closing:	Opening: Closing:	Opening: Closing:

Cleaning schedule

Task	Please tick boxes √	Mon	Tues	Wed	Thurs	Fri	Sat	Sun
Clean and sanitise refrigerators and freezers								
Clean and sanitise the sinks and taps								
Empty and clean the coffee machine								
Clean the grills,ovens,hobs,griddles and stoves								
Clean the fryers								
Brush the grill and clean out grease traps								
Clean and sanitise all kitchen preparation surfaces								
Clean and sanitise all cutting boards								
Clean the meat and cheese slicer,if used								
Sanitise the telephone and all surfaces								
Clean behind fridges,ovens and fryers								
Empty bins and clean the kitchen floor								
Any other Step(s):								

Supervisor signature: Date:

Weekly review-The Good,The Bad,The Ugly,Hirings and Firings

What went right:	What went wrong:

Notes:

Week Starting: Date/Month/Year	**Temperature recordings** Please tick boxes √ Week 2								
Monday	Time	Dish	Temp	Time	Dish	Temp	Time	Dish	Temp
Opening checks done ☐									
Issues: Yes ☐ No ☐									
Closing checks ☐									
Safe methods followed ☐									
Name:									
Signature:									
Tuesday	Time	Dish	Temp	Time	Dish	Temp	Time	Dish	Temp
Opening checks done ☐									
Issues: Yes ☐ No ☐									
Closing checks ☐									
Safe methods followed ☐									
Name:									
Signature:									
Wednesday	Time	Dish	Temp	Time	Dish	Temp	Time	Dish	Temp
Opening checks done ☐									
Issues: Yes ☐ No ☐									
Closing checks ☐									
Safe methods followed ☐									
Name:									
Signature:									
Thursday	Time	Dish	Temp	Time	Dish	Temp	Time	Dish	Temp
Opening checks done ☐									
Issues: Yes ☐ No ☐									
Closing checks ☐									
Safe methods followed ☐									
Name:									
Signature:									

Temperature recordings		Please tick boxes √								
Friday	Time	Dish		Temp	Time	Dish	Temp	Time	Dish	Temp
Opening checks done ☐										
Issues: Yes ☐ No ☐										
Closing checks ☐										
Safe methods followed ☐										
Name:										
Signature:										
Saturday	Time	Dish		Temp	Time	Dish	Temp	Time	Dish	Temp
Opening checks done ☐										
Issues: Yes ☐ No ☐										
Closing checks ☐										
Safe methods followed ☐										
Name:										
Signature:										
Sunday	Time	Dish		Temp	Time	Dish	Temp	Time	Dish	Temp
Opening checks done ☐										
Issues: Yes ☐ No ☐										
Closing checks ☐										
Safe methods followed ☐										
Name:										
Signature:										

Fridge/Freezer/Chiller Temperature records

Day	Frid/Frz/Chil 1	Frid/Frz/Chil 2	Frid/Frz/Chil 3	Frid/Frz/Chil 4	Frid/Frz/Chil 6	Frid/Frz/Chil 7
Monday	Opening: Closing:	Opening: Closing:	Opening: Closing:	Opening: Closing:	Opening: Closing:	Opening: Closing:
Tuesday	Opening: Closing:	Opening: Closing:	Opening: Closing:	Opening: Closing:	Opening: Closing:	Opening: Closing:
Wednesday	Opening: Closing:	Opening: Closing:	Opening: Closing:	Opening: Closing:	Opening: Closing:	Opening: Closing:
Thursday	Opening: Closing:	Opening: Closing:	Opening: Closing:	Opening: Closing:	Opening: Closing:	Opening: Closing:

Friday	Opening: Closing:	Opening: Closing:	Opening: Closing:	Opening: Closing:	Opening: Closing:	Opening: Closing:
Saturday	Opening: Closing:	Opening: Closing:	Opening: Closing:	Opening: Closing:	Opening: Closing:	Opening: Closing:
Sunday	Opening: Closing:	Opening: Closing:	Opening: Closing:	Opening: Closing:	Opening: Closing:	Opening: Closing:

Cleaning schedule

Task — Please tick boxes √	Mon	Tues	Wed	Thurs	Fri	Sat	Sun
Clean and sanitise refrigerators and freezers							
Clean and sanitise the sinks and taps							
Empty and clean the coffee machine							
Clean the grills,ovens,hobs,griddles and stoves							
Clean the fryers							
Brush the grill and clean out grease traps							
Clean and sanitise all kitchen preparation surfaces							
Clean and sanitise all cutting boards							
Clean the meat and cheese slicer,if used							
Sanitise the telephone and all surfaces							
Clean behind fridges,ovens and fryers							
Empty bins and clean the kitchen floor							
Any other Step(s):							

Supervisor signature: Date:

Weekly review-The Good,The Bad,The Ugly,Hirings and Firings

What went right:	**What went wrong:**

Notes:

Week Starting: Date/Month/Year	Temperature recordings			Please tick boxes √		Week 3			
Monday	Time	Dish	Temp	Time	Dish	Temp	Time	Dish	Temp
Opening checks done ☐									
Issues: Yes ☐ No ☐									
Closing checks ☐									
Safe methods followed ☐									
Name:									
Signature:									
Tuesday	Time	Dish	Temp	Time	Dish	Temp	Time	Dish	Temp
Opening checks done ☐									
Issues: Yes ☐ No ☐									
Closing checks ☐									
Safe methods followed ☐									
Name:									
Signature:									
Wednesday	Time	Dish	Temp	Time	Dish	Temp	Time	Dish	Temp
Opening checks done ☐									
Issues: Yes ☐ No ☐									
Closing checks ☐									
Safe methods followed ☐									
Name:									
Signature:									
Thursday	Time	Dish	Temp	Time	Dish	Temp	Time	Dish	Temp
Opening checks done ☐									
Issues: Yes ☐ No ☐									
Closing checks ☐									
Safe methods followed ☐									
Name:									
Signature:									

Temperature recordings   Please tick boxes √

Friday	Time	Dish	Temp	Time	Dish	Temp	Time	Dish	Temp
Opening checks done ☐									
Issues: Yes ☐ No ☐									
Closing checks ☐									
Safe methods followed ☐									
Name:									
Signature:									
Saturday	Time	Dish	Temp	Time	Dish	Temp	Time	Dish	Temp
Opening checks done ☐									
Issues: Yes ☐ No ☐									
Closing checks ☐									
Safe methods followed ☐									
Name:									
Signature:									
Sunday	Time	Dish	Temp	Time	Dish	Temp	Time	Dish	Temp
Opening checks done ☐									
Issues: Yes ☐ No ☐									
Closing checks ☐									
Safe methods followed ☐									
Name:									
Signature:									

Fridge/Freezer/Chiller Temperature records

Day	Frid/Frz/Chil 1	Frid/Frz/Chil 2	Frid/Frz/Chil 3	Frid/Frz/Chil 4	Frid/Frz/Chil 6	Frid/Frz/Chil 7
Monday	Opening: Closing:	Opening: Closing:	Opening: Closing:	Opening: Closing:	Opening: Closing:	Opening: Closing:
Tuesday	Opening: Closing:	Opening: Closing:	Opening: Closing:	Opening: Closing:	Opening: Closing:	Opening: Closing:
Wednesday	Opening: Closing:	Opening: Closing:	Opening: Closing:	Opening: Closing:	Opening: Closing:	Opening: Closing:
Thursday	Opening: Closing:	Opening: Closing:	Opening: Closing:	Opening: Closing:	Opening: Closing:	Opening: Closing:

Friday	Opening: Closing:	Opening: Closing:	Opening: Closing:	Opening: Closing:	Opening: Closing:	Opening: Closing:
Saturday	Opening: Closing:	Opening: Closing:	Opening: Closing:	Opening: Closing:	Opening: Closing:	Opening: Closing:
Sunday	Opening: Closing:	Opening: Closing:	Opening: Closing:	Opening: Closing:	Opening: Closing:	Opening: Closing:

Cleaning schedule

Task	Please tick boxes √	Mon	Tues	Wed	Thurs	Fri	Sat	Sun
Clean and sanitise refrigerators and freezers								
Clean and sanitise the sinks and taps								
Empty and clean the coffee machine								
Clean the grills,ovens,hobs,griddles and stoves								
Clean the fryers								
Brush the grill and clean out grease traps								
Clean and sanitise all kitchen preparation surfaces								
Clean and sanitise all cutting boards								
Clean the meat and cheese slicer,if used								
Sanitise the telephone and all surfaces								
Clean behind fridges,ovens and fryers								
Empty bins and clean the kitchen floor								
Any other Step(s):								

Supervisor signature: Date:

Weekly review-The Good,The Bad,The Ugly,Hirings and Firings

What went right:	went wrong:

Notes:

Week Starting: Date/Month/Year	Temperature recordings			Please tick boxes √			Week 4		
Monday	Time	Dish	Temp	Time	Dish	Temp	Time	Dish	Temp
Opening checks done ☐									
Issues: Yes ☐ No ☐									
Closing checks ☐									
Safe methods followed ☐									
Name:									
Signature:									
Tuesday	Time	Dish	Temp	Time	Dish	Temp	Time	Dish	Temp
Opening checks done ☐									
Issues: Yes ☐ No ☐									
Closing checks ☐									
Safe methods followed ☐									
Name:									
Signature:									
Wednesday	Time	Dish	Temp	Time	Dish	Temp	Time	Dish	Temp
Opening checks done ☐									
Issues: Yes ☐ No ☐									
Closing checks ☐									
Safe methods followed ☐									
Name:									
Signature:									
Thursday	Time	Dish	Temp	Time	Dish	Temp	Time	Dish	Temp
Opening checks done ☐									
Issues: Yes ☐ No ☐									
Closing checks ☐									
Safe methods followed ☐									
Name:									
Signature:									

Temperature recordings		Please tick boxes √								
Friday	Time	Dish		Temp	Time	Dish		Temp	Time	Dish	Temp
Opening checks done ☐										
Issues: Yes ☐ No ☐										
Closing checks ☐										
Safe methods followed ☐										
Name:										
Signature:										
Saturday	Time	Dish		Temp	Time	Dish		Temp	Time	Dish	Temp
Opening checks done ☐										
Issues: Yes ☐ No ☐										
Closing checks ☐										
Safe methods followed ☐										
Name:										
Signature:										
Sunday	Time	Dish		Temp	Time	Dish		Temp	Time	Dish	Temp
Opening checks done ☐										
Issues: Yes ☐ No ☐										
Closing checks ☐										
Safe methods followed ☐										
Name:										
Signature:										

Fridge/Freezer/Chiller Temperature records

Day	Frid/Frz/Chil 1	Frid/Frz/Chil 2	Frid/Frz/Chil 3	Frid/Frz/Chil 4	Frid/Frz/Chil 6	Frid/Frz/Chil 7
Monday	Opening: Closing:	Opening: Closing:	Opening: Closing:	Opening: Closing:	Opening: Closing:	Opening: Closing:
Tuesday	Opening: Closing:	Opening: Closing:	Opening: Closing:	Opening: Closing:	Opening: Closing:	Opening: Closing:
Wednesday	Opening: Closing:	Opening: Closing:	Opening: Closing:	Opening: Closing:	Opening: Closing:	Opening: Closing:
Thursday	Opening: Closing:	Opening: Closing:	Opening: Closing:	Opening: Closing:	Opening: Closing:	Opening: Closing:

Friday	Opening: Closing:	Opening: Closing:	Opening: Closing:	Opening: Closing:	Opening: Closing:	Opening: Closing:
Saturday	Opening: Closing:	Opening: Closing:	Opening: Closing:	Opening: Closing:	Opening: Closing:	Opening: Closing:
Sunday	Opening: Closing:	Opening: Closing:	Opening: Closing:	Opening: Closing:	Opening: Closing:	Opening: Closing:

Cleaning schedule

Task Please tick boxes √	Mon	Tues	Wed	Thurs	Fri	Sat	Sun
Clean and sanitise refrigerators and freezers							
Clean and sanitise the sinks and taps							
Empty and clean the coffee machine							
Clean the grills, ovens, hobs, griddles and stoves							
Clean the fryers							
Brush the grill and clean out grease traps							
Clean and sanitise all kitchen preparation surfaces							
Clean and sanitise all cutting boards							
Clean the meat and cheese slicer, if used							
Sanitise the telephone and all surfaces							
Clean behind fridges, ovens and fryers							
Empty bins and clean the kitchen floor							
Any other Step(s):							
Supervisor signature: Date:							

Kitchen hygiene: monthly cleaning

Task Please tick boxes √	When	Who	Comment
Wash kitchen walls and storage areas			
Clean and sanitise refrigerators and freezers			
Clean cooker hood and filters			
Supervisor signature:		**Date:**	

Always use appropriate personal protective equipment (PPE) when undertaking any cleaning task and follow the manufacturer's product use and, where relevant, dilution guidance.

4-weekly review

You should regularly review the methods used in your business to check that they are up to date, and still being followed by you and your staff.

You can use the checklist below to help you.
Look back over the past 4 weeks' diary entries. If you had a serious problem, or the same thing went wrong three times or more, make a note of it here, find out why and do something about it. Did you have a serious problem or did the same thing go wrong three times or more?
Yes ☐ No ☐
Details:

What did you do about it?

Did you get a new member of staff in the past 4 weeks? Yes ☐ No ☐

Were they trained in your methods? Yes ☐ No ☐

Have you changed your menu?

Have you reviewed your safe methods?

Any changes/new methods? Yes ☐ No ☐

Have you changed supplier/bought new ingredients? Yes ☐ No ☐

Do these affect any of your safe methods?

Other changes:

Notes:

Week Starting: Date/Month/Year	Temperature recordings			Please tick boxes √			Week 1		
Monday	Time	Dish	Temp	Time	Dish	Temp	Time	Dish	Temp
Opening checks done ☐									
Issues: Yes ☐ No ☐									
Closing checks ☐									
Safe methods followed ☐									
Name:									
Signature:									
Tuesday	Time	Dish	Temp	Time	Dish	Temp	Time	Dish	Temp
Opening checks done ☐									
Issues: Yes ☐ No ☐									
Closing checks ☐									
Safe methods followed ☐									
Name:									
Signature:									
Wednesday	Time	Dish	Temp	Time	Dish	Temp	Time	Dish	Temp
Opening checks done ☐									
Issues: Yes ☐ No ☐									
Closing checks ☐									
Safe methods followed ☐									
Name:									
Signature:									
Thursday	Time	Dish	Temp	Time	Dish	Temp	Time	Dish	Temp
Opening checks done ☐									
Issues: Yes ☐ No ☐									
Closing checks ☐									
Safe methods followed ☐									
Name:									
Signature:									

Temperature recordings   Please tick boxes √

Friday	Time	Dish	Temp	Time	Dish	Temp	Time	Dish	Temp
Opening checks done ☐									
Issues: Yes ☐ No ☐									
Closing checks ☐									
Safe methods followed ☐									
Name:									
Signature:									
Saturday	Time	Dish	Temp	Time	Dish	Temp	Time	Dish	Temp
Opening checks done ☐									
Issues: Yes ☐ No ☐									
Closing checks ☐									
Safe methods followed ☐									
Name:									
Signature:									
Sunday	Time	Dish	Temp	Time	Dish	Temp	Time	Dish	Temp
Opening checks done ☐									
Issues: Yes ☐ No ☐									
Closing checks ☐									
Safe methods followed ☐									
Name:									
Signature:									

Fridge/Freezer/Chiller Temperature records

Day	Frid/Frz/Chil 1	Frid/Frz/Chil 2	Frid/Frz/Chil 3	Frid/Frz/Chil 4	Frid/Frz/Chil 6	Frid/Frz/Chil 7
Monday	Opening: Closing:	Opening: Closing:	Opening: Closing:	Opening: Closing:	Opening: Closing:	Opening: Closing:
Tuesday	Opening: Closing:	Opening: Closing:	Opening: Closing:	Opening: Closing:	Opening: Closing:	Opening: Closing:
Wednesday	Opening: Closing:	Opening: Closing:	Opening: Closing:	Opening: Closing:	Opening: Closing:	Opening: Closing:
Thursday	Opening: Closing:	Opening: Closing:	Opening: Closing:	Opening: Closing:	Opening: Closing:	Opening: Closing:

Friday	Opening: Closing:	Opening: Closing:	Opening: Closing:	Opening: Closing:	Opening: Closing:	Opening: Closing:
Saturday	Opening: Closing:	Opening: Closing:	Opening: Closing:	Opening: Closing:	Opening: Closing:	Opening: Closing:
Sunday	Opening: Closing:	Opening: Closing:	Opening: Closing:	Opening: Closing:	Opening: Closing:	Opening: Closing:

Cleaning schedule

Task — Please tick boxes √	Mon	Tues	Wed	Thurs	Fri	Sat	Sun
Clean and sanitise refrigerators and freezers							
Clean and sanitise the sinks and taps							
Empty and clean the coffee machine							
Clean the grills, ovens, hobs, griddles and stoves							
Clean the fryers							
Brush the grill and clean out grease traps							
Clean and sanitise all kitchen preparation surfaces							
Clean and sanitise all cutting boards							
Clean the meat and cheese slicer, if used							
Sanitise the telephone and all surfaces							
Clean behind fridges, ovens and fryers							
Empty bins and clean the kitchen floor							
Any other Step(s):							

Supervisor signature: Date:

Weekly review-The Good, The Bad, The Ugly, Hirings and Firings

What went right:	What went wrong:

Notes:

Week Starting: Date/Month/Year	Temperature recordings			Please tick boxes √ Week 2					
Monday	Time	Dish	Temp	Time	Dish	Temp	Time	Dish	Temp
Opening checks done ☐									
Issues: Yes ☐ No ☐									
Closing checks ☐									
Safe methods followed ☐									
Name:									
Signature:									
Tuesday	Time	Dish	Temp	Time	Dish	Temp	Time	Dish	Temp
Opening checks done ☐									
Issues: Yes ☐ No ☐									
Closing checks ☐									
Safe methods followed ☐									
Name:									
Signature:									
Wednesday	Time	Dish	Temp	Time	Dish	Temp	Time	Dish	Temp
Opening checks done ☐									
Issues: Yes ☐ No ☐									
Closing checks ☐									
Safe methods followed ☐									
Name:									
Signature:									
Thursday	Time	Dish	Temp	Time	Dish	Temp	Time	Dish	Temp
Opening checks done ☐									
Issues: Yes ☐ No ☐									
Closing checks ☐									
Safe methods followed ☐									
Name:									
Signature:									

Temperature recordings   Please tick boxes √

Friday	Time	Dish	Temp	Time	Dish	Temp	Time	Dish	Temp
Opening checks done ☐									
Issues: Yes ☐ No ☐									
Closing checks ☐									
Safe methods followed ☐									
Name:									
Signature:									

Saturday	Time	Dish	Temp	Time	Dish	Temp	Time	Dish	Temp
Opening checks done ☐									
Issues: Yes ☐ No ☐									
Closing checks ☐									
Safe methods followed ☐									
Name:									
Signature:									

Sunday	Time	Dish	Temp	Time	Dish	Temp	Time	Dish	Temp
Opening checks done ☐									
Issues: Yes ☐ No ☐									
Closing checks ☐									
Safe methods followed ☐									
Name:									
Signature:									

Fridge/Freezer/Chiller Temperature records

Day	Frid/Frz/Chil 1	Frid/Frz/Chil 2	Frid/Frz/Chil 3	Frid/Frz/Chil 4	Frid/Frz/Chil 6	Frid/Frz/Chil 7
Monday	Opening: Closing:	Opening: Closing:	Opening: Closing:	Opening: Closing:	Opening: Closing:	Opening: Closing:
Tuesday	Opening: Closing:	Opening: Closing:	Opening: Closing:	Opening: Closing:	Opening: Closing:	Opening: Closing:
Wednesday	Opening: Closing:	Opening: Closing:	Opening: Closing:	Opening: Closing:	Opening: Closing:	Opening: Closing:
Thursday	Opening: Closing:	Opening: Closing:	Opening: Closing:	Opening: Closing:	Opening: Closing:	Opening: Closing:

Friday	Opening: Closing:	Opening: Closing:	Opening: Closing:	Opening: Closing:	Opening: Closing:	Opening: Closing:
Saturday	Opening: Closing:	Opening: Closing:	Opening: Closing:	Opening: Closing:	Opening: Closing:	Opening: Closing:
Sunday	Opening: Closing:	Opening: Closing:	Opening: Closing:	Opening: Closing:	Opening: Closing:	Opening: Closing:

Cleaning schedule

Task	Please tick boxes √	Mon	Tues	Wed	Thurs	Fri	Sat	Sun
Clean and sanitise refrigerators and freezers								
Clean and sanitise the sinks and taps								
Empty and clean the coffee machine								
Clean the grills,ovens,hobs,griddles and stoves								
Clean the fryers								
Brush the grill and clean out grease traps								
Clean and sanitise all kitchen preparation surfaces								
Clean and sanitise all cutting boards								
Clean the meat and cheese slicer,if used								
Sanitise the telephone and all surfaces								
Clean behind fridges,ovens and fryers								
Empty bins and clean the kitchen floor								
Any other Step(s):								
Supervisor signature:	Date:							

Weekly review-The Good,The Bad,The Ugly,Hirings and Firings

What went right:	What went wrong:

Notes:

Week Starting: Date/Month/Year	Temperature recordings			Please tick boxes √			Week 3		
Monday	Time	Dish	Temp	Time	Dish	Temp	Time	Dish	Temp
Opening checks done ☐									
Issues: Yes ☐ No ☐									
Closing checks ☐									
Safe methods followed ☐									
Name:									
Signature:									
Tuesday	Time	Dish	Temp	Time	Dish	Temp	Time	Dish	Temp
Opening checks done ☐									
Issues: Yes ☐ No ☐									
Closing checks ☐									
Safe methods followed ☐									
Name:									
Signature:									
Wednesday	Time	Dish	Temp	Time	Dish	Temp	Time	Dish	Temp
Opening checks done ☐									
Issues: Yes ☐ No ☐									
Closing checks ☐									
Safe methods followed ☐									
Name:									
Signature:									
Thursday	Time	Dish	Temp	Time	Dish	Temp	Time	Dish	Temp
Opening checks done ☐									
Issues: Yes ☐ No ☐									
Closing checks ☐									
Safe methods followed ☐									
Name:									
Signature:									

Temperature recordings   Please tick boxes √

Friday	Time	Dish	Temp	Time	Dish	Temp	Time	Dish	Temp
Opening checks done ☐									
Issues: Yes ☐ No ☐									
Closing checks ☐									
Safe methods followed ☐									
Name:									
Signature:									

Saturday	Time	Dish	Temp	Time	Dish	Temp	Time	Dish	Temp
Opening checks done ☐									
Issues: Yes ☐ No ☐									
Closing checks ☐									
Safe methods followed ☐									
Name:									
Signature:									

Sunday	Time	Dish	Temp	Time	Dish	Temp	Time	Dish	Temp
Opening checks done ☐									
Issues: Yes ☐ No ☐									
Closing checks ☐									
Safe methods followed ☐									
Name:									
Signature:									

Fridge/Freezer/Chiller Temperature records

Day	Frid/Frz/Chil 1	Frid/Frz/Chil 2	Frid/Frz/Chil 3	Frid/Frz/Chil 4	Frid/Frz/Chil 6	Frid/Frz/Chil 7
Monday	Opening: Closing:	Opening: Closing:	Opening: Closing:	Opening: Closing:	Opening: Closing:	Opening: Closing:
Tuesday	Opening: Closing:	Opening: Closing:	Opening: Closing:	Opening: Closing:	Opening: Closing:	Opening: Closing:
Wednesday	Opening: Closing:	Opening: Closing:	Opening: Closing:	Opening: Closing:	Opening: Closing:	Opening: Closing:
Thursday	Opening: Closing:	Opening: Closing:	Opening: Closing:	Opening: Closing:	Opening: Closing:	Opening: Closing:

Friday	Opening: Closing:	Opening: Closing:	Opening: Closing:	Opening: Closing:	Opening: Closing:	Opening: Closing:
Saturday	Opening: Closing:	Opening: Closing:	Opening: Closing:	Opening: Closing:	Opening: Closing:	Opening: Closing:
Sunday	Opening: Closing:	Opening: Closing:	Opening: Closing:	Opening: Closing:	Opening: Closing:	Opening: Closing:

Cleaning schedule

Task Please tick boxes √	Mon	Tues	Wed	Thurs	Fri	Sat	Sun
Clean and sanitise refrigerators and freezers							
Clean and sanitise the sinks and taps							
Empty and clean the coffee machine							
Clean the grills,ovens,hobs,griddles and stoves							
Clean the fryers							
Brush the grill and clean out grease traps							
Clean and sanitise all kitchen preparation surfaces							
Clean and sanitise all cutting boards							
Clean the meat and cheese slicer,if used							
Sanitise the telephone and all surfaces							
Clean behind fridges,ovens and fryers							
Empty bins and clean the kitchen floor							
Any other Step(s):							

Supervisor signature: Date:

Weekly review-The Good,The Bad,The Ugly,Hirings and Firings

What went right:	**What went wrong:**

Notes:

Week Starting: Date/Month/Year	Temperature recordings			Please tick boxes √		Week 4			
Monday	Time	Dish	Temp	Time	Dish	Temp	Time	Dish	Temp
Opening checks done ☐									
Issues: Yes ☐ No ☐									
Closing checks ☐									
Safe methods followed ☐									
Name:									
Signature:									
Tuesday	Time	Dish	Temp	Time	Dish	Temp	Time	Dish	Temp
Opening checks done ☐									
Issues: Yes ☐ No ☐									
Closing checks ☐									
Safe methods followed ☐									
Name:									
Signature:									
Wednesday	Time	Dish	Temp	Time	Dish	Temp	Time	Dish	Temp
Opening checks done ☐									
Issues: Yes ☐ No ☐									
Closing checks ☐									
Safe methods followed ☐									
Name:									
Signature:									
Thursday	Time	Dish	Temp	Time	Dish	Temp	Time	Dish	Temp
Opening checks done ☐									
Issues: Yes ☐ No ☐									
Closing checks ☐									
Safe methods followed ☐									
Name:									
Signature:									

Temperature recordings		Please tick boxes √								
Friday	Time	Dish	Temp	Time	Dish	Temp	Time	Dish	Temp
Opening checks done ☐									
Issues: Yes ☐ No ☐									
Closing checks ☐									
Safe methods followed ☐									
Name:									
Signature:									
Saturday	Time	Dish	Temp	Time	Dish	Temp	Time	Dish	Temp
Opening checks done ☐									
Issues: Yes ☐ No ☐									
Closing checks ☐									
Safe methods followed ☐									
Name:									
Signature:									
Sunday	Time	Dish	Temp	Time	Dish	Temp	Time	Dish	Temp
Opening checks done ☐									
Issues: Yes ☐ No ☐									
Closing checks ☐									
Safe methods followed ☐									
Name:									
Signature:									

Fridge/Freezer/Chiller Temperature records

Day	Frid/Frz/Chil 1	Frid/Frz/Chil 2	Frid/Frz/Chil 3	Frid/Frz/Chil 4	Frid/Frz/Chil 6	Frid/Frz/Chil 7
Monday	Opening: Closing:	Opening: Closing:	Opening: Closing:	Opening: Closing:	Opening: Closing:	Opening: Closing:
Tuesday	Opening: Closing:	Opening: Closing:	Opening: Closing:	Opening: Closing:	Opening: Closing:	Opening: Closing:
Wednesday	Opening: Closing:	Opening: Closing:	Opening: Closing:	Opening: Closing:	Opening: Closing:	Opening: Closing:
Thursday	Opening: Closing:	Opening: Closing:	Opening: Closing:	Opening: Closing:	Opening: Closing:	Opening: Closing:

Friday	Opening: Closing:	Opening: Closing:	Opening: Closing:	Opening: Closing:	Opening: Closing:	Opening: Closing:
Saturday	Opening: Closing:	Opening: Closing:	Opening: Closing:	Opening: Closing:	Opening: Closing:	Opening: Closing:
Sunday	Opening: Closing:	Opening: Closing:	Opening: Closing:	Opening: Closing:	Opening: Closing:	Opening: Closing:

Cleaning schedule

Task	Please tick boxes √	Mon	Tues	Wed	Thurs	Fri	Sat	Sun
Clean and sanitise refrigerators and freezers								
Clean and sanitise the sinks and taps								
Empty and clean the coffee machine								
Clean the grills,ovens,hobs,griddles and stoves								
Clean the fryers								
Brush the grill and clean out grease traps								
Clean and sanitise all kitchen preparation surfaces								
Clean and sanitise all cutting boards								
Clean the meat and cheese slicer,if used								
Sanitise the telephone and all surfaces								
Clean behind fridges,ovens and fryers								
Empty bins and clean the kitchen floor								
Any other Step(s):								
Supervisor signature:		Date:						

Kitchen hygiene: monthly cleaning

Task	Please tick boxes √	When	Who	Comment
Wash kitchen walls and storage areas				
Clean and sanitise refrigerators and freezers				
Clean cooker hood and filters				
Supervisor signature:		**Date:**		

Always use appropriate personal protective equipment (PPE) when undertaking any cleaning task and follow the manufacturer's product use and, where relevant, dilution guidance.

4-weekly review

You should regularly review the methods used in your business to check that they are up to date, and still being followed by you and your staff.

You can use the checklist below to help you.
Look back over the past 4 weeks' diary entries. If you had a serious problem, or the same thing went wrong three times or more, make a note of it here, find out why and do something about it. Did you have a serious problem or did the same thing go wrong three times or more?
Yes ☐ No ☐
Details:

What did you do about it?

Did you get a new member of staff in the past 4 weeks? Yes ☐ No ☐

Were they trained in your methods? Yes ☐ No ☐

Have you changed your menu?

Have you reviewed your safe methods?

Any changes/new methods?   Yes ☐ No ☐

Have you changed supplier/bought new ingredients? Yes ☐ No ☐

Do these affect any of your safe methods?

Other changes:

Notes:

Week Starting: Date/Month/Year	Temperature recordings			Please tick boxes √ Week 1					
Monday	Time	Dish	Temp	Time	Dish	Temp	Time	Dish	Temp
Opening checks done ☐									
Issues: Yes ☐ No ☐									
Closing checks ☐									
Safe methods followed ☐									
Name:									
Signature:									
Tuesday	Time	Dish	Temp	Time	Dish	Temp	Time	Dish	Temp
Opening checks done ☐									
Issues: Yes ☐ No ☐									
Closing checks ☐									
Safe methods followed ☐									
Name:									
Signature:									
Wednesday	Time	Dish	Temp	Time	Dish	Temp	Time	Dish	Temp
Opening checks done ☐									
Issues: Yes ☐ No ☐									
Closing checks ☐									
Safe methods followed ☐									
Name:									
Signature:									
Thursday	Time	Dish	Temp	Time	Dish	Temp	Time	Dish	Temp
Opening checks done ☐									
Issues: Yes ☐ No ☐									
Closing checks ☐									
Safe methods followed ☐									
Name:									
Signature:									

Temperature recordings   Please tick boxes √

Friday	Time	Dish	Temp	Time	Dish	Temp	Time	Dish	Temp
Opening checks done ☐									
Issues: Yes ☐ No ☐									
Closing checks ☐									
Safe methods followed ☐									
Name:									
Signature:									
Saturday	Time	Dish	Temp	Time	Dish	Temp	Time	Dish	Temp
Opening checks done ☐									
Issues: Yes ☐ No ☐									
Closing checks ☐									
Safe methods followed ☐									
Name:									
Signature:									
Sunday	Time	Dish	Temp	Time	Dish	Temp	Time	Dish	Temp
Opening checks done ☐									
Issues: Yes ☐ No ☐									
Closing checks ☐									
Safe methods followed ☐									
Name:									
Signature:									

Fridge/Freezer/Chiller Temperature records

Day	Frid/Frz/Chil 1	Frid/Frz/Chil 2	Frid/Frz/Chil 3	Frid/Frz/Chil 4	Frid/Frz/Chil 6	Frid/Frz/Chil 7
Monday	Opening: Closing:	Opening: Closing:	Opening: Closing:	Opening: Closing:	Opening: Closing:	Opening: Closing:
Tuesday	Opening: Closing:	Opening: Closing:	Opening: Closing:	Opening: Closing:	Opening: Closing:	Opening: Closing:
Wednesday	Opening: Closing:	Opening: Closing:	Opening: Closing:	Opening: Closing:	Opening: Closing:	Opening: Closing:
Thursday	Opening: Closing:	Opening: Closing:	Opening: Closing:	Opening: Closing:	Opening: Closing:	Opening: Closing:

Friday	Opening: Closing:	Opening: Closing:	Opening: Closing:	Opening: Closing:	Opening: Closing:	Opening: Closing:
Saturday	Opening: Closing:	Opening: Closing:	Opening: Closing:	Opening: Closing:	Opening: Closing:	Opening: Closing:
Sunday	Opening: Closing:	Opening: Closing:	Opening: Closing:	Opening: Closing:	Opening: Closing:	Opening: Closing:

Cleaning schedule

Task	Please tick boxes √	Mon	Tues	Wed	Thurs	Fri	Sat	Sun
Clean and sanitise refrigerators and freezers								
Clean and sanitise the sinks and taps								
Empty and clean the coffee machine								
Clean the grills,ovens,hobs,griddles and stoves								
Clean the fryers								
Brush the grill and clean out grease traps								
Clean and sanitise all kitchen preparation surfaces								
Clean and sanitise all cutting boards								
Clean the meat and cheese slicer,if used								
Sanitise the telephone and all surfaces								
Clean behind fridges,ovens and fryers								
Empty bins and clean the kitchen floor								
Any other Step(s):								
Supervisor signature:	Date:							

Weekly review-The Good,The Bad,The Ugly,Hirings and Firings

What went right:	What went wrong:

Notes:

Week Starting: Date/Month/Year	Temperature recordings								Please tick boxes √ Week 2	
Monday	Time	Dish	Temp	Time	Dish	Temp	Time	Dish	Temp
Opening checks done ☐									
Issues: Yes ☐ No ☐									
Closing checks ☐									
Safe methods followed ☐									
Name:									
Signature:									
Tuesday	Time	Dish	Temp	Time	Dish	Temp	Time	Dish	Temp
Opening checks done ☐									
Issues: Yes ☐ No ☐									
Closing checks ☐									
Safe methods followed ☐									
Name:									
Signature:									
Wednesday	Time	Dish	Temp	Time	Dish	Temp	Time	Dish	Temp
Opening checks done ☐									
Issues: Yes ☐ No ☐									
Closing checks ☐									
Safe methods followed ☐									
Name:									
Signature:									
Thursday	Time	Dish	Temp	Time	Dish	Temp	Time	Dish	Temp
Opening checks done ☐									
Issues: Yes ☐ No ☐									
Closing checks ☐									
Safe methods followed ☐									
Name:									
Signature:									

Temperature recordings		Please tick boxes √								
Friday	Time	Dish		Temp	Time	Dish		Temp	Time	Dish	Temp
Opening checks done ☐										
Issues: Yes ☐ No ☐										
Closing checks ☐										
Safe methods followed ☐										
Name:										
Signature:										
Saturday	Time	Dish		Temp	Time	Dish		Temp	Time	Dish	Temp
Opening checks done ☐										
Issues: Yes ☐ No ☐										
Closing checks ☐										
Safe methods followed ☐										
Name:										
Signature:										
Sunday	Time	Dish		Temp	Time	Dish		Temp	Time	Dish	Temp
Opening checks done ☐										
Issues: Yes ☐ No ☐										
Closing checks ☐										
Safe methods followed ☐										
Name:										
Signature:										

Fridge/Freezer/Chiller Temperature records

Day	Frid/Frz/Chil 1	Frid/Frz/Chil 2	Frid/Frz/Chil 3	Frid/Frz/Chil 4	Frid/Frz/Chil 6	Frid/Frz/Chil 7
Monday	Opening: Closing:	Opening: Closing:	Opening: Closing:	Opening: Closing:	Opening: Closing:	Opening: Closing:
Tuesday	Opening: Closing:	Opening: Closing:	Opening: Closing:	Opening: Closing:	Opening: Closing:	Opening: Closing:
Wednesday	Opening: Closing:	Opening: Closing:	Opening: Closing:	Opening: Closing:	Opening: Closing:	Opening: Closing:
Thursday	Opening: Closing:	Opening: Closing:	Opening: Closing:	Opening: Closing:	Opening: Closing:	Opening: Closing:

Friday	Opening: Closing:	Opening: Closing:	Opening: Closing:	Opening: Closing:	Opening: Closing:	Opening: Closing:
Saturday	Opening: Closing:	Opening: Closing:	Opening: Closing:	Opening: Closing:	Opening: Closing:	Opening: Closing:
Sunday	Opening: Closing:	Opening: Closing:	Opening: Closing:	Opening: Closing:	Opening: Closing:	Opening: Closing:

Cleaning schedule

Task	Please tick boxes √	Mon	Tues	Wed	Thurs	Fri	Sat	Sun
Clean and sanitise refrigerators and freezers								
Clean and sanitise the sinks and taps								
Empty and clean the coffee machine								
Clean the grills,ovens,hobs,griddles and stoves								
Clean the fryers								
Brush the grill and clean out grease traps								
Clean and sanitise all kitchen preparation surfaces								
Clean and sanitise all cutting boards								
Clean the meat and cheese slicer,if used								
Sanitise the telephone and all surfaces								
Clean behind fridges,ovens and fryers								
Empty bins and clean the kitchen floor								
Any other Step(s):								

Supervisor signature: Date:

Weekly review-The Good,The Bad,The Ugly,Hirings and Firings

What went right:	What went wrong:

Notes:

Week Starting: Date/Month/Year	Temperature recordings			Please tick boxes √ Week 3					
Monday	Time	Dish	Temp	Time	Dish	Temp	Time	Dish	Temp
Opening checks done ☐									
Issues: Yes ☐ No ☐									
Closing checks ☐									
Safe methods followed ☐									
Name:									
Signature:									
Tuesday	Time	Dish	Temp	Time	Dish	Temp	Time	Dish	Temp
Opening checks done ☐									
Issues: Yes ☐ No ☐									
Closing checks ☐									
Safe methods followed ☐									
Name:									
Signature:									
Wednesday	Time	Dish	Temp	Time	Dish	Temp	Time	Dish	Temp
Opening checks done ☐									
Issues: Yes ☐ No ☐									
Closing checks ☐									
Safe methods followed ☐									
Name:									
Signature:									
Thursday	Time	Dish	Temp	Time	Dish	Temp	Time	Dish	Temp
Opening checks done ☐									
Issues: Yes ☐ No ☐									
Closing checks ☐									
Safe methods followed ☐									
Name:									
Signature:									

Temperature recordings   Please tick boxes √

Friday	Time	Dish	Temp	Time	Dish	Temp	Time	Dish	Temp
Opening checks done ☐									
Issues: Yes ☐ No ☐									
Closing checks ☐									
Safe methods followed ☐									
Name:									
Signature:									
Saturday	Time	Dish	Temp	Time	Dish	Temp	Time	Dish	Temp
Opening checks done ☐									
Issues: Yes ☐ No ☐									
Closing checks ☐									
Safe methods followed ☐									
Name:									
Signature:									
Sunday	Time	Dish	Temp	Time	Dish	Temp	Time	Dish	Temp
Opening checks done ☐									
Issues: Yes ☐ No ☐									
Closing checks ☐									
Safe methods followed ☐									
Name:									
Signature:									

Fridge/Freezer/Chiller Temperature records

Day	Frid/Frz/Chil 1	Frid/Frz/Chil 2	Frid/Frz/Chil 3	Frid/Frz/Chil 4	Frid/Frz/Chil 6	Frid/Frz/Chil 7
Monday	Opening: Closing:	Opening: Closing:	Opening: Closing:	Opening: Closing:	Opening: Closing:	Opening: Closing:
Tuesday	Opening: Closing:	Opening: Closing:	Opening: Closing:	Opening: Closing:	Opening: Closing:	Opening: Closing:
Wednesday	Opening: Closing:	Opening: Closing:	Opening: Closing:	Opening: Closing:	Opening: Closing:	Opening: Closing:
Thursday	Opening: Closing:	Opening: Closing:	Opening: Closing:	Opening: Closing:	Opening: Closing:	Opening: Closing:

Friday	Opening: Closing:	Opening: Closing:	Opening: Closing:	Opening: Closing:	Opening: Closing:	Opening: Closing:
Saturday	Opening: Closing:	Opening: Closing:	Opening: Closing:	Opening: Closing:	Opening: Closing:	Opening: Closing:
Sunday	Opening: Closing:	Opening: Closing:	Opening: Closing:	Opening: Closing:	Opening: Closing:	Opening: Closing:

Cleaning schedule

Task	Please tick boxes √	Mon	Tues	Wed	Thurs	Fri	Sat	Sun
Clean and sanitise refrigerators and freezers								
Clean and sanitise the sinks and taps								
Empty and clean the coffee machine								
Clean the grills,ovens,hobs,griddles and stoves								
Clean the fryers								
Brush the grill and clean out grease traps								
Clean and sanitise all kitchen preparation surfaces								
Clean and sanitise all cutting boards								
Clean the meat and cheese slicer,if used								
Sanitise the telephone and all surfaces								
Clean behind fridges,ovens and fryers								
Empty bins and clean the kitchen floor								
Any other Step(s):								
Supervisor signature:	Date:							

Weekly review-The Good,The Bad,The Ugly,Hirings and Firings

What went right:	What went wrong:

Notes:

Week Starting: Date/Month/Year	Temperature recordings									Please tick boxes √ Week 4
Monday	Time	Dish	Temp	Time	Dish	Temp	Time	Dish	Temp
Opening checks done ☐									
Issues: Yes ☐ No ☐									
Closing checks ☐									
Safe methods followed ☐									
Name:									
Signature:									
Tuesday	Time	Dish	Temp	Time	Dish	Temp	Time	Dish	Temp
Opening checks done ☐									
Issues: Yes ☐ No ☐									
Closing checks ☐									
Safe methods followed ☐									
Name:									
Signature:									
Wednesday	Time	Dish	Temp	Time	Dish	Temp	Time	Dish	Temp
Opening checks done ☐									
Issues: Yes ☐ No ☐									
Closing checks ☐									
Safe methods followed ☐									
Name:									
Signature:									
Thursday	Time	Dish	Temp	Time	Dish	Temp	Time	Dish	Temp
Opening checks done ☐									
Issues: Yes ☐ No ☐									
Closing checks ☐									
Safe methods followed ☐									
Name:									
Signature:									

Temperature recordings		Please tick boxes √								
Friday	Time	Dish		Temp	Time	Dish		Temp	Time	Dish	Temp
Opening checks done ☐										
Issues: Yes ☐ No ☐										
Closing checks ☐										
Safe methods followed ☐										
Name:										
Signature:										
Saturday	Time	Dish		Temp	Time	Dish		Temp	Time	Dish	Temp
Opening checks done ☐										
Issues: Yes ☐ No ☐										
Closing checks ☐										
Safe methods followed ☐										
Name:										
Signature:										
Sunday	Time	Dish		Temp	Time	Dish		Temp	Time	Dish	Temp
Opening checks done ☐										
Issues: Yes ☐ No ☐										
Closing checks ☐										
Safe methods followed ☐										
Name:										
Signature:										

Fridge/Freezer/Chiller Temperature records

Day	Frid/Frz/Chil 1	Frid/Frz/Chil 2	Frid/Frz/Chil 3	Frid/Frz/Chil 4	Frid/Frz/Chil 6	Frid/Frz/Chil 7
Monday	Opening: Closing:	Opening: Closing:	Opening: Closing:	Opening: Closing:	Opening: Closing:	Opening: Closing:
Tuesday	Opening: Closing:	Opening: Closing:	Opening: Closing:	Opening: Closing:	Opening: Closing:	Opening: Closing:
Wednesday	Opening: Closing:	Opening: Closing:	Opening: Closing:	Opening: Closing:	Opening: Closing:	Opening: Closing:
Thursday	Opening: Closing:	Opening: Closing:	Opening: Closing:	Opening: Closing:	Opening: Closing:	Opening: Closing:

Friday	Opening: Closing:	Opening: Closing:	Opening: Closing:	Opening: Closing:	Opening: Closing:	Opening: Closing:
Saturday	Opening: Closing:	Opening: Closing:	Opening: Closing:	Opening: Closing:	Opening: Closing:	Opening: Closing:
Sunday	Opening: Closing:	Opening: Closing:	Opening: Closing:	Opening: Closing:	Opening: Closing:	Opening: Closing:

Cleaning schedule

Task	Please tick boxes √	Mon	Tues	Wed	Thurs	Fri	Sat	Sun
Clean and sanitise refrigerators and freezers								
Clean and sanitise the sinks and taps								
Empty and clean the coffee machine								
Clean the grills,ovens,hobs,griddles and stoves								
Clean the fryers								
Brush the grill and clean out grease traps								
Clean and sanitise all kitchen preparation surfaces								
Clean and sanitise all cutting boards								
Clean the meat and cheese slicer,if used								
Sanitise the telephone and all surfaces								
Clean behind fridges,ovens and fryers								
Empty bins and clean the kitchen floor								
Any other Step(s):								
Supervisor signature:		Date:						

Kitchen hygiene: monthly cleaning

Task	Please tick boxes √	When	Who	Comment
Wash kitchen walls and storage areas				
Clean and sanitise refrigerators and freezers				
Clean cooker hood and filters				
Supervisor signature:		**Date:**		

Always use appropriate personal protective equipment (PPE) when undertaking any cleaning task and follow the manufacturer's product use and, where relevant, dilution guidance.

4-weekly review

You should regularly review the methods used in your business to check that they are up to date, and still being followed by you and your staff.

You can use the checklist below to help you.
Look back over the past 4 weeks' diary entries. If you had a serious problem, or the same thing went wrong three times or more, make a note of it here, find out why and do something about it. Did you have a serious problem or did the same thing go wrong three times or more?
Yes ☐ No ☐
Details:

What did you do about it?

Did you get a new member of staff in the past 4 weeks? Yes ☐ No ☐

Were they trained in your methods? Yes ☐ No ☐

Have you changed your menu?

Have you reviewed your safe methods?

Any changes/new methods?   Yes ☐ No ☐

Have you changed supplier/bought new ingredients? Yes ☐ No ☐

Do these affect any of your safe methods?

Other changes:

Notes:

Week Starting: Date/Month/Year	Temperature recordings			Please tick boxes √			Week 1		
Monday	Time	Dish	Temp	Time	Dish	Temp	Time	Dish	Temp
Opening checks done ☐									
Issues: Yes ☐ No ☐									
Closing checks ☐									
Safe methods followed ☐									
Name:									
Signature:									
Tuesday	Time	Dish	Temp	Time	Dish	Temp	Time	Dish	Temp
Opening checks done ☐									
Issues: Yes ☐ No ☐									
Closing checks ☐									
Safe methods followed ☐									
Name:									
Signature:									
Wednesday	Time	Dish	Temp	Time	Dish	Temp	Time	Dish	Temp
Opening checks done ☐									
Issues: Yes ☐ No ☐									
Closing checks ☐									
Safe methods followed ☐									
Name:									
Signature:									
Thursday	Time	Dish	Temp	Time	Dish	Temp	Time	Dish	Temp
Opening checks done ☐									
Issues: Yes ☐ No ☐									
Closing checks ☐									
Safe methods followed ☐									
Name:									
Signature:									

Temperature recordings		Please tick boxes √									
Friday	Time	Dish		Temp	Time	Dish	Temp	Time	Dish		Temp
Opening checks done ☐											
Issues: Yes ☐ No ☐											
Closing checks ☐											
Safe methods followed ☐											
Name:											
Signature:											
Saturday	Time	Dish		Temp	Time	Dish	Temp	Time	Dish		Temp
Opening checks done ☐											
Issues: Yes ☐ No ☐											
Closing checks ☐											
Safe methods followed ☐											
Name:											
Signature:											
Sunday	Time	Dish		Temp	Time	Dish	Temp	Time	Dish		Temp
Opening checks done ☐											
Issues: Yes ☐ No ☐											
Closing checks ☐											
Safe methods followed ☐											
Name:											
Signature:											

Fridge/Freezer/Chiller Temperature records

Day	Frid/Frz/Chil 1	Frid/Frz/Chil 2	Frid/Frz/Chil 3	Frid/Frz/Chil 4	Frid/Frz/Chil 6	Frid/Frz/Chil 7
Monday	Opening: Closing:	Opening: Closing:	Opening: Closing:	Opening: Closing:	Opening: Closing:	Opening: Closing:
Tuesday	Opening: Closing:	Opening: Closing:	Opening: Closing:	Opening: Closing:	Opening: Closing:	Opening: Closing:
Wednesday	Opening: Closing:	Opening: Closing:	Opening: Closing:	Opening: Closing:	Opening: Closing:	Opening: Closing:
Thursday	Opening: Closing:	Opening: Closing:	Opening: Closing:	Opening: Closing:	Opening: Closing:	Opening: Closing:

Friday	Opening: Closing:	Opening: Closing:	Opening: Closing:	Opening: Closing:	Opening: Closing:	Opening: Closing:
Saturday	Opening: Closing:	Opening: Closing:	Opening: Closing:	Opening: Closing:	Opening: Closing:	Opening: Closing:
Sunday	Opening: Closing:	Opening: Closing:	Opening: Closing:	Opening: Closing:	Opening: Closing:	Opening: Closing:

Cleaning schedule

Task — Please tick boxes √	Mon	Tues	Wed	Thurs	Fri	Sat	Sun
Clean and sanitise refrigerators and freezers							
Clean and sanitise the sinks and taps							
Empty and clean the coffee machine							
Clean the grills,ovens,hobs,griddles and stoves							
Clean the fryers							
Brush the grill and clean out grease traps							
Clean and sanitise all kitchen preparation surfaces							
Clean and sanitise all cutting boards							
Clean the meat and cheese slicer,if used							
Sanitise the telephone and all surfaces							
Clean behind fridges,ovens and fryers							
Empty bins and clean the kitchen floor							
Any other Step(s):							

Supervisor signature: Date:

Weekly review-The Good,The Bad,The Ugly,Hirings and Firings

What went right:	What went wrong:

Notes:

Week Starting: Date/Month/Year	Temperature recordings			Please tick boxes √		Week 2			
Monday	Time	Dish	Temp	Time	Dish	Temp	Time	Dish	Temp
Opening checks done ☐									
Issues: Yes ☐ No ☐									
Closing checks ☐									
Safe methods followed ☐									
Name:									
Signature:									
Tuesday	Time	Dish	Temp	Time	Dish	Temp	Time	Dish	Temp
Opening checks done ☐									
Issues: Yes ☐ No ☐									
Closing checks ☐									
Safe methods followed ☐									
Name:									
Signature:									
Wednesday	Time	Dish	Temp	Time	Dish	Temp	Time	Dish	Temp
Opening checks done ☐									
Issues: Yes ☐ No ☐									
Closing checks ☐									
Safe methods followed ☐									
Name:									
Signature:									
Thursday	Time	Dish	Temp	Time	Dish	Temp	Time	Dish	Temp
Opening checks done ☐									
Issues: Yes ☐ No ☐									
Closing checks ☐									
Safe methods followed ☐									
Name:									
Signature:									

Temperature recordings			Please tick boxes √							
Friday	Time	Dish	Temp	Time	Dish	Temp	Time	Dish	Temp
Opening checks done ☐									
Issues: Yes ☐ No ☐									
Closing checks ☐									
Safe methods followed ☐									
Name:									
Signature:									
Saturday	Time	Dish	Temp	Time	Dish	Temp	Time	Dish	Temp
Opening checks done ☐									
Issues: Yes ☐ No ☐									
Closing checks ☐									
Safe methods followed ☐									
Name:									
Signature:									
Sunday	Time	Dish	Temp	Time	Dish	Temp	Time	Dish	Temp
Opening checks done ☐									
Issues: Yes ☐ No ☐									
Closing checks ☐									
Safe methods followed ☐									
Name:									
Signature:									

Fridge/Freezer/Chiller Temperature records

Day	Frid/Frz/Chil 1	Frid/Frz/Chil 2	Frid/Frz/Chil 3	Frid/Frz/Chil 4	Frid/Frz/Chil 6	Frid/Frz/Chil 7
Monday	Opening: Closing:	Opening: Closing:	Opening: Closing:	Opening: Closing:	Opening: Closing:	Opening: Closing:
Tuesday	Opening: Closing:	Opening: Closing:	Opening: Closing:	Opening: Closing:	Opening: Closing:	Opening: Closing:
Wednesday	Opening: Closing:	Opening: Closing:	Opening: Closing:	Opening: Closing:	Opening: Closing:	Opening: Closing:
Thursday	Opening: Closing:	Opening: Closing:	Opening: Closing:	Opening: Closing:	Opening: Closing:	Opening: Closing:

Friday	Opening: Closing:	Opening: Closing:	Opening: Closing:	Opening: Closing:	Opening: Closing:	Opening: Closing:
Saturday	Opening: Closing:	Opening: Closing:	Opening: Closing:	Opening: Closing:	Opening: Closing:	Opening: Closing:
Sunday	Opening: Closing:	Opening: Closing:	Opening: Closing:	Opening: Closing:	Opening: Closing:	Opening: Closing:

Cleaning schedule

Task	Please tick boxes √	Mon	Tues	Wed	Thurs	Fri	Sat	Sun
Clean and sanitise refrigerators and freezers								
Clean and sanitise the sinks and taps								
Empty and clean the coffee machine								
Clean the grills,ovens,hobs,griddles and stoves								
Clean the fryers								
Brush the grill and clean out grease traps								
Clean and sanitise all kitchen preparation surfaces								
Clean and sanitise all cutting boards								
Clean the meat and cheese slicer,if used								
Sanitise the telephone and all surfaces								
Clean behind fridges,ovens and fryers								
Empty bins and clean the kitchen floor								
Any other Step(s):								
Supervisor signature:	Date:							

Weekly review-The Good,The Bad,The Ugly,Hirings and Firings

What went right:	What went wrong:

Notes:

Week Starting: Date/Month/Year	Temperature recordings				Please tick boxes √			Week 3	
Monday	Time	Dish	Temp	Time	Dish	Temp	Time	Dish	Temp
Opening checks done ☐									
Issues: Yes ☐ No ☐									
Closing checks ☐									
Safe methods followed ☐									
Name:									
Signature:									
Tuesday	Time	Dish	Temp	Time	Dish	Temp	Time	Dish	Temp
Opening checks done ☐									
Issues: Yes ☐ No ☐									
Closing checks ☐									
Safe methods followed ☐									
Name:									
Signature:									
Wednesday	Time	Dish	Temp	Time	Dish	Temp	Time	Dish	Temp
Opening checks done ☐									
Issues: Yes ☐ No ☐									
Closing checks ☐									
Safe methods followed ☐									
Name:									
Signature:									
Thursday	Time	Dish	Temp	Time	Dish	Temp	Time	Dish	Temp
Opening checks done ☐									
Issues: Yes ☐ No ☐									
Closing checks ☐									
Safe methods followed ☐									
Name:									
Signature:									

Temperature recordings   Please tick boxes √

Friday	Time	Dish	Temp	Time	Dish	Temp	Time	Dish	Temp
Opening checks done ☐									
Issues: Yes ☐ No ☐									
Closing checks ☐									
Safe methods followed ☐									
Name:									
Signature:									

Saturday	Time	Dish	Temp	Time	Dish	Temp	Time	Dish	Temp
Opening checks done ☐									
Issues: Yes ☐ No ☐									
Closing checks ☐									
Safe methods followed ☐									
Name:									
Signature:									

Sunday	Time	Dish	Temp	Time	Dish	Temp	Time	Dish	Temp
Opening checks done ☐									
Issues: Yes ☐ No ☐									
Closing checks ☐									
Safe methods followed ☐									
Name:									
Signature:									

Fridge/Freezer/Chiller Temperature records

Day	Frid/Frz/Chil 1	Frid/Frz/Chil 2	Frid/Frz/Chil 3	Frid/Frz/Chil 4	Frid/Frz/Chil 6	Frid/Frz/Chil 7
Monday	Opening: Closing:	Opening: Closing:	Opening: Closing:	Opening: Closing:	Opening: Closing:	Opening: Closing:
Tuesday	Opening: Closing:	Opening: Closing:	Opening: Closing:	Opening: Closing:	Opening: Closing:	Opening: Closing:
Wednesday	Opening: Closing:	Opening: Closing:	Opening: Closing:	Opening: Closing:	Opening: Closing:	Opening: Closing:
Thursday	Opening: Closing:	Opening: Closing:	Opening: Closing:	Opening: Closing:	Opening: Closing:	Opening: Closing:

Friday	Opening: Closing:	Opening: Closing:	Opening: Closing:	Opening: Closing:	Opening: Closing:	Opening: Closing:
Saturday	Opening: Closing:	Opening: Closing:	Opening: Closing:	Opening: Closing:	Opening: Closing:	Opening: Closing:
Sunday	Opening: Closing:	Opening: Closing:	Opening: Closing:	Opening: Closing:	Opening: Closing:	Opening: Closing:

Cleaning schedule

Task — Please tick boxes √	Mon	Tues	Wed	Thurs	Fri	Sat	Sun
Clean and sanitise refrigerators and freezers							
Clean and sanitise the sinks and taps							
Empty and clean the coffee machine							
Clean the grills,ovens,hobs,griddles and stoves							
Clean the fryers							
Brush the grill and clean out grease traps							
Clean and sanitise all kitchen preparation surfaces							
Clean and sanitise all cutting boards							
Clean the meat and cheese slicer,if used							
Sanitise the telephone and all surfaces							
Clean behind fridges,ovens and fryers							
Empty bins and clean the kitchen floor							
Any other Step(s):							

Supervisor signature: Date:

Weekly review-The Good,The Bad,The Ugly,Hirings and Firings

What went right:	What went wrong:

Notes:

Week Starting: Date/Month/Year	Temperature recordings			Please tick boxes √			Week 4		
Monday	Time	Dish		Temp	Time	Dish	Temp	Time	Dish	Temp
Opening checks done ☐										
Issues: Yes ☐ No ☐										
Closing checks ☐										
Safe methods followed ☐										
Name:										
Signature:										
Tuesday	Time	Dish	Temp	Time	Dish	Temp	Time	Dish	Temp
Opening checks done ☐										
Issues: Yes ☐ No ☐										
Closing checks ☐										
Safe methods followed ☐										
Name:										
Signature:										
Wednesday	Time	Dish	Temp	Time	Dish	Temp	Time	Dish	Temp
Opening checks done ☐										
Issues: Yes ☐ No ☐										
Closing checks ☐										
Safe methods followed ☐										
Name:										
Signature:										
Thursday	Time	Dish	Temp	Time	Dish	Temp	Time	Dish	Temp
Opening checks done ☐										
Issues: Yes ☐ No ☐										
Closing checks ☐										
Safe methods followed ☐										
Name:										
Signature:										

Temperature recordings   Please tick boxes √

Friday	Time	Dish	Temp	Time	Dish	Temp	Time	Dish	Temp
Opening checks done ☐									
Issues: Yes ☐ No ☐									
Closing checks ☐									
Safe methods followed ☐									
Name:									
Signature:									
Saturday	Time	Dish	Temp	Time	Dish	Temp	Time	Dish	Temp
Opening checks done ☐									
Issues: Yes ☐ No ☐									
Closing checks ☐									
Safe methods followed ☐									
Name:									
Signature:									
Sunday	Time	Dish	Temp	Time	Dish	Temp	Time	Dish	Temp
Opening checks done ☐									
Issues: Yes ☐ No ☐									
Closing checks ☐									
Safe methods followed ☐									
Name:									
Signature:									

Fridge/Freezer/Chiller Temperature records

Day	Frid/Frz/Chil 1	Frid/Frz/Chil 2	Frid/Frz/Chil 3	Frid/Frz/Chil 4	Frid/Frz/Chil 6	Frid/Frz/Chil 7
Monday	Opening: Closing:	Opening: Closing:	Opening: Closing:	Opening: Closing:	Opening: Closing:	Opening: Closing:
Tuesday	Opening: Closing:	Opening: Closing:	Opening: Closing:	Opening: Closing:	Opening: Closing:	Opening: Closing:
Wednesday	Opening: Closing:	Opening: Closing:	Opening: Closing:	Opening: Closing:	Opening: Closing:	Opening: Closing:
Thursday	Opening: Closing:	Opening: Closing:	Opening: Closing:	Opening: Closing:	Opening: Closing:	Opening: Closing:

Friday	Opening: Closing:	Opening: Closing:	Opening: Closing:	Opening: Closing:	Opening: Closing:	Opening: Closing:
Saturday	Opening: Closing:	Opening: Closing:	Opening: Closing:	Opening: Closing:	Opening: Closing:	Opening: Closing:
Sunday	Opening: Closing:	Opening: Closing:	Opening: Closing:	Opening: Closing:	Opening: Closing:	Opening: Closing:

Cleaning schedule

Task	Please tick boxes √	Mon	Tues	Wed	Thurs	Fri	Sat	Sun
Clean and sanitise refrigerators and freezers								
Clean and sanitise the sinks and taps								
Empty and clean the coffee machine								
Clean the grills, ovens, hobs, griddles and stoves								
Clean the fryers								
Brush the grill and clean out grease traps								
Clean and sanitise all kitchen preparation surfaces								
Clean and sanitise all cutting boards								
Clean the meat and cheese slicer, if used								
Sanitise the telephone and all surfaces								
Clean behind fridges, ovens and fryers								
Empty bins and clean the kitchen floor								
Any other Step(s):								
Supervisor signature:		Date:						

Kitchen hygiene: monthly cleaning

Task	Please tick boxes √	When	Who	Comment
Wash kitchen walls and storage areas				
Clean and sanitise refrigerators and freezers				
Clean cooker hood and filters				
Supervisor signature:		**Date:**		

Always use appropriate personal protective equipment (PPE) when undertaking any cleaning task and follow the manufacturer's product use and, where relevant, dilution guidance.

4-weekly review

You should regularly review the methods used in your business to check that they are up to date, and still being followed by you and your staff.

You can use the checklist below to help you.
Look back over the past 4 weeks' diary entries. If you had a serious problem, or the same thing went wrong three times or more, make a note of it here, find out why and do something about it. Did you have a serious problem or did the same thing go wrong three times or more?
Yes ☐ No ☐
Details:

What did you do about it?

Did you get a new member of staff in the past 4 weeks? Yes ☐ No ☐

Were they trained in your methods? Yes ☐ No ☐

Have you changed your menu?

Have you reviewed your safe methods?

Any changes/new methods? Yes ☐ No ☐

Have you changed supplier/bought new ingredients? Yes ☐ No ☐

Do these affect any of your safe methods?

Other changes:

Notes:

Week Starting: Date/Month/Year	Temperature recordings			Please tick boxes √			Week 1		
Monday	Time	Dish	Temp	Time	Dish	Temp	Time	Dish	Temp
Opening checks done ☐									
Issues: Yes ☐ No ☐									
Closing checks ☐									
Safe methods followed ☐									
Name:									
Signature:									
Tuesday	Time	Dish	Temp	Time	Dish	Temp	Time	Dish	Temp
Opening checks done ☐									
Issues: Yes ☐ No ☐									
Closing checks ☐									
Safe methods followed ☐									
Name:									
Signature:									
Wednesday	Time	Dish	Temp	Time	Dish	Temp	Time	Dish	Temp
Opening checks done ☐									
Issues: Yes ☐ No ☐									
Closing checks ☐									
Safe methods followed ☐									
Name:									
Signature:									
Thursday	Time	Dish	Temp	Time	Dish	Temp	Time	Dish	Temp
Opening checks done ☐									
Issues: Yes ☐ No ☐									
Closing checks ☐									
Safe methods followed ☐									
Name:									
Signature:									

Temperature recordings   Please tick boxes √

Friday	Time	Dish	Temp	Time	Dish	Temp	Time	Dish	Temp
Opening checks done ☐									
Issues: Yes ☐ No ☐									
Closing checks ☐									
Safe methods followed ☐									
Name:									
Signature:									

Saturday	Time	Dish	Temp	Time	Dish	Temp	Time	Dish	Temp
Opening checks done ☐									
Issues: Yes ☐ No ☐									
Closing checks ☐									
Safe methods followed ☐									
Name:									
Signature:									

Sunday	Time	Dish	Temp	Time	Dish	Temp	Time	Dish	Temp
Opening checks done ☐									
Issues: Yes ☐ No ☐									
Closing checks ☐									
Safe methods followed ☐									
Name:									
Signature:									

Fridge/Freezer/Chiller Temperature records

Day	Frid/Frz/Chil 1	Frid/Frz/Chil 2	Frid/Frz/Chil 3	Frid/Frz/Chil 4	Frid/Frz/Chil 6	Frid/Frz/Chil 7
Monday	Opening: Closing:	Opening: Closing:	Opening: Closing:	Opening: Closing:	Opening: Closing:	Opening: Closing:
Tuesday	Opening: Closing:	Opening: Closing:	Opening: Closing:	Opening: Closing:	Opening: Closing:	Opening: Closing:
Wednesday	Opening: Closing:	Opening: Closing:	Opening: Closing:	Opening: Closing:	Opening: Closing:	Opening: Closing:
Thursday	Opening: Closing:	Opening: Closing:	Opening: Closing:	Opening: Closing:	Opening: Closing:	Opening: Closing:

Friday	Opening: Closing:	Opening: Closing:	Opening: Closing:	Opening: Closing:	Opening: Closing:	Opening: Closing:
Saturday	Opening: Closing:	Opening: Closing:	Opening: Closing:	Opening: Closing:	Opening: Closing:	Opening: Closing:
Sunday	Opening: Closing:	Opening: Closing:	Opening: Closing:	Opening: Closing:	Opening: Closing:	Opening: Closing:

Cleaning schedule

Task	Please tick boxes √	Mon	Tues	Wed	Thurs	Fri	Sat	Sun
Clean and sanitise refrigerators and freezers								
Clean and sanitise the sinks and taps								
Empty and clean the coffee machine								
Clean the grills,ovens,hobs,griddles and stoves								
Clean the fryers								
Brush the grill and clean out grease traps								
Clean and sanitise all kitchen preparation surfaces								
Clean and sanitise all cutting boards								
Clean the meat and cheese slicer,if used								
Sanitise the telephone and all surfaces								
Clean behind fridges,ovens and fryers								
Empty bins and clean the kitchen floor								
Any other Step(s):								

Supervisor signature: Date:

Weekly review-The Good,The Bad,The Ugly,Hirings and Firings

What went right:	What went wrong:

Notes:

Week Starting: Date/Month/Year	Temperature recordings			Please tick boxes √			Week 2		
Monday	Time	Dish	Temp	Time	Dish	Temp	Time	Dish	Temp
Opening checks done ☐									
Issues: Yes ☐ No ☐									
Closing checks ☐									
Safe methods followed ☐									
Name:									
Signature:									
Tuesday	Time	Dish	Temp	Time	Dish	Temp	Time	Dish	Temp
Opening checks done ☐									
Issues: Yes ☐ No ☐									
Closing checks ☐									
Safe methods followed ☐									
Name:									
Signature:									
Wednesday	Time	Dish	Temp	Time	Dish	Temp	Time	Dish	Temp
Opening checks done ☐									
Issues: Yes ☐ No ☐									
Closing checks ☐									
Safe methods followed ☐									
Name:									
Signature:									
Thursday	Time	Dish	Temp	Time	Dish	Temp	Time	Dish	Temp
Opening checks done ☐									
Issues: Yes ☐ No ☐									
Closing checks ☐									
Safe methods followed ☐									
Name:									
Signature:									

Temperature recordings			Please tick boxes √								
Friday	Time	Dish		Temp	Time	Dish		Temp	Time	Dish	Temp
Opening checks done ☐											
Issues: Yes ☐ No ☐											
Closing checks ☐											
Safe methods followed ☐											
Name:											
Signature:											
Saturday	Time	Dish		Temp	Time	Dish		Temp	Time	Dish	Temp
Opening checks done ☐											
Issues: Yes ☐ No ☐											
Closing checks ☐											
Safe methods followed ☐											
Name:											
Signature:											
Sunday	Time	Dish		Temp	Time	Dish		Temp	Time	Dish	Temp
Opening checks done ☐											
Issues: Yes ☐ No ☐											
Closing checks ☐											
Safe methods followed ☐											
Name:											
Signature:											

Fridge/Freezer/Chiller Temperature records

Day	Frid/Frz/Chil 1	Frid/Frz/Chil 2	Frid/Frz/Chil 3	Frid/Frz/Chil 4	Frid/Frz/Chil 6	Frid/Frz/Chil 7
Monday	Opening: Closing:	Opening: Closing:	Opening: Closing:	Opening: Closing:	Opening: Closing:	Opening: Closing:
Tuesday	Opening: Closing:	Opening: Closing:	Opening: Closing:	Opening: Closing:	Opening: Closing:	Opening: Closing:
Wednesday	Opening: Closing:	Opening: Closing:	Opening: Closing:	Opening: Closing:	Opening: Closing:	Opening: Closing:
Thursday	Opening: Closing:	Opening: Closing:	Opening: Closing:	Opening: Closing:	Opening: Closing:	Opening: Closing:

Friday	Opening: Closing:	Opening: Closing:	Opening: Closing:	Opening: Closing:	Opening: Closing:	Opening: Closing:
Saturday	Opening: Closing:	Opening: Closing:	Opening: Closing:	Opening: Closing:	Opening: Closing:	Opening: Closing:
Sunday	Opening: Closing:	Opening: Closing:	Opening: Closing:	Opening: Closing:	Opening: Closing:	Opening: Closing:

Cleaning schedule

Task Please tick boxes √	Mon	Tues	Wed	Thurs	Fri	Sat	Sun
Clean and sanitise refrigerators and freezers							
Clean and sanitise the sinks and taps							
Empty and clean the coffee machine							
Clean the grills,ovens,hobs,griddles and stoves							
Clean the fryers							
Brush the grill and clean out grease traps							
Clean and sanitise all kitchen preparation surfaces							
Clean and sanitise all cutting boards							
Clean the meat and cheese slicer,if used							
Sanitise the telephone and all surfaces							
Clean behind fridges,ovens and fryers							
Empty bins and clean the kitchen floor							
Any other Step(s):							

Supervisor signature: Date:

Weekly review-The Good,The Bad,The Ugly,Hirings and Firings

What went right:	What went wrong:

Notes:

Week Starting: Date/Month/Year	Temperature recordings			Please tick boxes √			Week 3		
Monday	Time	Dish	Temp	Time	Dish	Temp	Time	Dish	Temp
Opening checks done ☐									
Issues: Yes ☐ No ☐									
Closing checks ☐									
Safe methods followed ☐									
Name:									
Signature:									
Tuesday	Time	Dish	Temp	Time	Dish	Temp	Time	Dish	Temp
Opening checks done ☐									
Issues: Yes ☐ No ☐									
Closing checks ☐									
Safe methods followed ☐									
Name:									
Signature:									
Wednesday	Time	Dish	Temp	Time	Dish	Temp	Time	Dish	Temp
Opening checks done ☐									
Issues: Yes ☐ No ☐									
Closing checks ☐									
Safe methods followed ☐									
Name:									
Signature:									
Thursday	Time	Dish	Temp	Time	Dish	Temp	Time	Dish	Temp
Opening checks done ☐									
Issues: Yes ☐ No ☐									
Closing checks ☐									
Safe methods followed ☐									
Name:									
Signature:									

Temperature recordings   Please tick boxes √

Friday	Time	Dish	Temp	Time	Dish	Temp	Time	Dish	Temp
Opening checks done ☐									
Issues: Yes ☐ No ☐									
Closing checks ☐									
Safe methods followed ☐									
Name:									
Signature:									

Saturday	Time	Dish	Temp	Time	Dish	Temp	Time	Dish	Temp
Opening checks done ☐									
Issues: Yes ☐ No ☐									
Closing checks ☐									
Safe methods followed ☐									
Name:									
Signature:									

Sunday	Time	Dish	Temp	Time	Dish	Temp	Time	Dish	Temp
Opening checks done ☐									
Issues: Yes ☐ No ☐									
Closing checks ☐									
Safe methods followed ☐									
Name:									
Signature:									

Fridge/Freezer/Chiller Temperature records

Day	Frid/Frz/Chil 1	Frid/Frz/Chil 2	Frid/Frz/Chil 3	Frid/Frz/Chil 4	Frid/Frz/Chil 6	Frid/Frz/Chil 7
Monday	Opening: Closing:	Opening: Closing:	Opening: Closing:	Opening: Closing:	Opening: Closing:	Opening: Closing:
Tuesday	Opening: Closing:	Opening: Closing:	Opening: Closing:	Opening: Closing:	Opening: Closing:	Opening: Closing:
Wednesday	Opening: Closing:	Opening: Closing:	Opening: Closing:	Opening: Closing:	Opening: Closing:	Opening: Closing:
Thursday	Opening: Closing:	Opening: Closing:	Opening: Closing:	Opening: Closing:	Opening: Closing:	Opening: Closing:

Friday	Opening: Closing:	Opening: Closing:	Opening: Closing:	Opening: Closing:	Opening: Closing:	Opening: Closing:
Saturday	Opening: Closing:	Opening: Closing:	Opening: Closing:	Opening: Closing:	Opening: Closing:	Opening: Closing:
Sunday	Opening: Closing:	Opening: Closing:	Opening: Closing:	Opening: Closing:	Opening: Closing:	Opening: Closing:

Cleaning schedule

Task	Please tick boxes √	Mon	Tues	Wed	Thurs	Fri	Sat	Sun
Clean and sanitise refrigerators and freezers								
Clean and sanitise the sinks and taps								
Empty and clean the coffee machine								
Clean the grills,ovens,hobs,griddles and stoves								
Clean the fryers								
Brush the grill and clean out grease traps								
Clean and sanitise all kitchen preparation surfaces								
Clean and sanitise all cutting boards								
Clean the meat and cheese slicer,if used								
Sanitise the telephone and all surfaces								
Clean behind fridges,ovens and fryers								
Empty bins and clean the kitchen floor								
Any other Step(s):								
Supervisor signature:	Date:							

Weekly review-The Good,The Bad,The Ugly,Hirings and Firings

What went right:

What went wrong:

Notes:

Week Starting: Date/Month/Year	Temperature recordings			Please tick boxes √			Week 4		
Monday	Time	Dish	Temp	Time	Dish	Temp	Time	Dish	Temp
Opening checks done ☐									
Issues: Yes ☐ No ☐									
Closing checks ☐									
Safe methods followed ☐									
Name:									
Signature:									
Tuesday	Time	Dish	Temp	Time	Dish	Temp	Time	Dish	Temp
Opening checks done ☐									
Issues: Yes ☐ No ☐									
Closing checks ☐									
Safe methods followed ☐									
Name:									
Signature:									
Wednesday	Time	Dish	Temp	Time	Dish	Temp	Time	Dish	Temp
Opening checks done ☐									
Issues: Yes ☐ No ☐									
Closing checks ☐									
Safe methods followed ☐									
Name:									
Signature:									
Thursday	Time	Dish	Temp	Time	Dish	Temp	Time	Dish	Temp
Opening checks done ☐									
Issues: Yes ☐ No ☐									
Closing checks ☐									
Safe methods followed ☐									
Name:									
Signature:									

Temperature recordings			Please tick boxes √						
Friday	Time	Dish		Temp	Time	Dish	Temp	Time	Dish	Temp
Opening checks done ☐									
Issues: Yes ☐ No ☐									
Closing checks ☐									
Safe methods followed ☐									
Name:									
Signature:									
Saturday	Time	Dish		Temp	Time	Dish	Temp	Time	Dish	Temp
Opening checks done ☐									
Issues: Yes ☐ No ☐									
Closing checks ☐									
Safe methods followed ☐									
Name:									
Signature:									
Sunday	Time	Dish		Temp	Time	Dish	Temp	Time	Dish	Temp
Opening checks done ☐									
Issues: Yes ☐ No ☐									
Closing checks ☐									
Safe methods followed ☐									
Name:									
Signature:									

Fridge/Freezer/Chiller Temperature records

Day	Frid/Frz/Chil 1	Frid/Frz/Chil 2	Frid/Frz/Chil 3	Frid/Frz/Chil 4	Frid/Frz/Chil 6	Frid/Frz/Chil 7
Monday	Opening: Closing:	Opening: Closing:	Opening: Closing:	Opening: Closing:	Opening: Closing:	Opening: Closing:
Tuesday	Opening: Closing:	Opening: Closing:	Opening: Closing:	Opening: Closing:	Opening: Closing:	Opening: Closing:
Wednesday	Opening: Closing:	Opening: Closing:	Opening: Closing:	Opening: Closing:	Opening: Closing:	Opening: Closing:
Thursday	Opening: Closing:	Opening: Closing:	Opening: Closing:	Opening: Closing:	Opening: Closing:	Opening: Closing:

Friday	Opening: Closing:	Opening: Closing:	Opening: Closing:	Opening: Closing:	Opening: Closing:	Opening: Closing:
Saturday	Opening: Closing:	Opening: Closing:	Opening: Closing:	Opening: Closing:	Opening: Closing:	Opening: Closing:
Sunday	Opening: Closing:	Opening: Closing:	Opening: Closing:	Opening: Closing:	Opening: Closing:	Opening: Closing:

Cleaning schedule

Task	Please tick boxes √	Mon	Tues	Wed	Thurs	Fri	Sat	Sun
Clean and sanitise refrigerators and freezers								
Clean and sanitise the sinks and taps								
Empty and clean the coffee machine								
Clean the grills, ovens, hobs, griddles and stoves								
Clean the fryers								
Brush the grill and clean out grease traps								
Clean and sanitise all kitchen preparation surfaces								
Clean and sanitise all cutting boards								
Clean the meat and cheese slicer, if used								
Sanitise the telephone and all surfaces								
Clean behind fridges, ovens and fryers								
Empty bins and clean the kitchen floor								
Any other Step(s):								
Supervisor signature:		Date:						

Kitchen hygiene: monthly cleaning

Task	Please tick boxes √	When	Who	Comment
Wash kitchen walls and storage areas				
Clean and sanitise refrigerators and freezers				
Clean cooker hood and filters				
Supervisor signature:		**Date:**		

Always use appropriate personal protective equipment (PPE) when undertaking any cleaning task and follow the manufacturer's product use and, where relevant, dilution guidance.

4-weekly review

You should regularly review the methods used in your business to check that they are up to date, and still being followed by you and your staff.

You can use the checklist below to help you.
Look back over the past 4 weeks' diary entries. If you had a serious problem, or the same thing went wrong three times or more, make a note of it here, find out why and do something about it. Did you have a serious problem or did the same thing go wrong three times or more?
Yes ☐ No ☐
Details:

What did you do about it?

Did you get a new member of staff in the past 4 weeks? Yes ☐ No ☐

Were they trained in your methods? Yes ☐ No ☐

Have you changed your menu?

Have you reviewed your safe methods?

Any changes/new methods?   Yes ☐ No ☐

Have you changed supplier/bought new ingredients? Yes ☐ No ☐

Do these affect any of your safe methods?

Other changes:

Notes:

Week Starting: Date/Month/Year	Temperature recordings Please tick boxes √ Week 1								
Monday	Time	Dish	Temp	Time	Dish	Temp	Time	Dish	Temp
Opening checks done ☐									
Issues: Yes ☐ No ☐									
Closing checks ☐									
Safe methods followed ☐									
Name:									
Signature:									
Tuesday	Time	Dish	Temp	Time	Dish	Temp	Time	Dish	Temp
Opening checks done ☐									
Issues: Yes ☐ No ☐									
Closing checks ☐									
Safe methods followed ☐									
Name:									
Signature:									
Wednesday	Time	Dish	Temp	Time	Dish	Temp	Time	Dish	Temp
Opening checks done ☐									
Issues: Yes ☐ No ☐									
Closing checks ☐									
Safe methods followed ☐									
Name:									
Signature:									
Thursday	Time	Dish	Temp	Time	Dish	Temp	Time	Dish	Temp
Opening checks done ☐									
Issues: Yes ☐ No ☐									
Closing checks ☐									
Safe methods followed ☐									
Name:									
Signature:									

Temperature recordings			Please tick boxes √							
Friday	Time	Dish		Temp	Time	Dish		Temp	Time	Dish	Temp
Opening checks done ☐											
Issues: Yes ☐ No ☐											
Closing checks ☐											
Safe methods followed ☐											
Name:											
Signature:											
Saturday	Time	Dish		Temp	Time	Dish		Temp	Time	Dish	Temp
Opening checks done ☐											
Issues: Yes ☐ No ☐											
Closing checks ☐											
Safe methods followed ☐											
Name:											
Signature:											
Sunday	Time	Dish		Temp	Time	Dish		Temp	Time	Dish	Temp
Opening checks done ☐											
Issues: Yes ☐ No ☐											
Closing checks ☐											
Safe methods followed ☐											
Name:											
Signature:											

Fridge/Freezer/Chiller Temperature records

Day	Frid/Frz/Chil 1	Frid/Frz/Chil 2	Frid/Frz/Chil 3	Frid/Frz/Chil 4	Frid/Frz/Chil 6	Frid/Frz/Chil 7
Monday	Opening: Closing:	Opening: Closing:	Opening: Closing:	Opening: Closing:	Opening: Closing:	Opening: Closing:
Tuesday	Opening: Closing:	Opening: Closing:	Opening: Closing:	Opening: Closing:	Opening: Closing:	Opening: Closing:
Wednesday	Opening: Closing:	Opening: Closing:	Opening: Closing:	Opening: Closing:	Opening: Closing:	Opening: Closing:
Thursday	Opening: Closing:	Opening: Closing:	Opening: Closing:	Opening: Closing:	Opening: Closing:	Opening: Closing:

Friday	Opening: Closing:	Opening: Closing:	Opening: Closing:	Opening: Closing:	Opening: Closing:	Opening: Closing:
Saturday	Opening: Closing:	Opening: Closing:	Opening: Closing:	Opening: Closing:	Opening: Closing:	Opening: Closing:
Sunday	Opening: Closing:	Opening: Closing:	Opening: Closing:	Opening: Closing:	Opening: Closing:	Opening: Closing:

Cleaning schedule

Task — Please tick boxes √	Mon	Tues	Wed	Thurs	Fri	Sat	Sun
Clean and sanitise refrigerators and freezers							
Clean and sanitise the sinks and taps							
Empty and clean the coffee machine							
Clean the grills,ovens,hobs,griddles and stoves							
Clean the fryers							
Brush the grill and clean out grease traps							
Clean and sanitise all kitchen preparation surfaces							
Clean and sanitise all cutting boards							
Clean the meat and cheese slicer,if used							
Sanitise the telephone and all surfaces							
Clean behind fridges,ovens and fryers							
Empty bins and clean the kitchen floor							
Any other Step(s):							

Supervisor signature: Date:

Weekly review-The Good,The Bad,The Ugly,Hirings and Firings

What went right:	What went wrong:

Notes:

Week Starting: Date/Month/Year	Temperature recordings			Please tick boxes √			Week 2		
Monday	Time	Dish	Temp	Time	Dish	Temp	Time	Dish	Temp
Opening checks done ☐									
Issues: Yes ☐ No ☐									
Closing checks ☐									
Safe methods followed ☐									
Name:									
Signature:									
Tuesday	Time	Dish	Temp	Time	Dish	Temp	Time	Dish	Temp
Opening checks done ☐									
Issues: Yes ☐ No ☐									
Closing checks ☐									
Safe methods followed ☐									
Name:									
Signature:									
Wednesday	Time	Dish	Temp	Time	Dish	Temp	Time	Dish	Temp
Opening checks done ☐									
Issues: Yes ☐ No ☐									
Closing checks ☐									
Safe methods followed ☐									
Name:									
Signature:									
Thursday	Time	Dish	Temp	Time	Dish	Temp	Time	Dish	Temp
Opening checks done ☐									
Issues: Yes ☐ No ☐									
Closing checks ☐									
Safe methods followed ☐									
Name:									
Signature:									

Temperature recordings   Please tick boxes √

Friday	Time	Dish	Temp	Time	Dish	Temp	Time	Dish	Temp
Opening checks done ☐									
Issues: Yes ☐ No ☐									
Closing checks ☐									
Safe methods followed ☐									
Name:									
Signature:									
Saturday	Time	Dish	Temp	Time	Dish	Temp	Time	Dish	Temp
Opening checks done ☐									
Issues: Yes ☐ No ☐									
Closing checks ☐									
Safe methods followed ☐									
Name:									
Signature:									
Sunday	Time	Dish	Temp	Time	Dish	Temp	Time	Dish	Temp
Opening checks done ☐									
Issues: Yes ☐ No ☐									
Closing checks ☐									
Safe methods followed ☐									
Name:									
Signature:									

Fridge/Freezer/Chiller Temperature records

Day	Frid/Frz/Chil 1	Frid/Frz/Chil 2	Frid/Frz/Chil 3	Frid/Frz/Chil 4	Frid/Frz/Chil 6	Frid/Frz/Chil 7
Monday	Opening: Closing:	Opening: Closing:	Opening: Closing:	Opening: Closing:	Opening: Closing:	Opening: Closing:
Tuesday	Opening: Closing:	Opening: Closing:	Opening: Closing:	Opening: Closing:	Opening: Closing:	Opening: Closing:
Wednesday	Opening: Closing:	Opening: Closing:	Opening: Closing:	Opening: Closing:	Opening: Closing:	Opening: Closing:
Thursday	Opening: Closing:	Opening: Closing:	Opening: Closing:	Opening: Closing:	Opening: Closing:	Opening: Closing:

Friday	Opening: Closing:	Opening: Closing:	Opening: Closing:	Opening: Closing:	Opening: Closing:	Opening: Closing:
Saturday	Opening: Closing:	Opening: Closing:	Opening: Closing:	Opening: Closing:	Opening: Closing:	Opening: Closing:
Sunday	Opening: Closing:	Opening: Closing:	Opening: Closing:	Opening: Closing:	Opening: Closing:	Opening: Closing:

Cleaning schedule

Task	Please tick boxes √	Mon	Tues	Wed	Thurs	Fri	Sat	Sun
Clean and sanitise refrigerators and freezers								
Clean and sanitise the sinks and taps								
Empty and clean the coffee machine								
Clean the grills,ovens,hobs,griddles and stoves								
Clean the fryers								
Brush the grill and clean out grease traps								
Clean and sanitise all kitchen preparation surfaces								
Clean and sanitise all cutting boards								
Clean the meat and cheese slicer,if used								
Sanitise the telephone and all surfaces								
Clean behind fridges,ovens and fryers								
Empty bins and clean the kitchen floor								
Any other Step(s):								
Supervisor signature:	Date:							

Weekly review-The Good,The Bad,The Ugly,Hirings and Firings

What went right:	What went wrong:

Notes:

262

Week Starting: Date/Month/Year	Temperature recordings			Please tick boxes √			Week 3		
Monday	Time	Dish	Temp	Time	Dish	Temp	Time	Dish	Temp
Opening checks done ☐									
Issues: Yes ☐ No ☐									
Closing checks ☐									
Safe methods followed ☐									
Name:									
Signature:									
Tuesday	Time	Dish	Temp	Time	Dish	Temp	Time	Dish	Temp
Opening checks done ☐									
Issues: Yes ☐ No ☐									
Closing checks ☐									
Safe methods followed ☐									
Name:									
Signature:									
Wednesday	Time	Dish	Temp	Time	Dish	Temp	Time	Dish	Temp
Opening checks done ☐									
Issues: Yes ☐ No ☐									
Closing checks ☐									
Safe methods followed ☐									
Name:									
Signature:									
Thursday	Time	Dish	Temp	Time	Dish	Temp	Time	Dish	Temp
Opening checks done ☐									
Issues: Yes ☐ No ☐									
Closing checks ☐									
Safe methods followed ☐									
Name:									
Signature:									

Temperature recordings			Please tick boxes √							
Friday	Time	Dish		Temp	Time	Dish	Temp	Time	Dish	Temp
Opening checks done ☐										
Issues: Yes ☐ No ☐										
Closing checks ☐										
Safe methods followed ☐										
Name:										
Signature:										
Saturday	Time	Dish		Temp	Time	Dish	Temp	Time	Dish	Temp
Opening checks done ☐										
Issues: Yes ☐ No ☐										
Closing checks ☐										
Safe methods followed ☐										
Name:										
Signature:										
Sunday	Time	Dish		Temp	Time	Dish	Temp	Time	Dish	Temp
Opening checks done ☐										
Issues: Yes ☐ No ☐										
Closing checks ☐										
Safe methods followed ☐										
Name:										
Signature:										

Fridge/Freezer/Chiller Temperature records

Day	Frid/Frz/Chil 1	Frid/Frz/Chil 2	Frid/Frz/Chil 3	Frid/Frz/Chil 4	Frid/Frz/Chil 6	Frid/Frz/Chil 7
Monday	Opening: Closing:	Opening: Closing:	Opening: Closing:	Opening: Closing:	Opening: Closing:	Opening: Closing:
Tuesday	Opening: Closing:	Opening: Closing:	Opening: Closing:	Opening: Closing:	Opening: Closing:	Opening: Closing:
Wednesday	Opening: Closing:	Opening: Closing:	Opening: Closing:	Opening: Closing:	Opening: Closing:	Opening: Closing:
Thursday	Opening: Closing:	Opening: Closing:	Opening: Closing:	Opening: Closing:	Opening: Closing:	Opening: Closing:

Friday	Opening: Closing:	Opening: Closing:	Opening: Closing:	Opening: Closing:	Opening: Closing:	Opening: Closing:
Saturday	Opening: Closing:	Opening: Closing:	Opening: Closing:	Opening: Closing:	Opening: Closing:	Opening: Closing:
Sunday	Opening: Closing:	Opening: Closing:	Opening: Closing:	Opening: Closing:	Opening: Closing:	Opening: Closing:

Cleaning schedule

Task	Please tick boxes √	Mon	Tues	Wed	Thurs	Fri	Sat	Sun
Clean and sanitise refrigerators and freezers								
Clean and sanitise the sinks and taps								
Empty and clean the coffee machine								
Clean the grills,ovens,hobs,griddles and stoves								
Clean the fryers								
Brush the grill and clean out grease traps								
Clean and sanitise all kitchen preparation surfaces								
Clean and sanitise all cutting boards								
Clean the meat and cheese slicer,if used								
Sanitise the telephone and all surfaces								
Clean behind fridges,ovens and fryers								
Empty bins and clean the kitchen floor								
Any other Step(s):								

Supervisor signature: Date:

Weekly review-The Good,The Bad,The Ugly,Hirings and Firings

What went right:	What went wrong:

Notes:

Week Starting: Date/Month/Year	**Temperature recordings**			Please tick boxes √			Week 4		
Monday	Time	Dish	Temp	Time	Dish	Temp	Time	Dish	Temp
Opening checks done ☐									
Issues: Yes ☐ No ☐									
Closing checks ☐									
Safe methods followed ☐									
Name:									
Signature:									
Tuesday	Time	Dish	Temp	Time	Dish	Temp	Time	Dish	Temp
Opening checks done ☐									
Issues: Yes ☐ No ☐									
Closing checks ☐									
Safe methods followed ☐									
Name:									
Signature:									
Wednesday	Time	Dish	Temp	Time	Dish	Temp	Time	Dish	Temp
Opening checks done ☐									
Issues: Yes ☐ No ☐									
Closing checks ☐									
Safe methods followed ☐									
Name:									
Signature:									
Thursday	Time	Dish	Temp	Time	Dish	Temp	Time	Dish	Temp
Opening checks done ☐									
Issues: Yes ☐ No ☐									
Closing checks ☐									
Safe methods followed ☐									
Name:									
Signature:									

Temperature recordings   Please tick boxes √

Friday	Time	Dish	Temp	Time	Dish	Temp	Time	Dish	Temp
Opening checks done ☐									
Issues: Yes ☐ No ☐									
Closing checks ☐									
Safe methods followed ☐									
Name:									
Signature:									
Saturday	Time	Dish	Temp	Time	Dish	Temp	Time	Dish	Temp
Opening checks done ☐									
Issues: Yes ☐ No ☐									
Closing checks ☐									
Safe methods followed ☐									
Name:									
Signature:									
Sunday	Time	Dish	Temp	Time	Dish	Temp	Time	Dish	Temp
Opening checks done ☐									
Issues: Yes ☐ No ☐									
Closing checks ☐									
Safe methods followed ☐									
Name:									
Signature:									

Fridge/Freezer/Chiller Temperature records

Day	Frid/Frz/Chil 1	Frid/Frz/Chil 2	Frid/Frz/Chil 3	Frid/Frz/Chil 4	Frid/Frz/Chil 6	Frid/Frz/Chil 7
Monday	Opening: Closing:	Opening: Closing:	Opening: Closing:	Opening: Closing:	Opening: Closing:	Opening: Closing:
Tuesday	Opening: Closing:	Opening: Closing:	Opening: Closing:	Opening: Closing:	Opening: Closing:	Opening: Closing:
Wednesday	Opening: Closing:	Opening: Closing:	Opening: Closing:	Opening: Closing:	Opening: Closing:	Opening: Closing:
Thursday	Opening: Closing:	Opening: Closing:	Opening: Closing:	Opening: Closing:	Opening: Closing:	Opening: Closing:

Friday	Opening: Closing:	Opening: Closing:	Opening: Closing:	Opening: Closing:	Opening: Closing:	Opening: Closing:
Saturday	Opening: Closing:	Opening: Closing:	Opening: Closing:	Opening: Closing:	Opening: Closing:	Opening: Closing:
Sunday	Opening: Closing:	Opening: Closing:	Opening: Closing:	Opening: Closing:	Opening: Closing:	Opening: Closing:

Cleaning schedule

Task	Please tick boxes √	Mon	Tues	Wed	Thurs	Fri	Sat	Sun
Clean and sanitise refrigerators and freezers								
Clean and sanitise the sinks and taps								
Empty and clean the coffee machine								
Clean the grills, ovens, hobs, griddles and stoves								
Clean the fryers								
Brush the grill and clean out grease traps								
Clean and sanitise all kitchen preparation surfaces								
Clean and sanitise all cutting boards								
Clean the meat and cheese slicer, if used								
Sanitise the telephone and all surfaces								
Clean behind fridges, ovens and fryers								
Empty bins and clean the kitchen floor								
Any other Step(s):								
Supervisor signature:		Date:						

Kitchen hygiene: monthly cleaning

Task	Please tick boxes √	When	Who	Comment
Wash kitchen walls and storage areas				
Clean and sanitise refrigerators and freezers				
Clean cooker hood and filters				
Supervisor signature:		**Date:**		

Always use appropriate personal protective equipment (PPE) when undertaking any cleaning task and follow the manufacturer's product use and, where relevant, dilution guidance.

4-weekly review

You should regularly review the methods used in your business to check that they are up to date, and still being followed by you and your staff.

You can use the checklist below to help you.
Look back over the past 4 weeks' diary entries. If you had a serious problem, or the same thing went wrong three times or more, make a note of it here, find out why and do something about it. Did you have a serious problem or did the same thing go wrong three times or more?
Yes ☐ No ☐
Details:

What did you do about it?

Did you get a new member of staff in the past 4 weeks? Yes ☐ No ☐

Were they trained in your methods? Yes ☐ No ☐

Have you changed your menu?

Have you reviewed your safe methods?

Any changes/new methods?   Yes ☐ No ☐

Have you changed supplier/bought new ingredients? Yes ☐ No ☐

Do these affect any of your safe methods?

Other changes:

Notes:

Week Starting: Date/Month/Year	Temperature recordings			Please tick boxes √			Week 1		
Monday	Time	Dish	Temp	Time	Dish	Temp	Time	Dish	Temp
Opening checks done ☐									
Issues: Yes ☐ No ☐									
Closing checks ☐									
Safe methods followed ☐									
Name:									
Signature:									
Tuesday	Time	Dish	Temp	Time	Dish	Temp	Time	Dish	Temp
Opening checks done ☐									
Issues: Yes ☐ No ☐									
Closing checks ☐									
Safe methods followed ☐									
Name:									
Signature:									
Wednesday	Time	Dish	Temp	Time	Dish	Temp	Time	Dish	Temp
Opening checks done ☐									
Issues: Yes ☐ No ☐									
Closing checks ☐									
Safe methods followed ☐									
Name:									
Signature:									
Thursday	Time	Dish	Temp	Time	Dish	Temp	Time	Dish	Temp
Opening checks done ☐									
Issues: Yes ☐ No ☐									
Closing checks ☐									
Safe methods followed ☐									
Name:									
Signature:									

Temperature recordings   Please tick boxes √

Friday	Time	Dish	Temp	Time	Dish	Temp	Time	Dish	Temp
Opening checks done ☐									
Issues: Yes ☐ No ☐									
Closing checks ☐									
Safe methods followed ☐									
Name:									
Signature:									
Saturday	Time	Dish	Temp	Time	Dish	Temp	Time	Dish	Temp
Opening checks done ☐									
Issues: Yes ☐ No ☐									
Closing checks ☐									
Safe methods followed ☐									
Name:									
Signature:									
Sunday	Time	Dish	Temp	Time	Dish	Temp	Time	Dish	Temp
Opening checks done ☐									
Issues: Yes ☐ No ☐									
Closing checks ☐									
Safe methods followed ☐									
Name:									
Signature:									

Fridge/Freezer/Chiller Temperature records

Day	Frid/Frz/Chil 1	Frid/Frz/Chil 2	Frid/Frz/Chil 3	Frid/Frz/Chil 4	Frid/Frz/Chil 6	Frid/Frz/Chil 7
Monday	Opening: Closing:	Opening: Closing:	Opening: Closing:	Opening: Closing:	Opening: Closing:	Opening: Closing:
Tuesday	Opening: Closing:	Opening: Closing:	Opening: Closing:	Opening: Closing:	Opening: Closing:	Opening: Closing:
Wednesday	Opening: Closing:	Opening: Closing:	Opening: Closing:	Opening: Closing:	Opening: Closing:	Opening: Closing:
Thursday	Opening: Closing:	Opening: Closing:	Opening: Closing:	Opening: Closing:	Opening: Closing:	Opening: Closing:

Friday	Opening: Closing:	Opening: Closing:	Opening: Closing:	Opening: Closing:	Opening: Closing:	Opening: Closing:
Saturday	Opening: Closing:	Opening: Closing:	Opening: Closing:	Opening: Closing:	Opening: Closing:	Opening: Closing:
Sunday	Opening: Closing:	Opening: Closing:	Opening: Closing:	Opening: Closing:	Opening: Closing:	Opening: Closing:

Cleaning schedule

Task	Please tick boxes √	Mon	Tues	Wed	Thurs	Fri	Sat	Sun
Clean and sanitise refrigerators and freezers								
Clean and sanitise the sinks and taps								
Empty and clean the coffee machine								
Clean the grills,ovens,hobs,griddles and stoves								
Clean the fryers								
Brush the grill and clean out grease traps								
Clean and sanitise all kitchen preparation surfaces								
Clean and sanitise all cutting boards								
Clean the meat and cheese slicer,if used								
Sanitise the telephone and all surfaces								
Clean behind fridges,ovens and fryers								
Empty bins and clean the kitchen floor								
Any other Step(s):								

Supervisor signature: Date:

Weekly review-The Good,The Bad,The Ugly,Hirings and Firings

What went right:	**What went wrong:**

Notes:

Week Starting: Date/Month/Year	Temperature recordings			Please tick boxes √			Week 2		
Monday	Time	Dish	Temp	Time	Dish	Temp	Time	Dish	Temp
Opening checks done ☐									
Issues: Yes ☐ No ☐									
Closing checks ☐									
Safe methods followed ☐									
Name:									
Signature:									
Tuesday	Time	Dish	Temp	Time	Dish	Temp	Time	Dish	Temp
Opening checks done ☐									
Issues: Yes ☐ No ☐									
Closing checks ☐									
Safe methods followed ☐									
Name:									
Signature:									
Wednesday	Time	Dish	Temp	Time	Dish	Temp	Time	Dish	Temp
Opening checks done ☐									
Issues: Yes ☐ No ☐									
Closing checks ☐									
Safe methods followed ☐									
Name:									
Signature:									
Thursday	Time	Dish	Temp	Time	Dish	Temp	Time	Dish	Temp
Opening checks done ☐									
Issues: Yes ☐ No ☐									
Closing checks ☐									
Safe methods followed ☐									
Name:									
Signature:									

Temperature recordings		Please tick boxes √									
Friday	Time	Dish		Temp	Time	Dish		Temp	Time	Dish		Temp
Opening checks done ☐											
Issues: Yes ☐ No ☐											
Closing checks ☐											
Safe methods followed ☐											
Name:											
Signature:											
Saturday	Time	Dish		Temp	Time	Dish		Temp	Time	Dish		Temp
Opening checks done ☐											
Issues: Yes ☐ No ☐											
Closing checks ☐											
Safe methods followed ☐											
Name:											
Signature:											
Sunday	Time	Dish		Temp	Time	Dish		Temp	Time	Dish		Temp
Opening checks done ☐											
Issues: Yes ☐ No ☐											
Closing checks ☐											
Safe methods followed ☐											
Name:											
Signature:											

Fridge/Freezer/Chiller Temperature records

Day	Frid/Frz/Chil 1	Frid/Frz/Chil 2	Frid/Frz/Chil 3	Frid/Frz/Chil 4	Frid/Frz/Chil 6	Frid/Frz/Chil 7
Monday	Opening: Closing:	Opening: Closing:	Opening: Closing:	Opening: Closing:	Opening: Closing:	Opening: Closing:
Tuesday	Opening: Closing:	Opening: Closing:	Opening: Closing:	Opening: Closing:	Opening: Closing:	Opening: Closing:
Wednesday	Opening: Closing:	Opening: Closing:	Opening: Closing:	Opening: Closing:	Opening: Closing:	Opening: Closing:
Thursday	Opening: Closing:	Opening: Closing:	Opening: Closing:	Opening: Closing:	Opening: Closing:	Opening: Closing:

Friday	Opening: Closing:	Opening: Closing:	Opening: Closing:	Opening: Closing:	Opening: Closing:	Opening: Closing:
Saturday	Opening: Closing:	Opening: Closing:	Opening: Closing:	Opening: Closing:	Opening: Closing:	Opening: Closing:
Sunday	Opening: Closing:	Opening: Closing:	Opening: Closing:	Opening: Closing:	Opening: Closing:	Opening: Closing:

Cleaning schedule

Task	Please tick boxes √	Mon	Tues	Wed	Thurs	Fri	Sat	Sun
Clean and sanitise refrigerators and freezers								
Clean and sanitise the sinks and taps								
Empty and clean the coffee machine								
Clean the grills,ovens,hobs,griddles and stoves								
Clean the fryers								
Brush the grill and clean out grease traps								
Clean and sanitise all kitchen preparation surfaces								
Clean and sanitise all cutting boards								
Clean the meat and cheese slicer,if used								
Sanitise the telephone and all surfaces								
Clean behind fridges,ovens and fryers								
Empty bins and clean the kitchen floor								
Any other Step(s):								

Supervisor signature: Date:

Weekly review-The Good,The Bad,The Ugly,Hirings and Firings

What went right:

What went wrong:

Notes:

Week Starting: Date/Month/Year	Temperature recordings			Please tick boxes √			Week 3			
Monday	Time	Dish	Temp	Time	Dish	Temp	Time	Dish	Temp
Opening checks done ☐									
Issues: Yes ☐ No ☐									
Closing checks ☐									
Safe methods followed ☐									
Name:									
Signature:									
Tuesday	Time	Dish	Temp	Time	Dish	Temp	Time	Dish	Temp
Opening checks done ☐									
Issues: Yes ☐ No ☐									
Closing checks ☐									
Safe methods followed ☐									
Name:									
Signature:									
Wednesday	Time	Dish	Temp	Time	Dish	Temp	Time	Dish	Temp
Opening checks done ☐									
Issues: Yes ☐ No ☐									
Closing checks ☐									
Safe methods followed ☐									
Name:									
Signature:									
Thursday	Time	Dish	Temp	Time	Dish	Temp	Time	Dish	Temp
Opening checks done ☐									
Issues: Yes ☐ No ☐									
Closing checks ☐									
Safe methods followed ☐									
Name:									
Signature:									

Temperature recordings   Please tick boxes √

Friday	Time	Dish	Temp	Time	Dish	Temp	Time	Dish	Temp
Opening checks done ☐									
Issues: Yes ☐ No ☐									
Closing checks ☐									
Safe methods followed ☐									
Name:									
Signature:									

Saturday	Time	Dish	Temp	Time	Dish	Temp	Time	Dish	Temp
Opening checks done ☐									
Issues: Yes ☐ No ☐									
Closing checks ☐									
Safe methods followed ☐									
Name:									
Signature:									

Sunday	Time	Dish	Temp	Time	Dish	Temp	Time	Dish	Temp
Opening checks done ☐									
Issues: Yes ☐ No ☐									
Closing checks ☐									
Safe methods followed ☐									
Name:									
Signature:									

Fridge/Freezer/Chiller Temperature records

Day	Frid/Frz/Chil 1	Frid/Frz/Chil 2	Frid/Frz/Chil 3	Frid/Frz/Chil 4	Frid/Frz/Chil 6	Frid/Frz/Chil 7
Monday	Opening: Closing:	Opening: Closing:	Opening: Closing:	Opening: Closing:	Opening: Closing:	Opening: Closing:
Tuesday	Opening: Closing:	Opening: Closing:	Opening: Closing:	Opening: Closing:	Opening: Closing:	Opening: Closing:
Wednesday	Opening: Closing:	Opening: Closing:	Opening: Closing:	Opening: Closing:	Opening: Closing:	Opening: Closing:
Thursday	Opening: Closing:	Opening: Closing:	Opening: Closing:	Opening: Closing:	Opening: Closing:	Opening: Closing:

Friday	Opening: Closing:	Opening: Closing:	Opening: Closing:	Opening: Closing:	Opening: Closing:	Opening: Closing:
Saturday	Opening: Closing:	Opening: Closing:	Opening: Closing:	Opening: Closing:	Opening: Closing:	Opening: Closing:
Sunday	Opening: Closing:	Opening: Closing:	Opening: Closing:	Opening: Closing:	Opening: Closing:	Opening: Closing:

Cleaning schedule

Task	Please tick boxes √	Mon	Tues	Wed	Thurs	Fri	Sat	Sun
Clean and sanitise refrigerators and freezers								
Clean and sanitise the sinks and taps								
Empty and clean the coffee machine								
Clean the grills,ovens,hobs,griddles and stoves								
Clean the fryers								
Brush the grill and clean out grease traps								
Clean and sanitise all kitchen preparation surfaces								
Clean and sanitise all cutting boards								
Clean the meat and cheese slicer,if used								
Sanitise the telephone and all surfaces								
Clean behind fridges,ovens and fryers								
Empty bins and clean the kitchen floor								
Any other Step(s):								

Supervisor signature: Date:

Weekly review-The Good,The Bad,The Ugly,Hirings and Firings

What went right:

What went wrong:

Notes:

Week Starting: Date/Month/Year	Temperature recordings			Please tick boxes √			Week 4		
Monday	Time	Dish	Temp	Time	Dish	Temp	Time	Dish	Temp
Opening checks done ☐									
Issues: Yes ☐ No ☐									
Closing checks ☐									
Safe methods followed ☐									
Name:									
Signature:									
Tuesday	Time	Dish	Temp	Time	Dish	Temp	Time	Dish	Temp
Opening checks done ☐									
Issues: Yes ☐ No ☐									
Closing checks ☐									
Safe methods followed ☐									
Name:									
Signature:									
Wednesday	Time	Dish	Temp	Time	Dish	Temp	Time	Dish	Temp
Opening checks done ☐									
Issues: Yes ☐ No ☐									
Closing checks ☐									
Safe methods followed ☐									
Name:									
Signature:									
Thursday	Time	Dish	Temp	Time	Dish	Temp	Time	Dish	Temp
Opening checks done ☐									
Issues: Yes ☐ No ☐									
Closing checks ☐									
Safe methods followed ☐									
Name:									
Signature:									

Temperature recordings		Please tick boxes √								
Friday	Time	Dish		Temp	Time	Dish	Temp	Time	Dish	Temp
Opening checks done ☐										
Issues: Yes ☐ No ☐										
Closing checks ☐										
Safe methods followed ☐										
Name:										
Signature:										
Saturday	Time	Dish		Temp	Time	Dish	Temp	Time	Dish	Temp
Opening checks done ☐										
Issues: Yes ☐ No ☐										
Closing checks ☐										
Safe methods followed ☐										
Name:										
Signature:										
Sunday	Time	Dish		Temp	Time	Dish	Temp	Time	Dish	Temp
Opening checks done ☐										
Issues: Yes ☐ No ☐										
Closing checks ☐										
Safe methods followed ☐										
Name:										
Signature:										

Fridge/Freezer/Chiller Temperature records

Day	Frid/Frz/Chil 1	Frid/Frz/Chil 2	Frid/Frz/Chil 3	Frid/Frz/Chil 4	Frid/Frz/Chil 6	Frid/Frz/Chil 7
Monday	Opening: Closing:	Opening: Closing:	Opening: Closing:	Opening: Closing:	Opening: Closing:	Opening: Closing:
Tuesday	Opening: Closing:	Opening: Closing:	Opening: Closing:	Opening: Closing:	Opening: Closing:	Opening: Closing:
Wednesday	Opening: Closing:	Opening: Closing:	Opening: Closing:	Opening: Closing:	Opening: Closing:	Opening: Closing:
Thursday	Opening: Closing:	Opening: Closing:	Opening: Closing:	Opening: Closing:	Opening: Closing:	Opening: Closing:

Friday	Opening: Closing:	Opening: Closing:	Opening: Closing:	Opening: Closing:	Opening: Closing:	Opening: Closing:
Saturday	Opening: Closing:	Opening: Closing:	Opening: Closing:	Opening: Closing:	Opening: Closing:	Opening: Closing:
Sunday	Opening: Closing:	Opening: Closing:	Opening: Closing:	Opening: Closing:	Opening: Closing:	Opening: Closing:

Cleaning schedule

Task — Please tick boxes √	Mon	Tues	Wed	Thurs	Fri	Sat	Sun
Clean and sanitise refrigerators and freezers							
Clean and sanitise the sinks and taps							
Empty and clean the coffee machine							
Clean the grills, ovens, hobs, griddles and stoves							
Clean the fryers							
Brush the grill and clean out grease traps							
Clean and sanitise all kitchen preparation surfaces							
Clean and sanitise all cutting boards							
Clean the meat and cheese slicer, if used							
Sanitise the telephone and all surfaces							
Clean behind fridges, ovens and fryers							
Empty bins and clean the kitchen floor							
Any other Step(s):							

Supervisor signature:　　　　　　　　　　Date:

Kitchen hygiene: monthly cleaning

Task — Please tick boxes √	When	Who	Comment
Wash kitchen walls and storage areas			
Clean and sanitise refrigerators and freezers			
Clean cooker hood and filters			
Supervisor signature:		**Date:**	

Always use appropriate personal protective equipment (PPE) when undertaking any cleaning task and follow the manufacturer's product use and, where relevant, dilution guidance.

4-weekly review

You should regularly review the methods used in your business to check that they are up to date, and still being followed by you and your staff.

You can use the checklist below to help you.
Look back over the past 4 weeks' diary entries. If you had a serious problem, or the same thing went wrong three times or more, make a note of it here, find out why and do something about it. Did you have a serious problem or did the same thing go wrong three times or more?
Yes ☐　No ☐
Details:

What did you do about it?

Did you get a new member of staff in the past 4 weeks? Yes □ No □

Were they trained in your methods? Yes □ No □

Have you changed your menu?

Have you reviewed your safe methods?

Any changes/new methods?   Yes □ No □

Have you changed supplier/bought new ingredients? Yes □ No □

Do these affect any of your safe methods?

Other changes:

Notes:

Your diary is about to finish, order a new one now from Culinasalus.com

Week Starting: Date/Month/Year	Temperature recordings			Please tick boxes √			Week 1		
Monday	Time	Dish	Temp	Time	Dish	Temp	Time	Dish	Temp
Opening checks done ☐									
Issues: Yes ☐ No ☐									
Closing checks ☐									
Safe methods followed ☐									
Name:									
Signature:									
Tuesday	Time	Dish	Temp	Time	Dish	Temp	Time	Dish	Temp
Opening checks done ☐									
Issues: Yes ☐ No ☐									
Closing checks ☐									
Safe methods followed ☐									
Name:									
Signature:									
Wednesday	Time	Dish	Temp	Time	Dish	Temp	Time	Dish	Temp
Opening checks done ☐									
Issues: Yes ☐ No ☐									
Closing checks ☐									
Safe methods followed ☐									
Name:									
Signature:									
Thursday	Time	Dish	Temp	Time	Dish	Temp	Time	Dish	Temp
Opening checks done ☐									
Issues: Yes ☐ No ☐									
Closing checks ☐									
Safe methods followed ☐									
Name:									
Signature:									

Temperature recordings		Please tick boxes √									
Friday	Time	Dish		Temp	Time	Dish		Temp	Time	Dish		Temp
Opening checks done ☐											
Issues: Yes ☐ No ☐											
Closing checks ☐											
Safe methods followed ☐											
Name:											
Signature:											
Saturday	Time	Dish		Temp	Time	Dish		Temp	Time	Dish		Temp
Opening checks done ☐											
Issues: Yes ☐ No ☐											
Closing checks ☐											
Safe methods followed ☐											
Name:											
Signature:											
Sunday	Time	Dish		Temp	Time	Dish		Temp	Time	Dish		Temp
Opening checks done ☐											
Issues: Yes ☐ No ☐											
Closing checks ☐											
Safe methods followed ☐											
Name:											
Signature:											

Fridge/Freezer/Chiller Temperature records

Day	Frid/Frz/Chil 1	Frid/Frz/Chil 2	Frid/Frz/Chil 3	Frid/Frz/Chil 4	Frid/Frz/Chil 6	Frid/Frz/Chil 7
Monday	Opening: Closing:	Opening: Closing:	Opening: Closing:	Opening: Closing:	Opening: Closing:	Opening: Closing:
Tuesday	Opening: Closing:	Opening: Closing:	Opening: Closing:	Opening: Closing:	Opening: Closing:	Opening: Closing:
Wednesday	Opening: Closing:	Opening: Closing:	Opening: Closing:	Opening: Closing:	Opening: Closing:	Opening: Closing:
Thursday	Opening: Closing:	Opening: Closing:	Opening: Closing:	Opening: Closing:	Opening: Closing:	Opening: Closing:

Friday	Opening: Closing:	Opening: Closing:	Opening: Closing:	Opening: Closing:	Opening: Closing:	Opening: Closing:
Saturday	Opening: Closing:	Opening: Closing:	Opening: Closing:	Opening: Closing:	Opening: Closing:	Opening: Closing:
Sunday	Opening: Closing:	Opening: Closing:	Opening: Closing:	Opening: Closing:	Opening: Closing:	Opening: Closing:

Cleaning schedule

Task	Please tick boxes √	Mon	Tues	Wed	Thurs	Fri	Sat	Sun
Clean and sanitise refrigerators and freezers								
Clean and sanitise the sinks and taps								
Empty and clean the coffee machine								
Clean the grills,ovens,hobs,griddles and stoves								
Clean the fryers								
Brush the grill and clean out grease traps								
Clean and sanitise all kitchen preparation surfaces								
Clean and sanitise all cutting boards								
Clean the meat and cheese slicer,if used								
Sanitise the telephone and all surfaces								
Clean behind fridges,ovens and fryers								
Empty bins and clean the kitchen floor								
Any other Step(s):								

Supervisor signature: Date:

Weekly review-The Good,The Bad,The Ugly,Hirings and Firings

What went right:	What went wrong:

Notes:

Week Starting: Date/Month/Year	Temperature recordings			Please tick boxes √			Week 2		
Monday	Time	Dish	Temp	Time	Dish	Temp	Time	Dish	Temp
Opening checks done ☐									
Issues: Yes ☐ No ☐									
Closing checks ☐									
Safe methods followed ☐									
Name:									
Signature:									
Tuesday	Time	Dish	Temp	Time	Dish	Temp	Time	Dish	Temp
Opening checks done ☐									
Issues: Yes ☐ No ☐									
Closing checks ☐									
Safe methods followed ☐									
Name:									
Signature:									
Wednesday	Time	Dish	Temp	Time	Dish	Temp	Time	Dish	Temp
Opening checks done ☐									
Issues: Yes ☐ No ☐									
Closing checks ☐									
Safe methods followed ☐									
Name:									
Signature:									
Thursday	Time	Dish	Temp	Time	Dish	Temp	Time	Dish	Temp
Opening checks done ☐									
Issues: Yes ☐ No ☐									
Closing checks ☐									
Safe methods followed ☐									
Name:									
Signature:									

Temperature recordings   Please tick boxes √

Friday	Time	Dish	Temp	Time	Dish	Temp	Time	Dish	Temp
Opening checks done ☐									
Issues: Yes ☐ No ☐									
Closing checks ☐									
Safe methods followed ☐									
Name:									
Signature:									

Saturday	Time	Dish	Temp	Time	Dish	Temp	Time	Dish	Temp
Opening checks done ☐									
Issues: Yes ☐ No ☐									
Closing checks ☐									
Safe methods followed ☐									
Name:									
Signature:									

Sunday	Time	Dish	Temp	Time	Dish	Temp	Time	Dish	Temp
Opening checks done ☐									
Issues: Yes ☐ No ☐									
Closing checks ☐									
Safe methods followed ☐									
Name:									
Signature:									

Fridge/Freezer/Chiller Temperature records

Day	Frid/Frz/Chil 1	Frid/Frz/Chil 2	Frid/Frz/Chil 3	Frid/Frz/Chil 4	Frid/Frz/Chil 6	Frid/Frz/Chil 7
Monday	Opening: Closing:	Opening: Closing:	Opening: Closing:	Opening: Closing:	Opening: Closing:	Opening: Closing:
Tuesday	Opening: Closing:	Opening: Closing:	Opening: Closing:	Opening: Closing:	Opening: Closing:	Opening: Closing:
Wednesday	Opening: Closing:	Opening: Closing:	Opening: Closing:	Opening: Closing:	Opening: Closing:	Opening: Closing:
Thursday	Opening: Closing:	Opening: Closing:	Opening: Closing:	Opening: Closing:	Opening: Closing:	Opening: Closing:

Friday	Opening: Closing:	Opening: Closing:	Opening: Closing:	Opening: Closing:	Opening: Closing:	Opening: Closing:
Saturday	Opening: Closing:	Opening: Closing:	Opening: Closing:	Opening: Closing:	Opening: Closing:	Opening: Closing:
Sunday	Opening: Closing:	Opening: Closing:	Opening: Closing:	Opening: Closing:	Opening: Closing:	Opening: Closing:

Cleaning schedule

Task	Please tick boxes √	Mon	Tues	Wed	Thurs	Fri	Sat	Sun
Clean and sanitise refrigerators and freezers								
Clean and sanitise the sinks and taps								
Empty and clean the coffee machine								
Clean the grills,ovens,hobs,griddles and stoves								
Clean the fryers								
Brush the grill and clean out grease traps								
Clean and sanitise all kitchen preparation surfaces								
Clean and sanitise all cutting boards								
Clean the meat and cheese slicer,if used								
Sanitise the telephone and all surfaces								
Clean behind fridges,ovens and fryers								
Empty bins and clean the kitchen floor								
Any other Step(s):								
Supervisor signature:		Date:						

Weekly review-The Good,The Bad,The Ugly,Hirings and Firings

What went right:	What went wrong:

Notes:

Week Starting: Date/Month/Year	Temperature recordings			Please tick boxes √			Week 3		
Monday	Time	Dish	Temp	Time	Dish	Temp	Time	Dish	Temp
Opening checks done ☐									
Issues: Yes ☐ No ☐									
Closing checks ☐									
Safe methods followed ☐									
Name:									
Signature:									
Tuesday	Time	Dish	Temp	Time	Dish	Temp	Time	Dish	Temp
Opening checks done ☐									
Issues: Yes ☐ No ☐									
Closing checks ☐									
Safe methods followed ☐									
Name:									
Signature:									
Wednesday	Time	Dish	Temp	Time	Dish	Temp	Time	Dish	Temp
Opening checks done ☐									
Issues: Yes ☐ No ☐									
Closing checks ☐									
Safe methods followed ☐									
Name:									
Signature:									
Thursday	Time	Dish	Temp	Time	Dish	Temp	Time	Dish	Temp
Opening checks done ☐									
Issues: Yes ☐ No ☐									
Closing checks ☐									
Safe methods followed ☐									
Name:									
Signature:									

Temperature recordings			Please tick boxes √							
Friday	Time	Dish		Temp	Time	Dish	Temp	Time	Dish	Temp
Opening checks done ☐										
Issues: Yes ☐ No ☐										
Closing checks ☐										
Safe methods followed ☐										
Name:										
Signature:										
Saturday	Time	Dish		Temp	Time	Dish	Temp	Time	Dish	Temp
Opening checks done ☐										
Issues: Yes ☐ No ☐										
Closing checks ☐										
Safe methods followed ☐										
Name:										
Signature:										
Sunday	Time	Dish		Temp	Time	Dish	Temp	Time	Dish	Temp
Opening checks done ☐										
Issues: Yes ☐ No ☐										
Closing checks ☐										
Safe methods followed ☐										
Name:										
Signature:										

Fridge/Freezer/Chiller Temperature records

Day	Frid/Frz/Chil 1	Frid/Frz/Chil 2	Frid/Frz/Chil 3	Frid/Frz/Chil 4	Frid/Frz/Chil 6	Frid/Frz/Chil 7
Monday	Opening: Closing:	Opening: Closing:	Opening: Closing:	Opening: Closing:	Opening: Closing:	Opening: Closing:
Tuesday	Opening: Closing:	Opening: Closing:	Opening: Closing:	Opening: Closing:	Opening: Closing:	Opening: Closing:
Wednesday	Opening: Closing:	Opening: Closing:	Opening: Closing:	Opening: Closing:	Opening: Closing:	Opening: Closing:
Thursday	Opening: Closing:	Opening: Closing:	Opening: Closing:	Opening: Closing:	Opening: Closing:	Opening: Closing:

Friday	Opening: Closing:	Opening: Closing:	Opening: Closing:	Opening: Closing:	Opening: Closing:	Opening: Closing:
Saturday	Opening: Closing:	Opening: Closing:	Opening: Closing:	Opening: Closing:	Opening: Closing:	Opening: Closing:
Sunday	Opening: Closing:	Opening: Closing:	Opening: Closing:	Opening: Closing:	Opening: Closing:	Opening: Closing:

Cleaning schedule

Task — Please tick boxes √	Mon	Tues	Wed	Thurs	Fri	Sat	Sun
Clean and sanitise refrigerators and freezers							
Clean and sanitise the sinks and taps							
Empty and clean the coffee machine							
Clean the grills, ovens, hobs, griddles and stoves							
Clean the fryers							
Brush the grill and clean out grease traps							
Clean and sanitise all kitchen preparation surfaces							
Clean and sanitise all cutting boards							
Clean the meat and cheese slicer, if used							
Sanitise the telephone and all surfaces							
Clean behind fridges, ovens and fryers							
Empty bins and clean the kitchen floor							
Any other Step(s):							

Supervisor signature: Date:

Weekly review-The Good, The Bad, The Ugly, Hirings and Firings

What went right:	What went wrong:

Notes:

Week Starting: Date/Month/Year	Temperature recordings			Please tick boxes √			Week 4		
Monday	Time	Dish	Temp	Time	Dish	Temp	Time	Dish	Temp
Opening checks done ☐									
Issues: Yes ☐ No ☐									
Closing checks ☐									
Safe methods followed ☐									
Name:									
Signature:									
Tuesday	Time	Dish	Temp	Time	Dish	Temp	Time	Dish	Temp
Opening checks done ☐									
Issues: Yes ☐ No ☐									
Closing checks ☐									
Safe methods followed ☐									
Name:									
Signature:									
Wednesday	Time	Dish	Temp	Time	Dish	Temp	Time	Dish	Temp
Opening checks done ☐									
Issues: Yes ☐ No ☐									
Closing checks ☐									
Safe methods followed ☐									
Name:									
Signature:									
Thursday	Time	Dish	Temp	Time	Dish	Temp	Time	Dish	Temp
Opening checks done ☐									
Issues: Yes ☐ No ☐									
Closing checks ☐									
Safe methods followed ☐									
Name:									
Signature:									

Temperature recordings   Please tick boxes √

Friday	Time	Dish	Temp	Time	Dish	Temp	Time	Dish	Temp
Opening checks done ☐									
Issues: Yes ☐ No ☐									
Closing checks ☐									
Safe methods followed ☐									
Name:									
Signature:									

Saturday	Time	Dish	Temp	Time	Dish	Temp	Time	Dish	Temp
Opening checks done ☐									
Issues: Yes ☐ No ☐									
Closing checks ☐									
Safe methods followed ☐									
Name:									
Signature:									

Sunday	Time	Dish	Temp	Time	Dish	Temp	Time	Dish	Temp
Opening checks done ☐									
Issues: Yes ☐ No ☐									
Closing checks ☐									
Safe methods followed ☐									
Name:									
Signature:									

Fridge/Freezer/Chiller Temperature records

Day	Frid/Frz/Chil 1	Frid/Frz/Chil 2	Frid/Frz/Chil 3	Frid/Frz/Chil 4	Frid/Frz/Chil 6	Frid/Frz/Chil 7
Monday	Opening: Closing:	Opening: Closing:	Opening: Closing:	Opening: Closing:	Opening: Closing:	Opening: Closing:
Tuesday	Opening: Closing:	Opening: Closing:	Opening: Closing:	Opening: Closing:	Opening: Closing:	Opening: Closing:
Wednesday	Opening: Closing:	Opening: Closing:	Opening: Closing:	Opening: Closing:	Opening: Closing:	Opening: Closing:
Thursday	Opening: Closing:	Opening: Closing:	Opening: Closing:	Opening: Closing:	Opening: Closing:	Opening: Closing:

Friday	Opening: Closing:	Opening: Closing:	Opening: Closing:	Opening: Closing:	Opening: Closing:	Opening: Closing:
Saturday	Opening: Closing:	Opening: Closing:	Opening: Closing:	Opening: Closing:	Opening: Closing:	Opening: Closing:
Sunday	Opening: Closing:	Opening: Closing:	Opening: Closing:	Opening: Closing:	Opening: Closing:	Opening: Closing:

Cleaning schedule

Task	Please tick boxes √	Mon	Tues	Wed	Thurs	Fri	Sat	Sun
Clean and sanitise refrigerators and freezers								
Clean and sanitise the sinks and taps								
Empty and clean the coffee machine								
Clean the grills,ovens,hobs,griddles and stoves								
Clean the fryers								
Brush the grill and clean out grease traps								
Clean and sanitise all kitchen preparation surfaces								
Clean and sanitise all cutting boards								
Clean the meat and cheese slicer,if used								
Sanitise the telephone and all surfaces								
Clean behind fridges,ovens and fryers								
Empty bins and clean the kitchen floor								
Any other Step(s):								
Supervisor signature:	Date:							

Weekly review-The Good,The Bad,The Ugly,Hirings and Firings

What went right:	What went wrong:

Notes:

4-weekly review

You should regularly review the methods used in your business to check that they are up to date, and still being followed by you and your staff.

You can use the checklist below to help you.
Look back over the past 4 weeks' diary entries. If you had a serious problem, or the same thing went wrong three times or more, make a note of it here, find out why and do something about it. Did you have a serious problem or did the same thing go wrong three times or more?
Yes ☐ No ☐
Details:

What did you do about it?

Did you get a new member of staff in the past 4 weeks? Yes ☐ No ☐

Were they trained in your methods? Yes ☐ No ☐

Have you changed your menu?

Have you reviewed your safe methods?

Any changes/new methods?   Yes ☐ No ☐

Have you changed supplier/bought new ingredients? Yes ☐ No ☐

Do these affect any of your safe methods?

Other changes:

Notes:

Week Starting: Date/Month/Year	Temperature recordings			Please tick boxes √					
Monday	Time	Dish	Temp	Time	Dish	Temp	Time	Dish	Temp
Opening checks done ☐									
Issues: Yes ☐ No ☐									
Closing checks ☐									
Safe methods followed ☐									
Name:									
Signature:									
Tuesday	Time	Dish	Temp	Time	Dish	Temp	Time	Dish	Temp
Opening checks done ☐									
Issues: Yes ☐ No ☐									
Closing checks ☐									
Safe methods followed ☐									
Name:									
Signature:									
Wednesday	Time	Dish	Temp	Time	Dish	Temp	Time	Dish	Temp
Opening checks done ☐									
Issues: Yes ☐ No ☐									
Closing checks ☐									
Safe methods followed ☐									
Name:									
Signature:									
Thursday	Time	Dish	Temp	Time	Dish	Temp	Time	Dish	Temp
Opening checks done ☐									
Issues: Yes ☐ No ☐									
Closing checks ☐									
Safe methods followed ☐									
Name:									
Signature:									

Temperature recordings   Please tick boxes √

Friday	Time	Dish	Temp	Time	Dish	Temp	Time	Dish	Temp
Opening checks done ☐									
Issues: Yes ☐ No ☐									
Closing checks ☐									
Safe methods followed ☐									
Name:									
Signature:									

Saturday	Time	Dish	Temp	Time	Dish	Temp	Time	Dish	Temp
Opening checks done ☐									
Issues: Yes ☐ No ☐									
Closing checks ☐									
Safe methods followed ☐									
Name:									
Signature:									

Sunday	Time	Dish	Temp	Time	Dish	Temp	Time	Dish	Temp
Opening checks done ☐									
Issues: Yes ☐ No ☐									
Closing checks ☐									
Safe methods followed ☐									
Name:									
Signature:									

Fridge/Freezer/Chiller Temperature records

Day	Frid/Frz/Chil 1	Frid/Frz/Chil 2	Frid/Frz/Chil 3	Frid/Frz/Chil 4	Frid/Frz/Chil 6	Frid/Frz/Chil 7
Monday	Opening: Closing:	Opening: Closing:	Opening: Closing:	Opening: Closing:	Opening: Closing:	Opening: Closing:
Tuesday	Opening: Closing:	Opening: Closing:	Opening: Closing:	Opening: Closing:	Opening: Closing:	Opening: Closing:
Wednesday	Opening: Closing:	Opening: Closing:	Opening: Closing:	Opening: Closing:	Opening: Closing:	Opening: Closing:
Thursday	Opening: Closing:	Opening: Closing:	Opening: Closing:	Opening: Closing:	Opening: Closing:	Opening: Closing:

Friday	Opening: Closing:	Opening: Closing:	Opening: Closing:	Opening: Closing:	Opening: Closing:	Opening: Closing:
Saturday	Opening: Closing:	Opening: Closing:	Opening: Closing:	Opening: Closing:	Opening: Closing:	Opening: Closing:
Sunday	Opening: Closing:	Opening: Closing:	Opening: Closing:	Opening: Closing:	Opening: Closing:	Opening: Closing:

Cleaning schedule

Task	Please tick boxes √	Mon	Tues	Wed	Thurs	Fri	Sat	Sun
Clean and sanitise refrigerators and freezers								
Clean and sanitise the sinks and taps								
Empty and clean the coffee machine								
Clean the grills, ovens, hobs, griddles and stoves								
Clean the fryers								
Brush the grill and clean out grease traps								
Clean and sanitise all kitchen preparation surfaces								
Clean and sanitise all cutting boards								
Clean the meat and cheese slicer, if used								
Sanitise the telephone and all surfaces								
Clean behind fridges, ovens and fryers								
Empty bins and clean the kitchen floor								
Any other Step(s):								
Supervisor signature:		Date:						

Kitchen hygiene: monthly cleaning

Task	Please tick boxes √	When	Who	Comment
Wash kitchen walls and storage areas				
Clean and sanitise refrigerators and freezers				
Clean cooker hood and filters				
Supervisor signature:		**Date:**		

Always use appropriate personal protective equipment (PPE) when undertaking any cleaning task and follow the manufacturer's product use and, where relevant, dilution guidance.

4-weekly review

You should regularly review the methods used in your business to check that they are up to date, and still being followed by you and your staff.

You can use the checklist below to help you.
Look back over the past 4 weeks' diary entries. If you had a serious problem, or the same thing went wrong three times or more, make a note of it here, find out why and do something about it. Did you have a serious problem or did the same thing go wrong three times or more?
Yes ☐ No ☐
Details:

What did you do about it?

Did you get a new member of staff in the past 4 weeks? Yes ☐ No ☐

Were they trained in your methods? Yes ☐ No ☐

Have you changed your menu?

Have you reviewed your safe methods?

Any changes/new methods? Yes ☐ No ☐

Have you changed supplier/bought new ingredients? Yes ☐ No ☐

Do these affect any of your safe methods?

Other changes:

Notes:

Chef's allergen menu matrix sheets

The allergen menu recipe sheets that follow, will help all your kitchen kitchen staff, to log and check allergen information on dishes,items and all food products, you make and sell.

The 14 Allergens

1 Celery

2 Cereals containing gluten namely wheat like spelt and Khorasan, barley, rye and oats

3 Crustaceans like prawns, crabs, lobster and crayfish etc.

4 Eggs

5 Fish

6 Lupin

7 Milk.

8 Molluscs, examples are clams,scallops,squid,mussels,oysters and snails etc.

9 Mustard

10 Nuts such as Almonds,Hazelnuts,Walnuts,Pecan nuts,Brazil nuts,Pistachio,Cashew,Macadamia or Queensland nuts.

11 Peanuts

12 Sesame seeds

13 Soya

14 Sulphur dioxide often found in dried fruit and wine

Just tick off the allergens in your dishes/items/products,such as:

Meals

Cakes

Pies

Breads

Salad dressings

Pre-packed foods and snacks

Soups

Pasta

Curries

Marinades

Biscuits

Desserts

Oils

Meat products

Soft drinks

Wines

Vegetarian products

This list is not exhaustive

DISH ITEM PRODUCT	Celery	Cereals containing gluten	Crustaceans	Eggs	Fish	Lupin	Milk	Molluscs	Mustard	Nuts	Peanuts	Sesame Seeds	Soya	Sulphur Dioxide

DISH ITEM PRODUCT	Celery	Cereals containing gluten	Crustaceans	Eggs	Fish	Lupin	Milk	Molluscs	Mustard	Nuts	Peanuts	Sesame Seeds	Soya	Sulphur Dioxide

DISH ITEM PRODUCT	Celery	Cereals containing gluten	Crustaceans	Eggs	Fish	Lupin	Milk	Molluscs	Mustard	Nuts	Peanuts	Sesame Seeds	Soya	Sulphur Dioxide

DISH ITEM PRODUCT	Celery	Cereals containing gluten	Crustaceans	Eggs	Fish	Lupin	Milk	Molluscs	Mustard	Nuts	Peanuts	Sesame Seeds	Soya	Sulphur Dioxide

DISH ITEM PRODUCT	Celery	Cereals containing gluten	Crustaceans	Eggs	Fish	Lupin	Milk	Molluscs	Mustard	Nuts	Peanuts	Sesame Seeds	Soya	Sulphur Dioxide

DISH ITEM PRODUCT	Celery	Cereals containing gluten	Crustaceans	Eggs	Fish	Lupin	Milk	Molluscs	Mustard	Nuts	Peanuts	Sesame Seeds	Soya	Sulphur Dioxide

Printed in Poland
by Amazon Fulfillment
Poland Sp. z o.o., Wrocław